RAYMOND CHANDLER ON SCREEN:
His Novels Into Film

by
STEPHEN PENDO

The Scarecrow Press, Inc.
Metuchen, N.J.   1976

Library of Congress Cataloging in Publication Data

Pendo, Stephen, 1947–
   Raymond Chandler on screen.

   Bibliography: p.
   Includes index.
   1.   Chandler, Raymond, 1888-1959--Film adaptations.
2. Chandler, Raymond, 1888-1959--Characters--Philip
Marlowe. I.   Title.
PS3505. H3224Z8   813'. 5'2   76-9855
ISBN 0-8108-0931-1

Television, also, has not neglected the "Marlowe" detective or Chandler sleuth, as witnessed by the numerous private eye shows like "Mannix," "Cannon," "Barnaby Jones," "Harry O," and "The Rockford Files." Joe Mannix carbon copies the film image of Philip Marlowe. He is tough, ruggedly handsome, and has a strong desire to see justice done no matter what the personal risk. Cannon and Barnaby Jones emerge as variations of Chandler's hero. Both primarily concern themselves with justice, but each has an idiosyncrasy. Cannon likes food and is an expert chef, while Jones uses his age and "folksy" manner to fool criminals. Of greater interest, perhaps, than these detective shows, which have a loose relationship with Chandler, are two newer shows that display closer ties to the author. The style of "Harry O" has been described as "reminiscent of Raymond Chandler."[9] Not only is the character of Harry O much like Marlowe, (he is a rather down-and-out detective not very concerned with money) but also the program's style bears a similarity to previous Marlowe films. For example, the show uses narration in a way similar to Murder, My Sweet, and lines like "Homicide had come and gone, and left the empties" bear a distinct similarity to Chandler's dialogue.

Even closer to Chandler, however, is the other program, "The Rockford Files." Not only did one critic feel the series was done in a "Raymond Chandler tradition"[10] but also that the show may have been inspired by the television success of Marlowe and the acceptance of Garner's performance in that picture.[11] The opening episode of "The Rockford Files," in fact, used a Garner line, "Does your mother know what you do for a living?" that came directly from Marlowe. (This line seems well on its way to becoming a standard private eye show quip, for Mike Connors used it on a "Mannix" episode, "The Green Man." Nor is the line limited to detectives, for a hoodlum asked Sergeant Ed Brown the question on an "Ironside" episode.) Another "Rockford Files" episode put Garner in a classic Chandler situation. In Bay City on a case, Garner is harassed by the police and becomes involved in what looks like a police cover-up. This is classic Chandler, for his Marlowe receives continual harassment from the corrupt Bay City police.

There are, no doubt, several reasons for the renewed popularity of the fictional private detective (ironically at a time when the number of real-life private eyes is on the decline) but Clifford D. May postulated perhaps the most important one:

him, with the film character, as scriptwriters and directors
have interpreted him.   Marlowe is ideally suited to this type
of scrutiny.   No actor has played Marlowe more than once
in films and, therefore, the role has not been typecast to a
particular actor.   With very few exceptions, each film was
made by an entirely different group of people, and only two
were made by the same studio.   Each novel-film may be
looked upon as an independent entity, related to the other
novel-films but still unique.

Because such a study of the Marlowe character also
provides an interesting comparison between novels and films,
this analysis also examines this relationship, primarily in
the areas of plot and secondary characterizations.   The
screenwriter is the essential connection between a source
novel and its film.   All the available Marlowe film screenwriters were contacted by this writer in reference to their
work, and their comments help to illuminate the process by
which a novel is converted into a film.

Apart from being an exercise in characterization and
novel-film analysis, a study of Chandler's work helps to better understand the current mass media image of the private
eye.   Today more than ever before Chandler's influence can
be seen in motion pictures.   A wave of imitative Marlowe
films has appeared recently, not the least of which is the latest Chandler adaption, Farewell, My Lovely.   Other such
derivative movies include Gumshoe (1972), Hickey & Boggs
(1972), Shamus (1973), Pulp (1973), Lady Ice (1973), the
Shaft series (1971-1973), Chinatown (1974)--which some critics have compared to Chandler's work, Night Moves (1975),
and The Drowning Pool (1975), based on a Ross Macdonald
novel.   In some cases Chandler's influence is subtle; in others, it is more direct.   Hickey and Boggs, for example, are
characters in the Marlowe mold.   Each is a rugged individu-
alist, both are not too successful private detectives, and both
see justice done by the film's end.   The film Shamus has
two scenes lifted from Howard Hawks' The Big Sleep, the
most famous Marlowe film.   In particular, the scene in the
bookstore in which Burt Reynolds beds the proprietress directly copies a similar scene in The Big Sleep.   Also, the
interview Reynolds has with a millionaire in a cold room
matches the hot house sequence in The Big Sleep.   In Chinatown, the 1930's atmosphere of Los Angeles comes straight
out of Chandler, even if the detective hero does not (he
handles divorce cases and fails to see justice done in the
end).

and The Long Goodbye (The Long Goodbye).

Two other Chandler films were made in 1942, but
neither of these featured Philip Marlowe. The Falcon Takes
Over (MGM) was adapted by Lynn Root and Frank Fenton from
Farewell, My Lovely, with the character of Marlowe replaced
by Michael Arlen's detective, the Falcon, played by George
Sanders. [1]* Time to Kill (Twentieth Century-Fox) was adapted
by Clarence Upson Young from The High Window. Here Marlowe was replaced by Brett Halliday's Michael Shayne, played
by Lloyd Nolan. [2] In addition, one critic thought the Frank
Sinatra film Tony Rome (1967) was "an un-acknowledged remake of The Big Sleep,"[3] and another that its sequel, Lady
in Cement (1968), used for its model Farewell, My Lovely. [4]
Television, too, has not neglected Marlowe. Dick Powell
starred in a version of The Long Goodbye, which ran on CBS
on October 7, 1954, as the opening episode of the melodrama
series "Climax!"[5] In 1957 Chandler undertook negotiations
with Goodson-Todman Enterprises for the development of a
Philip Marlowe television show. [6] Perhaps as a result of the
writer's efforts, Marlowe did make it to the small screen.
An ABC network television series, "Philip Marlowe," debuted
on October 6, 1959, with Philip Carey in the role of Marlowe, but did not last into a second season. [7]

The six Chandler novels that were filmed provide an
interesting basis on which to examine Chandler's contribution
to the private detective film genre. Chandler's vivid characterizations, as well as his complex and, at times, nearly in-
comprehensible, plots provide a stiff challenge to any screenwriter's ingenuity. The screenwriter must work hard to keep
the plot line simple enough for screen audiences yet retain
Chandler's fascinating character studies. In addition, the director and cinematographer must strive to recreate the atmosphere present in the Marlowe novels. The director must
orchestrate the interplay between characters, the pace of the
action, the overall effect of the film, in order to accurately
reflect Chandler's style, while the cinematographer endeavors
to reproduce Chandler's vivid descriptions in visual terms.
In the cases of Marlowe, The Long Goodbye, and Farewell,
My Lovely, this involved shooting on location in Los Angeles. [8]

The purpose of this book primarily lies in comparing
the literary character of Philip Marlowe, as Chandler created

*See Notes, beginning on page 207.

INTRODUCTION

The private detective has long been a staple of both literature and films. From the pages of numerous stories and the celluloid of a host of films, countless detectives have gone forth to solve murders and seek justice. The best way to study this group of private eyes is to examine the prototypes from which most of them came. Two of the most famous private detective prototypes in literature and film are Sam Spade and Philip Marlowe. Their creators, Dashiell Hammett and Raymond Chandler, were among the most popular fiction writers of their day. And two films starring their creations, The Maltese Falcon and The Big Sleep, remain today the two best private detective adventures ever produced. The problem lay in deciding which of these offered the best opportunity for examining the private eye in novels and films.

Hammett's The Maltese Falcon is one of the classic detective stories of all time. The film version of the famous story also is considered by many film historians and critics to be the best detective film ever made. But Hammett chose to feature Sam Spade in only this one adventure. Raymond Chandler, on the other hand, developed Philip Marlowe in seven novels. In addition, six of these novels have been made into films, thereby making Marlowe one of the most popular screen detectives in recent film history. In addition, a study of Marlowe offers not only the opportunity to investigate the private detective character in film and fiction, but also a chance to compare the original novels with the film adaptions.

To date, six of Chandler's seven novels, but none of his twenty-four short stories, have been made directly into films. In addition, one novel has been filmed twice. The study is, therefore, limited to these six novels (and seven films): Farewell, My Lovely (made into Murder, My Sweet and remade as Farewell, My Lovely); The Big Sleep (The Big Sleep); The Lady in the Lake (Lady in the Lake); The High Window (The Brasher Doubloon); The Little Sister (Marlowe);

LIST OF TABLES

TABLE OF CONTENTS

v

many of the rough spots from this study. Additional credit goes to the proofreaders, Vonetta Lapidow, Elaine LaRosa, and Millyn Moore, and the typist, Nan Sue Walker.

The last person cited, Dr. Frank Manchel, is also the individual deserving the most thanks. From the beginning he guided this project, supplying information I would have not otherwise discovered and offering invaluable advice. He deserves credit for much of what is good in this book, and it is not too much to say that almost every page reflects at least one of his perceptive critical comments. More than any other person, I owe him a debt of gratitude hardly repaid by a few lines in this acknowledgment.

ACKNOWLEDGMENTS

This book is not the result of a single person's efforts, but rather the product of many people's time and talents. Without these individuals,
my efforts would have been far less effective, if,
indeed, this study could have been completed at
all. Although not all of these individuals are
recognized here, I wish to express my thanks to
all involved in this effort with particular appre-
ciation going to the persons cited below.

Several people were instrumental in aiding
the research of this book. The staff of the University of Vermont Bailey Library Interlibrary
Loan and Reference departments greatly facili-
tated the research, as did the Museum of Modern Art. Doug Lemza of Films Incorporated provided urgently needed prints of Murder, My Sweet
and The Brasher Doubloon. Avco Embassy Pictures furnished me with material on Farewell,
My Lovely. Additional gratitude goes to American Cinematographer, Houghton Mifflin, Take
One, and the University of North Carolina
Press for their permission to quote.

A special group of individuals contributed invaluable firsthand information to this book. All
the available screenwriters of the "Marlowe" pic-
tures--Leigh Brackett, Steve Fisher, David Zelag
Goodman, John Paxton, and Stirling Silliphant--
displayed kindness and interest in this project,
despite their often busy schedules. The personal
accounts of their script-writing experience on the
"Marlowe" pictures immeasurably added to this
study. In addition, Stirling Silliphant deserves
special thanks for supplying a copy of his script
for The Long Goodbye.

Thanks also go to two editors of this work,
Dr. John K. Worden and Dr. Ralph H. Orth.
Their valuable critical suggestions helped remove

> The prototypical private eye grew out of the
> 1920s, an age whose disposition was marked by post-
> war, post-Wilsonian disenchantment, by the hypocrisy
> and gangsterism of Prohibition, by the labor unions'
> battles for rights and recognition and often bloody
> repression of them, and by the Harding era corrup-
> tion.
>   These influences shaped a hero who was cynical,
> knew how to live with violence, and most significant
> of all, was divorced from and mistrustful of the offi-
> cial appendages of law and authority.
>   It should not be surprising that the private eye
> is being welcomed back by the present generation, a
> generation which has also been raised amid postwar
> disenchantment, excessive and repressive violence,
> the prohibition of a popular intoxicant, ubiquitous
> gangsterism, governmental corruption, and the failure
> of institutional morality. [12]

This study has several limitations, besides being con-
fined to the six novels and seven films mentioned. It does
not attempt to analyze any other Chandler writings. Furthermore, the seven films are not compared specifically with any
other detective movies and no effort is made to analyze the
films as part of any one filmmaker's total output. For example, the chapter dealing with The Big Sleep analyzes no
other imitative films and no attempt is undertaken to compare
that film with others made by Howard Hawks. To repeat,
this book primarily examines the Philip Marlowe character
and only general comparisons are made with other fictional
detectives. Also, very little background material is provided
on the studios, producers, writers, directors, and actors
that combined to make the Marlowe films. Readers wishing
further information of this nature are referred to the compre-
hensive resource work, Film Study: A Resource Guide, by
Frank Manchel (Cranbury, N. J.: Associated University Press,
1973).

Although the six novels discussed here bear no plot
relation to each other (i.e., the novels are in no way linked
by events or secondary characters), they are very similar in
style and form. Each one begins with two parallel plots, one
important, one unimportant. As the book progresses, the
secondary plot grows in importance at the other plot's expense. For example, in The Big Sleep, Marlowe is asked to
investigate a blackmail case. The fact that Rusty Regan has
disappeared is mentioned. By the end of the book, the black-

mail case is forgotten and the critical question becomes,
"What happened to Regan?" Each novel has several similar,
and in some cases, identical characters (in everything but
name): e.g., the tough and generally honest Los Angeles
police; the tough and generally dishonest Bay City police; the
shady doctors who serve the rich; the super-rich young or
elderly clients of Marlowe; and the big-time gamblers and
racketeers. And always there are the beautiful but deadly
women.

Because this book primarily deals with film, the chapters are arranged according to the domestic release dates of
the films under discussion. This presents no problem in
treating the literary character of Marlowe and enables the
reader to follow the chronological development of the hero in
the Marlowe films.

Each chapter opens with introductory statements about
the book under discussion. A brief plot synopsis of the novel
follows. This serves to refresh the reader's memory of the
plot or provide a reference point for understanding the chapter if he has not read the book. A critical examination of
the novel is then given. (This opening section is omitted in
Chapter 8, because the novel under study in that chapter is
discussed in Chapter 2.)

Statements concerning the script and production of the
film under discussion are given. Following these are critical reactions to the film and discussion of the film's secondary characters. Each chapter concludes with an analysis
of the fiction and film Marlowe characters and a summary
paragraph about the film. Each chapter contains two tables.
The first details the film's cast and credits. It should be
noted that the release dates on these tables should be taken,
like popcorn, with a grain of salt. Release dates often vary
depending upon their source and sometimes do not coincide
with the first major showing of a film. For example, The
Long Goodbye was released in March, 1973, was quickly with-
drawn from distribution, and re-released in October of the
same year.

The second table compares the novel, script (where
applicable), and film plots. The various plot events generally follow major developments in the action. They are as
complete an explanation of the plot as possible without including extraneous information. Because the selection of these
events was somewhat arbitrary, no statistical analysis based

on them is attempted. Plot events that appear in the same
row are identical. Those not in the same row differ from
the events in the preceding row. An examination of the table
will reveal the similarities and differences in the compared
plots. It should be recognized that these plot comparison
tables have limitations, and that even the most dedicated
Chandler fan would probably not want to wade through every
word of each one. It would, however, be extremely awkward
to compare these plots in the text, so the tables are provided as a somewhat more convenient method of plot comparison.

The material presented and conclusions reached in
this book should prove useful to cinema students interested
in private detective films as well as those interested in popular film heroes. Furthermore, the analysis should prove
useful to people concerned with comparing and contrasting the
literary sources of major private detective novels. Even
further, this book should be helpful to anyone studying the
results of one writer's works when these works are dealt
with by several different filmmakers, each of whom has his
own interpretation of that writer.

Chapter 1

BACKGROUND

Before we begin the investigation of Raymond Chandler
and the development of his hero, a short history of the detective in literature and film is in order.   This will help to
better define Chandler's place in the detective story genre,
and show that Philip Marlowe was not created out of a vac-
uum, but rather developed at least partly from his antecedents.
This discussion does not attempt, however, to completely
trace the history of the literary and film detective.   Readers
interested in a more thorough chronology are urged to con-
sult other sources, particularly Howard Haycraft's Murder
for Pleasure,[1] which discusses the mystery novel up to Chandler, and William K. Everson's The Detective in Film.[2]   A
heavy reliance has been placed on The Detective in Film in
this study because it is, to date, the most complete work on
the cinematic sleuth and the only one which contains a detailed history of detective films.   The purpose of this book
does not warrant extensive research into detective film history, and Everson's book adequately substitutes for such research.

The detective story comes rather late in the history
of literature, being a mere 135 years old.   The simple reason for the late appearance of this story form lies in the
fact that, before the early 1800's, there were no detectives.
Earlier civilizations did not have police forces as we think
of them today.   As George Bates stated: "The cause of
Chaucer's silence on the subject of airplanes was because he
had never seen one.   You cannot write about policemen before policemen exist to be written of."[3]   This condition
changed in the early 1800's.   In Paris, policemen formed
the Sureté, "the first police division organized solely and
purposely for the criminal investigation,"[4] and in London
they comprised the Bow Street Runners, later to be followed
by Scotland Yard.   (These men were not at first called detectives; the earliest appearance of that word in print did not
come until 1843.[5])   The exploits of the Sureté probably inspired Poe to set the world's first detective story in Paris.

1

To Edgar Allan Poe goes the honor of inventing not
only the detective story, but also the literary private detective as well. His hero, C. Auguste Dupin, first appeared
in "The Murders in the Rue Morgue," and later in "The Mystery of Marie Roget" and "The Purloined Letter." Dupin's
use of deductive reasoning places him in a different school
from the private eye of nearly one hundred years later, but
his reason for investigating crimes proves to be the prime
motivation behind Philip Marlowe. Dupin says, "My ultimate
object is only the truth."[6] As will be shown later, one of
Marlowe's primary concerns is to discover the truth and see
justice done.

In 1850, nine years after the publication of "The Murders in the Rue Morgue," Allan Pinkerton established the
first detective agency in the United States. Its trademark of
an open eye, along with the motto "We Never Sleep," was the
source of the term "private eye." As Clifford D. May
stated: "The Pinkertons pursued Jesse James, spied for
Lincoln (himself a detective-fiction fan), and smashed the
heads of striking steel workers for Andrew Carnegie before
settling down to become a reputable multimillion-dollar cor-
poration...."[7]

The next major advance in the literary private detective came from Arthur Conan Doyle. Doyle, of course,
created the most famous literary detective, Sherlock Holmes.
Holmes was, like Dupin, a private detective, working outside
the police and outguessing them at every turn. Doyle's first
story, "A Study in Scarlet," was published in 1887. After
a shaky start, Doyle's stories caught on and for almost the
next forty years Holmes' adventures flowed from Doyle's
imaginzation.

Of interest here is that readers remember Doyle far
more for his characterizations than plots. Howard Haycraft
said: "The Study in Scarlet ... violates two of the most
sacred tenets of the detective story: the culprit is revealed
to be one who has not, properly speaking, appeared previously in the story; and the solution is in large part based on
information acquired secretly by the detective and not revealed
to the reader until after the denouement. The latter fault, in
fact, tends to crop out in an embarrassing degree in many of
the [Holmes] narratives."[8] It is the vivid character of Holmes,
then, that makes the stories stand out. (Letters are, in fact,
still being sent to "Mr. Sherlock Holmes, 221-B Baker Street,
London.") In Chandler, too, the characterizations make the
story, not the plots.

One element of Sherlock Holmes' character was carried over into Philip Marlowe. Holmes takes no interest in
the opposite sex. As Watson puts it, "All emotions, and
that one (love) particularly, were abhorrent to his cold, pre-
cise but admirably balanced mind. ... He never spoke of the
softer passions, save with a gibe and sneer."[9] Marlowe's
attitude toward sex bears similarities towards Holmes', although Marlowe's viewpoint falls short of this extreme.

Following Doyle, the detective story genre expanded
greatly both in England and America. World War I brought
a change to this type of literature. According to Haycraft,
"Before 1914, the difference between detection and mere mystery was clear in the minds of only a few. After 1918, we
find a new and distinct cleavage, with the tinseled trappings
of romanticism relegated for the most part to the sphere of
mystery, and a fresher, sharper detective story making bold
and rapid strides on its own stout legs."[10] After the war,
the once astute amateur detective in England slowly developed
into a police investigator. In America, however, the golden
age of the private detective was just starting.

For some unexplained reason the quality of the American detective story lagged behind the British, and it was not
until 1926 that a major breakthrough in the genre came. In
that year, S. S. Van Dine (Willard Huntington Wright) produced the first Philo Vance novel, The Benson Murder Case.
Two factors favored the Philo Vance novels: their great lit-
eracy and their verisimilitude.[11] The Philo Vance novels,
in fact "raised the detective story to a new peak of excellence
and popularity."[12] But also at this time, other developments
in the private detective hero occurred outside the realm of
"respectable" literature.

The tough Marlowe-type private eye first developed
in the pulp magazines of the 1920's and '30's, particularly
Black Mask. Race Williams proved to be one of the first of
the new breed of detective hero. Created by Carroll John
Daly in 1923, Williams was tough, cynical, and had a code
of ethics all his own. As Philip Durham said: "Carroll
John Daly was a careless writer and a muddy thinker who
created the hard-boiled detective, the prototype for number-
less writers to follow."[13] Fortunately for the private eye,
a clearer thinker was also writing for Black Mask.

In 1923 Dashiell Hammett wrote the first Continental
Op story about a nameless first person narrator who worked

for the Continental Detective Agency in San Francisco.
Hammett had once been a Pinkerton operative, and this
helped provide the backgrounds and characters for his
stories. William F. Nolan said: "the Op described himself as 'a busy, middle-aged detective' more interested in
crime than in 'feminine beauty.' From the outset, he was
anti-woman when it came to a case; the Op was all business."[14] Hammett created a new hero, Sam Spade, for his
1929 Black Mask serial, "The Maltese Falcon." Published
as a novel in 1930, The Maltese Falcon is considered by
some to be one of the all time classic detective novels,
primarily because of its excellent plot and characters and
Hammett's deft blending of these two elements.   Spade
epitomized the tough private eye and started a whole new
sub-genre of detective heroes.   Spade's terse dialogue and
moral code would partially be incorporated into Philip Marlowe.

          It is important to understand that a crucial relation-
ship exists between detective literature and detective films,
for most popular screen sleuths originated in literature.
The detective film genre began shortly after the beginning
of the 1900's. Logically enough, the most popular literary
detective of the day, Sherlock Holmes, became the first
screen detective hero. As Everson discovered, "The first
known Holmes film was Sherlock Holmes Baffled, made by
the American Biograph Company, and since it was copy-
righted in February of 1903, chances are that it was made
at the end of 1902."[15] Other Sherlock Holmes films followed at various times throughout the silent era, and the
questionable quality of these pictures serves to illustrate
the problems of the silent detective film. The very nature
of the detective story, for example, requires a good deal of
verbal explanation throughout the tale.

          The whole language and construction of the si-
     lent film worked against a figure who needed con-
     versation and interrogation. In the earlier days
     of film, the stress was on action or at least physi-
     cal movement, often backed up by lengthy subti-
     tles. In the twenties, when the movies rapidly
     achieved increasing sophistication, the pace
     slowed, meaning was expressed via visual subtle-
     ties, and the title was used less and less. Neither
     made the detective an easier character to handle.[16]

Everson found the silent film detective fell into four

categories, which are not necessarily mutually exclusive.
The first category concerned films built around famous detective heroes like Sherlock Holmes.   The second dealt
with the use of a detective like Holmes because he was already a familiar figure to the audience.   Consequently, no
time was needed to explain the character to the audience.
The third category consisted of the quickly-made films.
Mercifully, these numbered only a few.   Such pictures often
had long subtitles that explained the action, thereby saving
a great deal of filming.   The last, and major, group of silent detective films had the sleuth as a secondary character.
Here, the detective usually served as a threat to the hero,
often someone trying to go straight or a person wrongly
suspected of a crime. [17]

     Other factors contributed to make the silent detective
film generally unexciting.   The American detective story,
for example, did not show a major creative burst until
1926.   Thus, in Everson's words, "the silent period was not
able to draw upon the great bulk of detective fiction heroes--
Philo Vance, Hercule Poirot, Sam Spade, Thatcher Colt,
Nick Charles, Nero Wolfe, and so many others--because
they just didn't exist until virtually the end of the silent
period, and in many cases not until much later."[18]   Furthermore, the private detective in the silent era was often
slighted in favor of characters who functioned as detectives,
but generally from outside the law. [19]   Thus silent detective
films were far from outstanding, partially because of the
limitations of the medium and partially from lack of suitable
literary characters.

     The coming of sound brought with it a tremendous
boost for the detective film.   The novelty of talking movies
spurred, of course, great interest in films that simply
talked; this alone could hold an audience.   So movies which
featured long dialogue scenes came into demand.   Thus the
very thing that limited the detective film in the silent era,
the need for verbal explanations, helped to make it a popular
sound film category.   By this time, too, many of the detectives mentioned above had been created, supplying more
material for the detective film. [20]

     Most early sound detective films, however, offered
little in the way of great mystery.   Usually they relied "on
the popularity of the genre and star, and on the novelty of
sound itself.   Cinematically, they were static and seemingly
welcomed the plot contrivances that caused the detective and

suspects to sit around in offices and drawing rooms and
just talk."[21]   But even this talk often failed to be satisfac-
tory.   Actors, anxious to look good in the new medium of
sound, delivered their lines with the utmost care.   The resulting dialogue sounded anything but natural.[22]

The detective film soon improved, however, and the
whole genre exploded in the thirties.   Quickly the detective
film went the way of the western and became staple fare
for the "B" movies.   Perhaps the major detective film trend
in the thirties lay in the series picture, although the films
in a particular series were not always made by the same
studio or had the same stars.   Ranking high among these
series was Philo Vance.   This series began in 1929 with
The Canary Murder Case, made in both a silent and sound
version.[23]   It starred William Powell as the first and best
of the Vances.   He continued in the role in The Greene
Murder Case (1929), The Benson Murder Case (1930), and
The Kennel Murder Case (1933).   Other actors took the role
of Vance, while Powell went on to play in The Thin Man
(1934).   Based on Dashiell Hammett's 1934 novel of the same
name, this film, made in fourteen days and earning over
$2 million,[24] teamed Powell with Myrna Loy.   They formed
perhaps the most popular detective film team.   This series,
with its "unpretentious blend of screwball comedy and murder mystery"[25] ran through 1947--with After the Thin Man
(1936), Another Thin Man (1939), Shadow of the Thin Man
(1941), The Thin Man Goes Home (1944), and Song of the
Thin Man (1947)--and gained great popularity.   Other series
of the times included Bulldog Drummond, Charlie Chan, Mr.
Moto, the Saint, and the Lone Wolf.   These private eyes,
however, were of a more gentlemanly nature than Philip
Marlowe.   Slightly more closely related film detectives
were Bill Crane, Nero Wolfe, and Ellery Queen.

In 1941 John Huston directed The Maltese Falcon.
The picture did for the detective film what the novel had
done for the detective story twelve years earlier: infuse
the genre with new blood and bring the "hard-boiled" detective into sharp focus.   Humphrey Bogart's portrayal of Sam
Spade became one of the classic detective performances,
seldom, if ever, surpassed.

In short, the private detective story to the time of
Chandler and the first Philip Marlowe movie was in a de-
veloping and expanding state.

Raymond Chandler was born in Chicago on July 23, 1888. His mother took him to England when he was eight, after having divorced her husband. Chandler attended Dulwich College (a secondary school) for nine years, spent a few months in France and Germany, and returned to England. He worked briefly for the Admiralty and wrote an occasional poem or review for some literary magazines. In 1912, he returned to the United States and then enlisted in the Gordon Highlanders in Canada, serving in France and England in 1917-1918. He was discharged in 1919 and returned to California with his mother. Soon after her death in 1924, Chandler, now 36, married Pearl Cecile ("Cissy") Bowen, 53. Chandler became an executive with the Dabney Oil Syndicate and moved upward as the company grew, handling several jobs within the Syndicate. [26] But the Depression hurt the oil business, and by 1933 Chandler was out of it altogether. He elected to turn his hand to writing.

In 1933, Chandler decided to see if he could write stories of the kind he had been reading in the pulp magazines, feeling this might be a way to learn the writer's craft. In five months he had produced a story, "Blackmailers Don't Shoot," and sold it to Black Mask for $180. During the next few years, Chandler continued to write for magazines. From December 1933 to October 14, 1939, eleven of his stories appeared in Black Mask, seven in Dime Detective Magazine, and one each in Detective Fiction Weekly and the Saturday Evening Post. [27] In 1939 The Big Sleep was published, much of it being a synthesis of Chandler's previous short stories. Following rapidly came Farewell, My Lovely (1940), The High Window (1942), and The Lady in the Lake (1943). Chandler went to Hollywood in 1942 and by 1943 he was writing screenplays, some original, some in collaboration. His most successful original effort was The Blue Dahlia (1946), which received an Academy Award nomination for best screenplay. But Chandler was outspoken about Hollywood and its writers and, in January, 1946, Paramount technically suspended him for refusing to perform under contract. [28]

Chandler returned to novel writing with The Little Sister in 1949 and The Long Goodbye in 1953. Cissy's death in 1954 completely broke Chandler up and he became something like the writer character he had created for The Long Goodbye. He made a feeble attempt to commit suicide and began drinking heavily. His writing ambition declined in the last five years of his life and he produced very few

manuscripts. His last novel, Playback, was published in
1958. Based on an unproduced screenplay he had written
much earlier, it was a poor effort at best. The Marlowe
of this novel was one scarcely recognizable to avid Chandler
fans (he even used a stethoscope to listen at a wall!) and
"was hardly more than a caricature of Marlowe in his
prime."[29] Chandler died of bronchial pneumonia in La Jolla,
California on March 26, 1959.

One main concern of this book is the development and
character of Philip Marlowe. A knowledge of his origin and
personality is necessary in discussing the changes Marlowe
has undergone from literature to film. Marlowe did not
spring into being in a single story, but rather developed in
many stories over a period of years.

Marlowe began as Mallory in "Blackmailers Don't
Shoot," where he was little different from many stock
heroes. He was strong, tough, unafraid of the police, and
ready to kill if the situation warranted it. But by Chandler's
third and fourth stories, his hero, who was now a nameless
first person narrator, had begun to change. He had become
concerned with social injustice and the mobsters that had
taken over city politics. He now governed his actions on
the basis of morality; he would pursue a course of action
he felt was morally right even if it went against the law.
Chandler's hero had become a knight and this is what he
was to remain.[30]

By 1937 Chandler's detective had graduated from simple investigations and now became involved in tangled affairs
in which he always tried to look out for his clients. In
"Try the Girl," the detective (named "Carmady") relied on
his own financial resources to correct a bad situation. In
"Mandarin's Jade," John Dalmas consistently refused to take
money he felt he did not deserve. "Red Wind" showed that
Dalmas worked not for money but for justice when he pro-
tected a suspect until he could get more facts. "Bay City
Blues" proved that the hero was a match for the violent world
he lived in, even if he found violence personally distasteful.
Like Sherlock Holmes and the Continental Op before him,
Chandler's hero rejected sex. Chandler explained why he
felt romance did not belong in a mystery story:

> Love interest nearly always weakens a mystery
> because it introduces a type of suspense that is
> antagonistic to the detective's struggle to solve the

problem. It stacks the cards, and, in nine cases
out of ten, it eliminates at least two useful suspects. The only effective kind of love interest
is that which creates a personal hazard for the
detective--but which, at the same time, you in-
stinctively feel to be a mere episode. A really
good detective never gets married. [31]

Durham found more specific reasons why the detective could
not become involved in romance. The hero could not marry
because he could not risk being killed on a case and leave
his family destitute. Yet he cannot indulge in non-marital
sex because of his moral code. As Durham put it, "Almost
any aspect of the code could, under certain conditions, be
forgiven except that of 'violating' a white woman."[32] And
so Dalmas, in "Trouble Is My Business," ultimately rejects
a romantic encounter. [33]

This, then, describes the Chandler hero who finally
became Philip Marlowe in The Big Sleep. He was tough
and able to hold his own in a violent situation. His strong
moral code kept him broke, but his honor was more pre-
cious than money. His sense of morality at times allowed
him to lie to the police, for he believed that until they
played fair in all their investigations, he had the right to
protect his client. Sex and a case did not mix, no matter
how tempting the offer. As Marlowe says after kissing
Vivian Regan, "I work at it [being a detective], lady. I
don't play at it. "[34]

Although his writings vividly presented his hero,
Chandler further defined him in "The Simple Art of Murder":

But down these mean streets a man must go
who is not himself mean, who is neither tarnished
or afraid. . . . He is the hero; he is everything.
He must be a complete man and a common man
and yet an unusual man. He must be, to use a
rather weathered phrase, a man of honor--by
instinct, by inevitability, without thought of it,
and certainly without saying it. He must be the
best man in his world and a good enough man for
any world. I do not care much about his private
life; he is neither a eunuch nor a satyr; I think
he might seduce a duchess and I am quite sure he
would not spoil a virgin; if he is a man of honor
in one thing, he is that in all things.

He is a relatively poor man, or he could not
be a detective at all. He is a common man or he
could not go among common people; he has a sense
of character, or he would not know his job. He
will take no man's money dishonestly and no man's
insolence without a due and dispassionate revenge;
he is a lonely man and his pride is that you will
treat him as a proud man or be very sorry that
you ever saw him. He talks as the man of his
age talks--that is, with rude wit, a lively sense
of the grotesque, a disgust for sham, and a contempt for pettiness.

The story is this man's adventure in search of
a hidden truth, and it would be no adventure if it
did not happen to a man fit for adventure. [35]

This, then, is a profile of Chandler's hero. But the
description remains incomplete, for it does not take into account the filmic image of Philip Marlowe. We shall see in
the following chapters how filmmakers have treated this
popular hero. At some times they have enhanced him; at
others detracted from him. But always they have kept the
ideas of honor and justice alive in the character. Marlowe
stands out as an important hero in both literature and film.

Chapter 2

FAREWELL, MY LOVELY:
MURDER, MY SWEET

Chandler obviously felt at home with Farewell, My
Lovely, his second novel. He had experienced difficulties
in putting the plot together for his first novel, The Big
Sleep, but these troubles were over by the time of Farewell,
My Lovely. Here Chandler constructed his best plot, free
from the irregularities that plagued his first novel. Here,
too, Chandler enlarged upon and improved the character base
begun in The Big Sleep. Added to the big-time gambler,
elderly millionaire, and other character types of the first
novel were several new ones: the beautiful, rich, deadly
blonde, the corrupt Bay City police, and the disreputable
dope doctor (a physician who illegally dispenses narcotics,
particularly to rich clients with bad hangovers). Chandler's
well-constructed plot and expert characterizations combined
to make Farewell, My Lovely the best of the writer's novels.

Soon after the publication of The Big Sleep, Chandler
began to plan his next several novels. Farewell, My Lovely
was born as a book entitled Law Is Where You Buy It. The
theme was to deal with the relationship between corrupt police and racketeers operating in a small California town
(Bay City) which appeared on the surface to be a respectable
community. (As the novel developed, however, this theme
took a back seat to the other story elements.) By August,
1939, Chandler, who was having some difficulty straightening
out the novel's conclusion, had decided on a title change.
The novel was to be called The Second Murderer (in reference to King Richard III, I, iv) and Chandler finished it in
June, 1940. By the time Chandler had decided he did not
like that title, the book had already been announced by Alfred A. Knopf, the publishers, under that label. When the
author turned in a completed draft of this latest Marlowe
adventure, he insisted on the title of Farewell, My Lovely,
although Knopf was not happy with it, feeling that it was not
a fitting title for a mystery novel. But they gave in, still

11

feeling the title was a liability rather than the asset Chandler
considered it. [1] (As we shall see later, a similar process of
title change occurred when it came time to title the first
film version of the novel.)

The novel opens when Marlowe, in the black section
of Los Angeles on a case, is forcibly dragged into an all-
black bar, Florian's, by a large man, Moose Malloy. Malloy is looking for his old sweetheart, Velma, but the people
at Florian's don't know her. Malloy's murder of Florian's
manager makes him a fugitive from the police. Marlowe
becomes interested in Malloy and goes looking for Velma.
Her trail leads to Jesse Florian. Marlowe gets little help
from her, however, only the news that Velma is dead and a
photograph, supposedly of the woman.

Lindsay Marriott hires Marlowe to go with him to buy
back a jade necklace stolen from a lady friend. The outing
results in the murder of Marriott and Marlowe's introduction
to Anne Riordan. Anne discovers a Mrs. Grayle owns the
necklace. Cigarettes taken from Marriott's body put Marlowe on the trail of a psychic consultant named Jules Amthor, who may be the head of a jewel robbery gang.

A visit with Mrs. Grayle, a beautiful blonde, reveals
that Marriott blackmailed women. A visit with Amthor earns
Marlowe a berth in Dr. Sonderborg's establishment, courtesy
of the Bay City police. Marlowe spots Malloy at Sonderborg's
and realizes the dope doctor also hides men on the run.
Marlowe escapes. He and Detective-Lieutenant Randall go to
Jessie Florian's to find she has been murdered by Malloy.

Marlowe goes to Bay City after the policemen who
took him to Sonderborg's. From one of these men, Galbraith, Marlowe learns Malloy may be hiding on a gambling
ship owned by Laird Brunette, the gangster who owns Bay
City. Through Brunette, Marlowe gets a message to Malloy.
Malloy comes to Marlowe's apartment shortly before Mrs.
Grayle. Marlowe tells her the necklace was never stolen.
Marriott thought he was going to kill Marlowe, but Mrs.
Grayle set Marriott up so she could kill him. Mrs. Grayle
is Velma. She kills Malloy and gets away, but later shoots
herself.

Farewell, My Lovely was published in 1940. Like
The Big Sleep, Farewell, My Lovely was constructed out of
several of Chandler's previous short stories. (Chandler's

TABLE 1.   MURDER, MY SWEET

Cast

Philip Marlowe	Dick Powell
Mrs. Grayle	Claire Trevor
Ann Grayle	Anne Shirley
Amthor	Otto Kruger
Moose Malloy	Mike Mazurki
Mr. Grayle	Miles Mander
Marriott	Douglas Walton
Lieut. Randall	Don Douglas
Dr. Sonderborg	Ralf Harolde
Mrs. Florian	Esther Howard

Released by RKO Radio Pictures, Inc.

Running time: 95 minutes

Release date: January 10, 1945

Credits

Produced by	Adrian Scott
Directed by	Edward Dmytryk
Screenplay by	John Paxton
Based on novel by	Raymond Chandler
Dir. of Photog.	Harry J. Wild, A.S.C.
Special Effects by	Vernon L. Walker, A.S.C.
Art Directors	Albert S. D'Agostino
	Carroll Clark
Set Decorations	Darrell Silvera
	Michael Ohrenbach
Recorded by	Bailey Fesler
Montage by	Douglas Travers
Music by	Roy Webb
Musical Director	C. Bakaleinikoff
Gowns by	Edward Stevenson
Edited by	Joseph Noriega
Asst. Director	William Dorfman
Rerecording by	James G. Stewart
Dialogue Director	Leslie Urbach

method for expanding his stories is detailed in the next chapter.) The major portions came from "The Man Who Liked Dogs" (Black Mask, March, 1936), "Try the Girl" (Black Mask, January, 1937), and "Mandarin's Jade" (Dime Detective Magazine, November, 1937). In addition, a small part grew out of "Trouble Is My Business" (Dime Detective Magazine, August, 1939).[2] "The Man Who Liked Dogs" supplied material for most of chapters 25-27, 32, and 35-37. From "Try the Girl," Chandler extracted chapters 1-5 and part of chapter 39. "Mandarin's Jade" contributed most of chapters 7-15, 18-22, 28, and 39. The remaining thirteen chapters were almost entirely new material.

As to characters, "The Man Who Liked Dogs" provided all of Dr. Sonderborg, Galbraith, Chief John Wax, and Red, as well as a very small part of Malloy. "Try the Girl" furnished Jessie Florian, Lieutenant Nulty, the manager, bouncer, and bartender from Florian's, the desk clerk at the Hotel San Souci, most of Moose Malloy, and the seamier side of Velma. Anne Riordan, Lindsay Marriott, Lieutenant Randall, Jules Amthor, Second Planting and the elegant part of Velma came from "Mandarin's Jade." The first of these stories gave the novel the Dr. Sonderborg and gambling ship subplots. The second story provided the

Malloy-Velma relationship.   And the third supplied the jewel
robbery gang subplot, as well as the adventure with Amthor.

Critical reaction to Farewell, My Lovely was guarded-
ly enthusiastic.   Reviewers, who were more kind than they
had been with The Big Sleep, praised the writing as being
"picturesque and vivid" and called Chandler "a neat craftsman. "[3]   But they still felt the novel was "swift and savage"
and "loose-jointed in spots. "[4]   The novel is ranked by
Chandler buffs, including Chandler himself, as the author's
best work. [5]

The novel clearly merits the praise it has received.
In no other novel did Chandler have such a command over
the English language.   His descriptions of people, things,
and feelings are brilliantly done.   For example, Moose
Malloy was "not more than six feet five inches tall and not
wider than a beer truck. "[6]   His clothes made him look
"about as inconspicuous as a tarantula on a slice of angel
food. "[7]   And the bouncer at Florian's had "a face that had
nothing to fear.   Everything had been done to it that anybody
could think of. "[8]   Objects, too, received tightly written descriptions.   The Grayle house "was not much.   It was
smaller than Buckingham Palace, rather gray for California,
and probably had fewer windows than the Chrysler Building. "[9]
Equally expert were Chandler's succinct descriptions of his
character's feelings.   Marlowe, for instance, felt "as cold
as Finnegan's feet, the day they buried him" when he was
interrupted in the act of kissing Mrs. Grayle. [10]

The plot of Farewell, My Lovely is Chandler's best.
It is complex enough to hold the reader, while containing no
ambiguities about either the action or the relationships between characters.   Chandler deftly leads his audience
throughout the novel and springs a surprise at the end.   He
carefully makes the reader believe the key to the story is
a jewel robbery gang, that, in reality, has nothing at all to
do with the plot.   The lesser subplots, such as Sonderborg's
dope racket and Brunette's criminal activities, dovetail
beautifully with the major storyline of Malloy and Velma to
form a complete, well-integrated whole.   The minor con-
necting links that hold the story together are masterful.
For example, Marlowe gives Jesse Florian one of his cards
and she puts her wet glass on top of it.   Later, when one of
Marlowe's cards turns up on the body of Lindsay Marriott,
Marlowe remarks to himself how the messy appearance of
the card does not fit in with Marriott's immaculate nature.

By the novel's end, of course, Marlowe has realized Marriott had got the card from Jesse Florian.   This and the
other instances cited above show a true craftsman at work.

In spite of Chandler's deft technique, the novel has
one flaw that is more a sign of his, and white society's,
social attitude than a literary lapse.   This is the racism
that pervades the early portion of the book, for here exists
a very definite bias against blacks.   The first major instance
of this bias occurs after the killing of Montgomery, the
black manager of Florian's.   Detective-Lieutenant Nulty is
not pleased at being assigned to the case: "'Shines.   Another
shine killing.   That's what I rate after eighteen years in
this man's police department.   No pix, no space, not even
four lines in the want-ad section.'"[11]   The police assign
only Nulty to investigate because a "shine" killing does not
rate space in the newspapers.   Nulty recalls: "'One time
there was five smokes carved Harlem sunsets on each other
down on East Eighty-four....   [A] newshawk ... makes a
face at us and says, 'Aw, hell, shines,'....   Don't even go
in the house.'"[12]

Interestingly enough, Philip Durham attributes the
inclusion of these incidents solely to Chandler's desire to
depict a bad side of the police.   Durham says, "The author,
with careful objectivity, allowed Nulty to express a repre-
hensible attitude."[13]   But Durham errs in his assessment
of Chandler's "careful objectivity."   Not only does Marlowe
label blacks "niggers" but also the novel contains the stereo-
typic black who rolls his eyes.   All the book's blacks are
loud dressers (one wears a stickpin with a green stone "not
quite as large as an apple"[14] and another a lilac-colored
suit) and we never meet an admirable black although the
other characters, no matter how unsavory, usually have
some admirable side to their nature.

The reception of Farewell, My Lovely caused Chandler some concern.   Although most reviews were favorable
and the book well publicized, first sales were not encourag-
ing, causing Chandler to wonder if he wasn't wasting his
time writing.   He felt that he might be encouraged if the
book sold over ten thousand copies.   Farewell, My Lovely
eventually sold over a million.[15]

RKO purchased the novel, for about $2000,[16] filmed
it in 1942 as The Falcon Takes Over (see p. x), and forgot about it.   But in 1944 Adrian Scott, who had just become

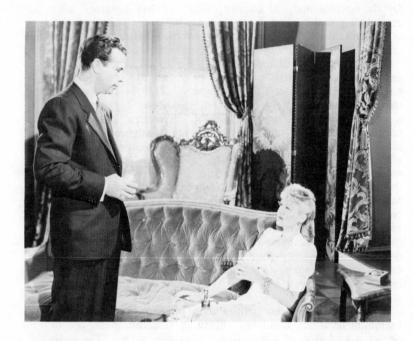

Marlowe (Dick Powell) meets Mrs. Grayle (Claire Trevor).
All photos in this chapter are from Murder, My Sweet
(RKO, 1945).

---

a producer at RKO, discovered the novel among the studio's
discarded properties.   He thought it would make a "'good,
gritty movie'" and persuaded the studio to let him work on
it. [17]   He contacted another newcomer at RKO, John Paxton,
and gave him the book.   Paxton read it the morning he came
to work. [18]   Hardly an easy way to begin a screenwriting
career!

        Both Scott and Paxton had come to Hollywood from
the New York theatre and both were on trial, working in
the "B" movie department of the studio.   From this unit
the bosses expected "strong stories" and "solid entertainment."[19]   These two factors, as well as Scott's and Paxton's respect for the "well-made play," governed their approach to adapting the novel. [20]

        Paxton wrote the screenplay in close collaboration

An unconscious Marlowe (Powell) is taken from Amthor's apartment by Moose Malloy (Mike Mazurki, center).

with Scott.   Paxton characterizes three elements he and
Scott considered in doing the script: condensation; simplification; and intensification.   Condensation and simplification
reduced many of the novel's complexities.   Paxton illustrates this by pointing out that, in the novel, Marlowe is in
conflict with both the Los Angeles and Bay City police, and
these two groups are in conflict with each other.   "This is
too complex to handle in ninety-odd minutes of film."[21]
Intensification figures heavily in Paxton's and Scott's attack
on many of Chandler's long passages.   These were "too
narrative, too aimless, too unresolved for the film [we] had
in mind."[22]   The substance of these passages was, at
times, used for "connective tissue."[23]

The main results of the scripting effort were simplification of the plot and a closer ordering of the relationship
between characters.   The film's plot is compared to that of
the novel in Table 2 at the end of this chapter.   Both plots
are quite similar in terms of key scenes.   As mentioned
above, the film eliminates all the book sections dealing with
the Bay City police and considerably reduces the role of the
Los Angeles police.   In addition, the gambler who owns Bay
City, Laird Brunette, has been dropped from the movie.
The importance of the jade has been increased in the picture
and the ending altered in terms of who killed whom.   Nevertheless, the film's plot is a fairly careful rendition of that
of the novel.

To enable Paxton and Scott to use as much of the
spirit of Chandler as possible, the two decided to let narration play an important part in the film.   But it was "narration with a difference."[24]   As Paxton puts it, the narration
served "not so much for the purposes of direct story-telling,
[but] in a subjective way[;] ... [it was] what I choose to
think of as syncopated narration, or narration that is not
directly related to the images one is seeing on the screen
at the time."[25]   For example, when Marlowe wakes up after
being knocked out next to Marriott's car, he tells the audience, in a line from the book, that he "felt like an ampu-
tated leg."   And when he tells Malloy to wait outside the
beach house, the audience learns it "was like lighting a
stick of dynamite and telling it not to go off."

The use of narration resulted in the framing of the
film by opening and closing sequences at the police station,
for Marlowe tells his story to both the audience and the police.   This narration helps to preserve the first-person

Publicity still showing Marlowe (Powell) during his drug-induced dream at Dr. Sonderborg's.

point of view which is maintained throughout the picture, except for the framing sequences in which the audience sees what the blinded Marlowe cannot. Other devices are used throughout the film to reinforce the first-person point of view. When Marlowe is beaten and drugged, the audience experiences his dream right along with him. And when the drugged Marlowe awakes, we see the motionless smoke that clouds his vision.

The film went into production with Edward Dmytryk as director. Dmytryk sought a film to help his sagging career. He had begun in 1931 as a film editor, later moving to the director's chair. But Dmytryk had consistently been assigned "B" films. By 1942 he had left Columbia and

signed a contract with RKO hoping for better films to direct. His assignments improved, and a new seven-year
contract followed, but not until Murder, My Sweet did he
receive serious critical recognition. [26]

Murder, My Sweet, which cost $500,000 and took
forty-four days to complete, [27] garnered more favorable
criticism than any other "Marlowe" film except The Big
Sleep. Reviewers praised the direction, photography, and
acting with comments such as a "superior piece of melodrama...."[28] A few negative comments concentrated on
the narration, photography, and story (certain critics found
the film confusing, but they had yet to experience The Big
Sleep). But these comments were generally in the context
of favorable reviews. Chandler himself liked the film, for
he wrote a complimentary note to Paxton after seeing the
film saying he had "considered the book untranslatable to
the screen."[29]

The film certainly deserves praise. The filmmakers
accurately captured the Chandler mood, not only in the
screenplay but also in the use of sets. Marlowe's office
projects just the right touch of shabbiness while the Grayle
mansion is bathed in elegance. Most of the film was un-
doubtably shot on a sound stage, but enough exterior and
process shots are included to make the viewer feel he has
been to Marlowe's Los Angeles. Particularly effective is
the use of the city's lights. Through the police station windows we see the gaudy neon of L. A. Marlowe's office window becomes an intermittent mirror on which the image of
Moose Malloy is projected as a neon light flickers on and
off. And from the penthouse perch of Jules Amthor, the
lights of the city stretch to the horizon. (Duplication of
this shot occurred in The Long Goodbye, showing that although Amthor and Marty Augustine lie three decades apart,
they have the same view of the city they prey upon.) These
examples help to explain why Murder, My Sweet stands out
as the most lavish-looking forties "Marlowe" film in terms
of set design. Both The Big Sleep and Lady in the Lake
relied heavily on obvious interior shots and The Brasher
Doubloon scarcely improved on the "sound-stage" look.

The film's characters differ somewhat from those of
the novel. It was Adrian Scott's idea to change Anne Riordan's character to that of Ann Grayle. Instead of being involved in the case as a free-lance journalist, as in the
book, she is a member of the family and thus has a personal

Ann Grayle (Anne Shirley): "What is it?" Marlowe (Powell): "It's a funny thing. About every third day I get hun-
gry. Always have to stop to eat something."

interest in the case.[30] Interestingly enough, Anne of the
novel finds Marlowe attractive and works at attempting to
be his girl friend. Ann of the film, on the other hand,
doesn't at first care for Marlowe and only develops a
strong attraction for him at the end of the picture. The
Malloy character also underwent alteration and enlarge-
ment. Paxton said:

> We liked him and wanted to use him more, so
> he took on some of the functions of some of the
> other assorted cop-goons hanging about the
> story.... I intensified him in several ways: I
> made him more simple-minded than Chandler did,
> less articulate, more monosyllabic, more unpre-
> dictable--and consequently, I think, more menac-
> ing....[31]

Ann's father received more of a part in the film than in the

novel, and a good number of minor characters have been
eliminated from the picture, including the blacks which
Chandler so unflatteringly described.

The acting of the supporting players is of high quality, with honors going to Claire Trevor as Mrs. Grayle.
Although the film did nothing for her career,[32] she played
her role well. The careful way she says her lines, coupled
with the self-assured manner in which she moves, effectively conveys the calm self-assurance of the novel's character. She tells Marlowe she wants him to help her kill
Amthor without batting an eyelash, while Marlowe spills his
drink in surprise. And when she reveals to Marlowe that
the necklace was never stolen, it is with the satisfied
naughty look of a child who has just played a joke on a
group of adults and gotten away with it. She stands out,
perhaps, as the most effective female character of any
Marlowe film. Claire Trevor's performance comes straight
out of Chandler; the epitome of the beautiful, deceitful,
rotten-to-the-core blonde that the author was so fond of
describing.

The main concern here, of course, lies with Dick
Powell's Marlowe. Murder, My Sweet remains the only
Marlowe film that advanced the career of the actor who
played Chandler's detective. The next four Marlowe films
merely helped to establish the stars more solidly in their
respective careers, as did the latest Marlowe picture. And
although The Long Goodbye did help the career of its star,
it was nothing to the boost Powell received.

Powell began in motion pictures as a song-and-dance
man and during the 1930's he made more than thirty musi-
cals for Warner Bros. and other studios. By 1940 his
constant urging for Warner to cast him in dramatic roles
had not borne fruit. He purchased his contract release
from Warner and free-lanced. But even then he could not
get the roles he wanted and took a year off from acting. In
1942 he was under contract to Paramount, and, although his
singing parts decreased and he got some dramatic roles,
Powell still wanted something to break his musical-comedy
star screen image. Paramount purchased Double Indemnity
(Chandler co-authored the screenplay) and Powell pushed for
the lead role. Paramount refused him the part and he left
the studio to sign a contract with RKO in May, 1944.[33]

Preparation of Murder, My Sweet naturally included

Marlowe (Powell) and Ann (Anne Shirley) find Mr. Grayle
(Miles Mander) on the edge of desperation.

finding an actor to play Marlowe. Paxton and Scott had
given much thought to using Bogart, but he was unavailable.
(Bogart was, in fact, just finishing his acting chores for
the first version of The Big Sleep, to be discussed in the
next chapter.) The two were willing to settle for John Gar-
field, who had just finished a couple of films for the studio.
But the head of RKO, who had not read the script, gave the
screenplay to Dick Powell. Besides Powell's eagerness for
a better part, he was also in demand because he had been
excused from military service. [34] Powell got the part and
"figured it would be my best or my last picture.... It
turned out to be the best." [35]

The studio sympathized with Powell's image problem,
even changing the name of the film for him.   The picture
originally used the novel's title and was "produced, previewed, and even advertised under" it. [36]   But RKO execu-
tives thought the title, <u>Farewell, My Lovely</u>, coupled with
Dick Powell's presence, would make the audience think this
was another musical.   Some work by Audience Research Inc.
confirmed this suspicion and a new title hurriedly emerged. [37]
<u>Murder, My Sweet</u> did for Powell what he had hoped, and
he went on to play "tough guys" in his subsequent films.
(An "in" joke about Powell's musical reputation occurs in
the film when Powell does a dance step in the musical-
stage-like marble hall of the Grayle mansion.)

Powell is a superb Marlowe.   He manages to blend
his own slightly boyish charm and innocence perfectly into
the character.   His terse narration and dialogue composed
of Chandler and Chandler-type lines effectively captures the
spirit of Chandler's hero.   For example, Powell remarks
that suddenly Jessie Florian "was cool.   Like someone making funeral arrangements for a murder, not yet committed."
And later when Marriott says he doesn't like Marlowe's
manner, Powell replies, in a line partially from the book,
"I've had complaints about it, but it keeps getting worse."
Perhaps the best aspect of Powell's Marlowe is the way
he treads the fine line between the hero's code of honor and
corruption.   This becomes particularly well illustrated when
one examines the handling of money throughout the film.
Several times throughout the picture Powell receives money
from his clients.   His clients then assume he is corruptible
and can be bought.   He astonishes them, subsequently, with
his sense of ethics.

Several bits of business add depth to Powell's characterization.   Marlowe retrieves the bottle from which he
supplied Jessie Florian with liquor, demonstrating his frugal-
ity.   His smooth forcefulness with police is indicated when
Lieutenant Randall takes out a pack of cigarettes.   Powell
takes the pack, helps himself, gives Randall a cigarette, and
puts the pack in his pocket.   Powell's boyish, mischievous
nature manifests itself when he strikes a match on the back-
side of a cupid statue.   Finally, his frequent sniffing of
cigarettes keeps his hands in motion, demonstrating his
curiosity to examine things.

<u>Murder, My Sweet</u> certainly emerges as an excellent
film that wears well thirty years after its production.

Everson credits it with starting a private eye film cycle,[38] and it is unquestionably one of the best private eye films ever made.

TABLE 2.   PLOT COMPARISON

Farewell, My Lovely / Murder, My Sweet

NOVEL	FILM
1.	A blinded Marlowe is being questioned by the police about his involvement in several murders. He tells Lieutenants Randall and Nulty his story.
2. Marlowe is dragged into Florian's, an all-black bar, by a large man, Moose Malloy. Malloy is looking for a girl named Velma, whom he hasn't seen since he went to prison eight years ago. Velma used to sing at Florian's when it was white. No one remembers Velma and Malloy runs into trouble. He kills the owner of the bar and leaves. Marlowe calls the police. A detective lieutenant named Nulty gets the case. Nulty asks Marlowe to look for Velma and Marlowe agrees.	
3.	A large man named Moose Malloy hires Marlowe to find a girl. Malloy takes Marlowe to Florian's, the bar where the girl, Velma, used to work. Malloy hasn't seen her since he went to prison eight years ago. Florian's has changed hands and no one remembers Velma. Malloy runs into trouble and he and Marlowe leave. Malloy tells Marlowe to keep looking for Velma and he will be in contact with Marlowe.

4.   Marlowe learns that the former owner of Florian's is dead but his widow, Jessie, is still alive. Marlowe goes to see Jessie and finds she is a drunk. He plies her with liquor and asks her about Velma. She gives Marlowe some photographs but tries to hide a picture of Velma. She refuses to say why she hid it and says Velma is dead.

Marlowe learns that the former owner of Florian's is dead but his widow, Jessie, is still alive. Marlowe goes to see Jessie and finds she is a drunk. He plies her with liquor and asks her about Velma. She gives Marlowe some photographs but tries to hide a picture of Velma. She refuses to say why she hid it and says Velma is dead.

5.

Marlowe leaves, but waits outside the door. He sees Jessie calling someone.

6.   Marlowe sees Nulty and tells what happened with Jessie. Marlowe suggests Nulty should find out who turned Malloy in for the reward when he was sent to jail. Nulty asks Marlowe if Jessie paid him to lay off.

7.   Marlowe goes to his office and gets a call from a man named Lindsay Marriott, asking him to come and see Marriott. Marlowe agrees.

8.

Marlowe goes to his office and finds a man named Marriott there. Marriott says he got Marlowe's name from the classified ads. He wants Marlowe to go with him to buy back some jewels that were stolen. Marlowe says he can't do anything for Marriott, but that he'll go along anyway.

9.   Nulty calls and says Malloy went to see Jessie. He asks Marlowe for more help, but Marlowe refuses.

10.   Marlowe goes to see Marriott. Marriott says a

(TABLE 2 cont.)

very rare jade necklace was
stolen in a hold-up from
one of his friends.   He is
going to buy it back and
wants Marlowe to go along.
He says he picked Mar-
lowe's name out of the
phone book.   Marlowe
says he doesn't think he
can help Marriott, but that
he'll go along anyway.

11.   Marlowe and Marriott drive   Marlowe and Marriott drive to
        to the rendezvous and find   the rendezvous spot and find it
        it deserted.   Marlowe   deserted.   Marlowe leaves the
        leaves the car to investi-   car to investigate, but finds
        gate, but finds no one.   no one.   He returns to the car
        He returns to the car and   and is knocked out.
        is knocked out.

12.   Marlowe awakes to find
        the car gone.   He follows
        its tracks and finds it
        empty.   A girl comes.
        She tells Marlowe that
        Marriott is dead and leads
        him to the body.   Mar-
        riott has been beaten to
        death.   Marlowe searches
        the body and finds an ex-
        tra cigarette case.   The
        girl, Anne Riordan, tells
        Marlowe she happened to
        be driving by and spotted
        Marlowe's flashlight.   Mar-
        lowe tells Anne to take him
        back to his car.

13.   Marlowe awakes to find a flash-
                                             light shining in his face.   A
                                             girl asks if he is all right,
                                             gets a good look at Marlowe's
                                             face, and runs away before he
                                             can stop her.   Marlowe finds
                                             Marriott dead in the car.   He
                                             has been beaten to death.

14.   Marlowe goes to the police
        and is questioned by Lieu-
        tenant Randall.   Randall
        suggests Marriott planned

to steal the money but was
killed by an accomplice.
Marlowe doesn't like that
idea. Randall shows Mar-
lowe the extra cigarette
case. The cigarettes that
were in it are gone.

15.

Marlowe calls the police and
is questioned by Randall and
Nulty. Randall suggests Marlowe is a contact for a jewel
robbery mob. They ran out of
uses for him and are trying to
pin a murder on him. The
police are skeptical of Marlowe's story but let him go,
after warning him to stay away
from one of Marriott's friends,
Jules Amthor.

16. Marlowe goes to his office
and finds Anne waiting for
him. She says she knows
who the necklace belongs
to. She says her father
was Bay City police chief
until a mob of gamblers led
by Laird Brunette had him
fired. The necklace be-
longs to the very rich
Mrs. Lewin Lockridge
Grayle. Anne says Mrs.
Grayle will talk with Marlowe. Marlowe says the
jade is probably lost be-
cause of Marriott's death.
Anne gives Marlowe the
cigarettes she took from
Marriott's cigarette case.

17.

Marlowe finds a girl waiting in
his office. She says she is a
newspaper woman and wants
information about Marriott and
the jade necklace. Marlowe is
suspicious and learns the girl
is really Ann Grayle. Ann
says the necklace was stolen
from her stepmother. Marlowe wants to see her father
and stepmother.

(TABLE 2 cont.)

18.   Marlowe finds a card that
       says "Jules Amthor Psy-
       chic Consultant" in Mar-
       riott's cigarette's mouth-
       piece.   Marlowe calls
       Amthor and arranges to
       see him.   Marlowe learns
       Marriott holds a trust deed
       to Jessie Florian's house.

19.   Marlowe goes to see Jes-
       sie.   A neighbor tells
       Marlowe that Jessie gets a
       registered letter every
       month.   Marlowe tells
       Jessie he knows about Mar-
       riott's trust deed.   She
       pulls a gun on Marlowe
       and he leaves.

20.   Marlowe gets a call asking
       him to come to the Grayle
       house.

21.   Marlowe sees Mrs. Grayle.
       She explains about the rob-
       bery and says Marriott was
       a blackmailer of women.

22.   Marlowe and Ann go to her
                                         father's house. Mr. Grayle is
                                         a rich old man who collects
                                         jade. He tells Marlowe the
                                         necklace was very valuable and
                                         he wants it back without pub-
                                         licity. Marlowe questions
                                         Mrs. Grayle. She says the
                                         necklace was stolen from her
                                         and that she knows Amthor
                                         slightly. Marlowe asks her to
                                         locate Amthor for him. The
                                         butler announces Amthor. Mar-
                                         lowe says he wants to talk to
                                         Amthor later.

23.   Marlowe goes to his apartment.
                                         Mrs. Grayle comes, gives
                                         Marlowe a retainer, and takes
                                         him to a night club. She leaves
                                         him on an excuse and Marlowe
                                         meets Ann in a booth. She

says her stepmother is leading
Marlowe off the track and tries
to buy Marlowe off the case.
Marlowe spots Malloy. Malloy
says he wants Marlowe to meet
someone.

24. An Indian named Second
     Planting takes Marlowe to
     see Amthor.   Marlowe
     asks why Amthor's cards
     were in the cigarette
     holders but Amthor says
     he doesn't know.   Mar-
     lowe suggests Amthor told
     Marriott what women to
     date so they could be set
     up for robbery.   Amthor
     and Planting beat up Mar-
     lowe.

25.   Malloy takes Marlowe to see
                                   Amthor, who has told Malloy
                                   that Marlowe knows where
                                   Velma is.   Marlowe says Mar-
                                   riott was a blackmailer of
                                   women and a jewel robber and
                                   that Amthor told Marriott which
                                   women to cultivate.   Amthor
                                   says he wants the necklace.
                                   Marlowe says he hasn't got it.
                                   Malloy and Amthor beat up
                                   Marlowe.

26. When Marlowe comes to,
     two Bay City policemen
     are there.   They drive him
     away from Amthor's and
     knock him out.

27. Marlowe wakes up three   Marlowe wakes up three days
     days later to find himself   later to find himself in a
     in a locked room, drugged.   locked room, drugged.   He
     He regains his senses and   regains his senses and breaks
     breaks out of the room.   out of the room.

28. Marlowe discovers Malloy
     in another room but doesn't
     let Malloy see him.

29. Marlowe confronts the man
     in charge, Dr. Sonderborg,
     who says the Bay City po-
     lice brought him there.
     Marlowe goes to Anne's.

(TABLE 2 cont.)

30.   Marlowe confronts the man in
                                       charge, Dr. Sonderborg, but
                                       learns nothing. He leaves and
                                       meets Malloy. Malloy says
                                       Amthor was lying to him and
                                       Malloy wants Marlowe to keep
                                       looking for Velma. Marlowe
                                       goes to see Ann.

31. Marlowe tells Anne what
     happened and says he
     doesn't think Amthor is
     the leader of a jewl rob-
     bery gang.

32.   Ann doesn't want to see Mar-
                                       lowe, but he forces his way in.
                                       Marlowe tells her what hap-
                                       pened and realizes she was the
                                       one who turned the flashlight
                                       on him when he was with Mar-
                                       riott. Marlowe says she
                                       thought he was her father and
                                       that her father could have
                                       killed Marriott out of jealousy.
                                       Randall and Nulty come. Mar-
                                       lowe tells them about Sonder-
                                       borg. They have been to the
                                       Grayle house but Mrs. Grayle
                                       wasn't there.

33. Randall comes to see
     Marlowe and he tells Ran-
     dall what happened. Mar-
     lowe tells Randall that
     Marriott blackmailed women
     and was the finger man for
     a jewel mob. Marriott was
     killed because he had out-
     lived his usefulness. Ran-
     dall knows that Marriott
     held the trust deed and
     has found out about Mar-
     lowe's interest about Mal-
     loy and Velma. Marlowe
     tells Randall he saw Malloy
     at Sonderborg's.

34.   Marlowe and Ann go to see
                                       Ann's father. He is desper-
                                       ately loading a gun. He says

the police came and asked
about the beach house Marriott
rented.   Mr. Grayle wants
Marlowe to stop investigating
and Marlowe agrees.   Marlowe
tells Ann he is going to the
beach house and that he can't
stop his investigation.

35.   Marlowe and Randall go to
      see Jessie Florian and find
      her dead.   Her neck has
      been broken by Malloy, but
      Marlowe says Malloy didn't
      mean to kill her.   Randall
      says Amthor and Sonder-
      borg have left town.

36.   Marlowe and Ann go to the
                                            beach house and find Mrs.
                                            Grayle.   Ann leaves.   Mrs.
                                            Grayle says Amthor is black-
                                            mailing her.   He has found
                                            out she has seen other men
                                            and she doesn't want her hus-
                                            band to know.   Amthor wanted
                                            the jade as blackmail payment
                                            but before she could give it to
                                            him, it was stolen.   She says
                                            Amthor thought Marriott stole
                                            the jade, so he killed Marriott.
                                            Perhaps Marlowe would be
                                            blamed for the murder.   Mrs.
                                            Grayle wants Marlowe to help
                                            her kill Amthor.   Marlowe
                                            agrees and says he will bring
                                            Amthor to the beach house the
                                            next evening.

37.   Marlowe goes to the Bay
      City police chief to find
      the two men, Blane and
      Galbraith, who took him
      to Sonderborg's.   Gal-
      braith tells Marlowe he
      and Blane kept people from
      bothering Amthor and he
      doesn't know what Sonder-
      borg's racket is.   But
      Galbraith thinks and Mar-
      lowe agrees, Sonderborg
      hid men on the run.   Mar-
      lowe wants to know where

(TABLE 2 cont.)

a man on the run might go
after leaving Sonderborg's.
Galbraith suggests the
gambling ships Laird
Brunette owns.

38.
                                 Marlowe goes to see Amthor
                                 and finds him dead. Malloy
                                 has broken his neck. Malloy
                                 comes to Marlowe's office.
                                 Marlowe says Malloy didn't
                                 mean to kill Amthor, but just
                                 shook him too hard. Malloy
                                 asks if the police have Velma.
                                 Marlowe shows Malloy the pic-
                                 ture he got from Jessie Flori-
                                 an.   The photo is a fake; it
                                 isn't Velma. Marlowe tells
                                 Malloy to come back the next
                                 evening and he'll take him to
                                 Velma.

39.   After some difficulty,
      Marlowe gets on board
      one of Brunette's gambling
      ships. He confronts Brun-
      ette, tells him some of
      what has happened, and
      says he wants to see Mal-
      loy. Brunette denies know-
      ing Malloy but agrees to
      see that Malloy gets a
      message from Marlowe.

40.   Marlowe returns to his
      apartment and calls Mrs.
      Grayle. She agrees to
      come over. Malloy comes
      and Marlowe says he didn't
      mean to kill Jessie Florian.
      Mrs. Grayle comes and
      Malloy hides in another
      room.

41.
                                 Marlowe and Malloy go to the
                                 beach house. Marlowe tells
                                 Malloy to wait outside. Mar-
                                 lowe goes in. Mrs. Grayle is
                                 there. Marlowe says Amthor
                                 is coming. Mrs. Grayle gives
                                 Marlowe the jade. It was

Mrs. Grayle (Claire Trevor) gets the drop on Marlowe (Powell).
She says: "I could like you, I could like you a lot. It's too bad
it has to be like this."

never stolen. Mrs. Grayle
said it was to keep Amthor
from getting it.

42. Marlowe tells Mrs. Grayle
     that he doesn't think Mar-
     riott was involved with
     jewel robbers and that the
     jade necklace was never
     stolen. Marriott went to
     the rendezvous spot think-
     ing he was going to kill
     Marlowe. Marlowe says
     Jessie and Marriott knew
     about Mrs. Grayle's past.
     Marriott was dangerous to
     Mrs. Grayle, so she killed
     him. Mrs. Grayle draws
     a gun on Marlowe.

43.   Marlowe says Mrs. Grayle

(TABLE 2 cont.)

killed Marriott.   Marriott
thought he was taking Marlowe
to be killed.   Jessie told Marriott about Marlowe.   Mrs.
Grayle planned to kill both
Marriott and Marlowe, but Ann
came.   Mrs. Grayle wants
help, but Marlowe refuses.
He says she asked help from
Malloy eight years ago.   She
and Malloy did something that
could send her to jail and
that's what Amthor was using
to blackmail her.   She pulls a
gun on Marlowe.

44.   Malloy enters the room.
      Mrs. Grayle is Velma.
      She shoots Malloy and tries
      to shoot Marlowe, but the
      gun is empty. She leaves.
      Marlowe calls the police
      and Malloy dies.

45.

Ann and her father come.   Mr.
Grayle takes Marlowe's gun.
Marlowe inadvertently tells
Mrs. Grayle that Amthor is
dead.   She is going to shoot
Marlowe but Mr. Grayle shoots
her.   Marlowe calls the police.
Malloy enters and sees Mrs.
Grayle, who is Velma, dead.
He goes to Mr. Grayle.   Marlowe tries to stop Mr. Grayle
from shooting Malloy, but he
is blinded by the gun's smoke
and, as he passes out, he
hears shots.

46.   Marlowe is with Anne.
      Mrs. Grayle has escaped.
      The photo Jessie gave Mar-
      lowe was false.   Velma
      had turned Malloy in eight
      years ago.   Amthor was
      an international con man
      but had nothing to do with
      the murders or Sonderborg.
      Velma is discovered by a
      detective in Baltimore.

She kills him and shoots
herself. She never could
have been prosecuted, but
Marlowe says she shot herself to spare her husband
the trial.

47.

At the police station Randall
and Nulty let Marlowe go because Ann has backed up Marlowe's story. Malloy was shot
twice by Mr. Grayle and they
fought for the gun. The third
shot killed Mr. Grayle. Marlowe expresses his admiration
for Ann and they go off together.

Chapter 3

THE BIG SLEEP

Chandler experienced trouble with his first novel,
The Big Sleep, and this novel illustrates many of the
strengths and weaknesses of his writing. The book contains
many of Chandler's classic characters: the big-time gambler; the elderly millionaire; the corrupt rich women; and
the petty hoods. Seldom does Chandler better describe
these and other characters. But the plot of The Big Sleep
is a confused tangle that demonstrates Chandler's problem
of producing a cohesive story line. The novel, therefore,
should be looked upon as a beginning; an expert character
study that gave the author a chance to experiment with plotting techniques.

The narrative opens when General Sternwood hires
Marlowe to investigate the blackmail of one of his daughters,
Carmen, by Arthur Geiger. Previously, Carmen had been
blackmailed by Joe Brody. The General also expresses his
displeasure that Rusty Regan, his friend and the husband of
his other daughter, Vivian, abruptly left the household.

Marlowe investigates Geiger and learns he runs a
pornographic book racket. An evening session at Geiger's
house leaves Geiger dead, Carmen naked and drugged, and
photographs of Carmen missing. Marlowe takes Carmen
home and returns to Geiger's to find his body gone. A
homicide man, Bernie Ohls, informs Marlowe that the Sternwood's chauffeur, Owen Taylor, has been found dead in the
ocean. Marlowe learns that Taylor was in love with Carmen.

Vivian tells Marlowe of a blackmail attempt on her
by someone who has the photographs of Carmen. She can
raise the blackmail payment by borrowing it from Eddie
Mars, the gambler whose wife Rusty Regan was supposed to
have run off with. Marlowe goes to see Brody and explains
how Brody is taking over Geiger's blackmail racket. Marlowe

TABLE 3.   THE BIG SLEEP

Cast*

Philip Marlowe	Humphrey Bogart
Vivian	Lauren Bacall
Carmen	Martha Vickers
General Sternwood	Charles Waldron
Eddie Mars	John Ridgely
Norris	Charles D. Brown
Bernie Ohls	Regis Toomey
Joe Brody	Louis Jean Heydt
Harry Jones	Elisha Cook, Jr.
Canino	Bob Steele
Agnes	Sonia Darrin
Arthur Geiger	Theadore Von Eltz
Mona Mars	Peggy Knudsen
Girl in Bookshop	Dorothy Malone
Girl Taxi Driver	Joy Barlowe
Carol Lundgren	Tom Rafferty
Sidney	Tom Fadden
Pete	Ben Welden
Art Huck	Trevor Bardette

*Also included in an early cast list
were James Flavin as Captain Cron-
jager, Thomas Jackson as District
Attorney Wilde and Dan Wallace as
Owen Taylor. Their parts were
eliminated when the picture was
shortened.

Credits

Produced by	Howard Hawks
Directed by	Howard Hawks
Screenplay by	William Faulkner
	Leigh Brackett
	Jules Furthman
Based on novel by	Raymond Chandler
Dir. of Photog.	Sid Hickox, A.S.C.
Special Effects by	Warren E. Lynch,
	A.S.C. (Dir.)
	E. Roy Davidson
Art Director	Carl Jules Weyl
Set Decorations	Fred M. MacLean
Sound by	Robert B. Lee
Music by	Max Steiner
Musical Director	Leo F. Forbstein
Wardrobe by	Leah Rhodes
Edited by	Christian Nyby
Asst. Director	Robert Vreeland
Makeup Artist	Perc Westmore
Unit Manager	Chuck Hansen
Unit Publicist	Jack Diamond

A Warner Brothers-First National picture
Running time: 114 minutes
Release date: August 31, 1946

---

knows Brody has the photographs of Carmen.   Brody stole
the photographs from Taylor.   Carol Lundgren, Geiger's
homosexual partner, kills Brody and Marlowe turns him into
the police.   Carol moved Geiger's body so his relationship
with Geiger wouldn't be discovered.

Marlowe goes to Mars' gambling club.   Vivian is
there.   Mars and Vivian try to make it look as if there is
nothing between them, but Marlowe doesn't buy it.   Vivian
refuses to tell Marlowe what Mars has on her.   Marlowe
returns to his apartment to find Carmen naked in his bed.
He throws her out.

Harry Jones, a friend of Brody's girl, Agnes, says
Agnes can tell Marlowe where Eddie Mars' wife is.   Mars'
man, Canino, murders Jones, but fails to find Agnes.
Agnes tells Marlowe where Mona Mars is hiding.   Marlowe
goes there and is captured by Canino, but Marlowe kills
Canino.   Marlowe solves the case when he discovers Car-
men, an epileptic, killed Regan because he rejected her.
Mars knew Vivian and was blackmailing her.

Chandler wrote The Big Sleep in three months in
1938 and it was published in early 1939. However, much of
the novel existed long before that. Two of his short stories
comprised the bulk of the text: "Killer in the Rain" (Black
Mask, January, 1935); and "The Curtain" (Black Mask,
September, 1936). In addition, "Finger Man" (Black Mask,
October, 1934) and "Mandarin's Jade" (Dime Detective
Magazine, November, 1937) supplied two small portions of
the story. From "Killer in the Rain" came material for
chapters 4, 6-10, and 12-16. "The Curtain" supplied most
of the chapters 1-3, 20, and 27-32. "Mandarin's Jade" furnished a small part of chapter 11 while "Finger Man" contributed chapter 22 and a small section of chapter 23. New
material comprised chapters 5, 17-19, 21, part of 23, and
24-26.[1] To put it another way, "Roughly, one third of the
novel drew from 'The Curtain', one third from 'Killer in
the Rain', and one third was entirely new."[2]

According to Durham, "Of the twenty-one characters
in The Big Sleep, seven were drawn directly from 'The Curtain,' six were taken from 'Killer in the Rain,' four were
composites from the two stories, and four were new creations."[3] Among the more important characters, "The Curtain" provided General Sternwood, Mona Mars, Vivian Regan, Rusty Regan, Art Huck, Norris, and Canino. "Killer
in the Rain" furnished all or part of characters such as
Carmen Sternwood, Owen Taylor, Joe Brody, Bernie Ohls,
Eddie Mars, Arthur Geiger, and Agnes. From "Killer in
the Rain" came the blackmail plot against Carmen, Geiger's
pornographic book racket, Owen Taylor's death, and the
confrontation in Joe Brody's apartment. "The Curtain" gave
the Sternwood greenhouse, the shoot-out at Huck's, and the
book's denouement.

Durham used The Big Sleep as a representative example of Chandler's short story expansion technique:

> At times Chandler lifted whole passages, chang-
> ing only a word here and there to improve syntax
> or vary a mood. More frequently, however, he
> blew up scenes for the novel. An example is the
> greenhouse scene, which accounts for approximately
> 1100 words in 'The Curtain,' but is enlarged to
> 2500 words in The Big Sleep.
>   In miniature, the transformation developed as
> follows: forty-two words from 'The Curtain':
>   The air steamed. The walls and ceiling of

the glass house dripped. In the half light enor-
mous tropical plants spread their blooms and
branches all over the place, and the smell of
them was almost as overpowering as the smell
of boiling alcohol.

became eighty-two words in The Big Sleep:
The air was thick, wet, steamy and larded with
the cloying smell of tropical orchids in bloom.
The glass walls and roof were heavily misted
and big drops of moisture splashed down on the
plants. The light had an unreal greenish color,
like light filtered through an aquarium tank.
The plants filled the place, a forest of them,
with nasty meaty leaves and stalks like the
newly washed fingers of dead men. They
smelled as overpowering as boiling alcohol under a blanket. [4]

Mixed critical reaction awaited Chandler's first novel.
Some reviewers praised the book, citing it for its "subtle
workmanship.... "[5] Others compared it to Dashiell Hammett's work, characterizing Chandler as "an author who
makes Dashiell Hammett seem as innocuous as Winnie-the-
Pooh. "[6] But most important to Chandler were the reviews
which dealt with "the depravity and unpleasantness of the
book. "[7] These upset the author, who remarked, "I do not
want to write depraved books.... I was more intrigued by
a situation where the mystery is solved more by the exposi-
tion of a single character, always in evidence, than by the
slow and sometimes long-winded concentration of circumstances. "[8] The negative reviews may have had their effect
on Chandler in terms of violence and his hero. In The Big
Sleep, as well as in Chandler's short stories, the hero
metes out as much violence as he receives. But in the five
novels following The Big Sleep, Marlowe never shoots anyone; indeed, only once fires a gun.

The Big Sleep contains strengths and weaknesses.
The novel neatly outlines many character types that appeared in later books: the big-time gambler; the decadent
rich; the flashy but deadly women; the tough hoods; and the
tough but basically honest L. A. police. And, of course,
the hardboiled but honest detective, for the novel introduced
Marlowe to the reading public. Furthermore, The Big Sleep
defines Marlowe's role in society. / As the cynical detective
states in an oft-quoted passage: "I looked down at the
chessboard. The move with the knight was wrong. I put it

back where I had moved it from.   Knights had no meaning
in this game.   It wasn't a game for knights. "9   But, of
course, Marlowe will himself function in all the Chandler
novels as such a knight, playing games where his moral and
ethical standards don't belong and where his opponents cannot understand him because they don't subscribe to these
ideals.   And yet, because of these standards, Marlowe sees
these games through.   But the plotting weaknesses, which
range from the trivial (labeling the same car both a Buick
and a Packard) to the serious (the unsatisfactory explanation
of Owen Taylor's death), serve to detract from The Big
Sleep's strengths.   Chandler himself recognized the novel's
faults and where he was headed.

> [The novel was] very uniquely written.   There
> are scenes that are all right, but there are other
> scenes still much too pulpy.   Insofar as I am
> able I want to develop the objective method--but
> slowly--to the point where I can carry the audi-
> ence over into a genuine dramatic, even melo-
> dramatic novel, written in a very vivid and pun-
> gent style, but not slangy or overly vernacular. 10

The Big Sleep can best be summed up in Chandler's
own words.   He called it a "detective yarn that happens to
be more interested in people than in plot. "11

Warner Bros. began production of The Big Sleep in
1944 and the cast and crew roster looked something like a
reuinion program for To Have and Have Not (1944), a new-
ly-completed Warner film.   Howard Hawks, known for his
fast-paced comedies and action-adventure films, signed to
direct.   Warner cast their most popular box-office duo,
Humphrey Bogart and Lauren Bacall, in the picture.   Scripting chores went to two veterans, William Faulkner and
Jules Furthman, and a newcomer, Leigh Brackett.   All of
these except Brackett had worked on To Have and Have Not.

Brackett was new to scriptwriting.   A friend saw to
it that one of her mystery novels got into the hands of
Hawks.   Hawks liked the novel's dialogue and hired Brackett, although he was somewhat shaken to learn she was a

---

Facing page: (top) Marlowe (Humphrey Bogart) meets Carmen
Sternwood (Martha Vickers) at the Sternwood mansion.   (Bottom) Librarian (Carole Douglas): "You know, you don't look
like a man who'd be interested in first editions. "   Marlowe
(Bogart): "I collect blondes in bottles, too. "   All photos in
this chapter are from The Big Sleep (Warner Bros. , 1946).

woman.   Brackett and Faulkner worked independent of each
other and of director-producer Hawks.   Faulkner, high man
on the writing totem pole, marked alternate sets of chapters
in the book; he did one set and Brackett the other.   Neither
of them saw what the other wrote, with finished portions of
the screenplay going directly to Hawks. [12]   The filmmakers
struggled through Chandler's complex plot and the scripting
produced the now-legendary query to Chandler concerning
who killed Owen Taylor.   (The filmmakers were confused
over the manner of Owen Taylor's death, so they telegraphed
or telephoned Chandler.   Because the author had not himself
satisfactorily explained the chauffeur's death in the novel,
he could not provide them an answer.)

The resultant long script became even longer with
Hawks' additions to it, and Jules Furthman got the task of
rewriting or cutting the unshot portions of the screenplay. [13]
This resulted in the wholesale lopping off of the script's
last twenty-eight pages, shortening the screenplay about 15
per cent.   Table 4 compares the novel, script, and film
plots.   (The script used here was published in Film Scripts
One. [14]   A later one that includes revisions made during
filming is on file in the Lincoln Center Theatre Research
Library.)   The film follows the book quite closely both in
terms of plot and characterizations.   Film censorship
caused the pornographic nature of Geiger's book store, the
homosexual relationship between Geiger and Lundgren, and
Carmen's nudity to be eliminated, although the context in
which these were used was not.   This helped to confuse the
plot even further.   For example, Geiger's book store appears in the film almost as it is described in the novel.
But without the knowledge that Geiger rents out pornographic
books, the mystery surrounding the store remains unexplained.

Much of the film more closely resembles the book
than the script, as though Hawks and Furthman decided to
work directly from the novel in their shortening efforts.
Interestingly enough, the film has two endings: one when
Marlowe explains about Carmen, as in the novel; and the

Facing page: (top) referring to a key to Geiger's house,
Marlowe (Bogart) says: "How'd you happen to have one?"
Eddie Mars (John Ridgely): "Is that any of your business?"
Marlowe: "I could make it my business."   Mars: "I could
make your business mine."   Marlowe: "You wouldn't like
it, the pay's too small."   (Bottom) two of Mars' men, Sid-
ney (Tom Fadden, left) and Pete (Bed Welden) search Marlowe (Bogart).

second when Mars dies in a hail of bullets from his own men
and Marlowe tells the police Mars killed Regan. This
second ending is somewhat ambiguous, for Marlowe may be
protecting Carmen by letting Mars take the blame for the
murder. The evidence seems to be against this, however,
for if Mars didn't kill Regan the violent end forced upon him
by an enraged Marlowe hardly seems justified.

It is interesting to note that one scene in the film
came uncredited from Chandler. Hawks stated: "The main
idea was to try and make every scene fun to look at. A
place where Bogart was to walk into a book store I said,
'This is an awfully ordinary scene. Can't you think of
something to do?' And he just pushed up his hat brim, put
on glasses and got a little effeminate. The moment he did
that, I said, 'O.K., come on, we're off, I'll write some
new dialogue when we're inside.' But just going in that way
made it fun...."[15] But Chandler, not Hawks or Bogart,
originated this effeminate touch, for Marlowe says, "I had
my horn-rimmed glasses on. I put my voice high and let a
bird twitter in it."[16]

The production history of The Big Sleep almost
matches the novel itself for involvement. Warner Bros.
shipped an early version of the picture to servicemen overseas in the early fall of 1944. (This previewing of films
overseas was, apparently, a common practice during the
war.[17]) Eight months after completion of the picture,
Warner called for more scenes between Bogart and Bacall.[18]
Not only were they very popular at this time, but their
May 21, 1945, marriage made them an even more successful box-office team. In addition, the actress who originally
played Mona Mars (name unknown) may have been replaced
by someone Hawks presumably liked better. Paxton Davis
maintains the Bogart/Bacall scene additions resulted in
slight differences in both the age and clothes of these actors
in different parts of the picture.[19]

Domestic release of The Big Sleep came in August,
1946. Just as Chandler's novel had been compared to Hammett's, so too was the film compared with a Hammett film,
The Maltese Falcon, in which Bogart played Sam Spade.
Initially it was not the critics that made this comparison,
but Warner Bros. themselves in a trailer advertising the
picture, the dialogue of which ran:

Girl: 'Can I help you, sir?'

Joe Brody (Louis Jean Heydt) is losing command of the situation in his own apartment.   Under the gun are Marlowe
(Bogart) and Vivian Sternwood (Lauren Bacall).

Bogart: 'Oh, yeah.   I'm looking for a good
mystery on something off the beaten track, like
The Maltese Falcon. '
Girl: 'Oh that was a fascinating story.   But
here's one that has everything the Falcon had and
more.   It's Raymond Chandler's latest [this is
seven years after the novel's publication, remem-
ber], The Big Sleep.   What a picture that'll make. '
Bogart: 'Mind if I look at it?   Huh.   "Sometimes I wonder what strange fate brought me out
of the storm to that house that stood alone in the
shadows.   As I probed into its mysteries, every
clue told me a different story.   But each had the
same ending: murder.   Every instinct warned me

to beware that something more dangerous, more
deadly than I'd ever known before was in that
room. And suddenly--'"[20]

   The picture was criticized on two counts: a confused
plot and violence. Bosley Crowther, who had not read the
novel before he saw the film summed up the frustration of
some critics: "... it's likely to leave you confused and
dissatisfied. And, by the way, would someone tell us the
meaning of the title, 'The Big Sleep. '"[21] (The title means,
of course, death, and interestingly enough was explained in
the script, but not in the film.) Even Howard Hawks wasn't
sure what the title meant and himself could not figure out
the plot. "I never figured out what was going on, but I
thought the basic thing had great scenes in it and it was
good entertainment. After that got by, I said, 'I'm never
going to worry about being logical again. '"[22] At least one
critic, however, found the intricate plot an asset to The Big
Sleep and said it is a "uniquely American classic. The fast
pace of the movie, which entailed loose ends criticized by
many reviewers, seems in retrospect a significant asset that
anticipates the emphasis on action rather than logic and
scene rather than transition evident in both avant garde and
popular work of the sixties--Blow-up, for example, and the
television series Mission Impossible."[23] The plot is confusing, perhaps being the most complex plot ever filmed. But
the most important aspect of the plot is that it reflects the
novel's style exactly. The film, in fact can be summed up
in the same words Chandler used to describe the novel: a
"detective yarn that happens to be more interested in people
than in plot."

   These 1946 reviewers had more success grappling with
the plot than more recent ones. Robin Wood, for example,
in his treatment of Howard Hawks, states: "The film follows Chandler's plot fairly closely until the book's last
chapter, then suddenly opts for a different killer. To have
Bacall turn out to be the killer would certainly have gone
against the whole spirit of the film, but the last-minute
switch doesn't make for clarity."[24] Bacall, of course,
played Vivian Rutledge, and there is no possibility she
murdered anyone. Ted Sennett produced an inaccurate
synopsis for his history of Warner Bros. It begins, "Dis-
solute young heiress Carmen Sternwood (Martha Vickers)
murders her father's bodyguard-companion Sean Regan and
is blackmailed by big-time hood Eddie Marx [sic] (John
Ridgely) who has a photograph of the crime. (To get the

To his surprise, Marlowe (Bogart) finds Vivian (Bacall) at Mars' gambling club.

---

photo, he has killed the original blackmailer, a disreputable book dealer named Geiger.)"[25] In the film Carmen may have killed Regan, but there is no photograph of the crime, and Owen Taylor, not Mars killed Geiger.

The second area of criticism concerned the film's violence, and this matched the criticism against the unpleasantness of the novel. Calling the picture "brutal and ... sinister," James Agee felt the film had reached "a new high in viciousness."[26] Other critics shared his concern. The film is, in fact, quite violent which at times reaches a cold sadism not again depicted in a Marlowe film until The Long Goodbye. The picture contains more violence than the novel; Marlowe is not beat up in the book, for instance, and the movie pointed the way toward the violent private-eye adventures of later years.

Suggestive sex laced the film. This was not, for the most part, the nymphomania, homosexuality, or pornographic book racket of Chandler's novel, but rather risqué dialogue for the Bogart/Bacall fan club. An example is the sequence using race track dialogue added to give the stars more film time together. Hawks said, "It was during the racing season at Santa Anita and I had some horses out there and so I made them talk about riding a horse, and so it ended with 'It all depends on who's in the saddle.' And it was just that I was thinking about racing and I thought, well, I'll do a scene about a little love argument about racing."[27] Critics did not fail to comment on the film's sexuality, although they did not generally criticize it. The Big Sleep remained, in fact, the sexiest Marlowe film until Marlowe in 1969, although it was a different kind of sex than Chandler had discussed.

The Big Sleep clearly bears the Howard Hawks trademark. Firstly, the film's entire shooting apparently took place on a sound stage. This, coupled with the fact that almost every exterior scene takes place at night and/or in rain or fog, gives the film a misty mood that reflects the atmosphere of Chandler's novel. The landscape, like the plot, is a clouded and obscured setting through which the characters must hesitatingly make their physical and emotional ways. Secondly, the photography, like the sets, is well done. Even in long scenes it never reaches the static level of Lady in the Lake, for the characters or the camera are always moving. For example, when Marlowe questions Joe Brody, Brody, seated in a chair, continually turns his head away from Marlowe forcing him to slowly walk around the chair if he wants to keep his eyes on Brody's face. And finally, Hawks' magnificent use of rapid-fire and overlapping dialogue makes the Chandler and non-Chandler lines crackle as they do in no other Marlowe picture.

In addition, The Big Sleep stands out as the best-cast "Marlowe" film. Warners had a sturdy stable of contract players to draw from, and they used them wisely. The sexuality of Carmen, the uneasiness of Brody, the suavity of Mars, the likeableness of Jones, and the controlled evil of Canino all come straight from Chandler. The only character poorly cast is General Sternwood, played by Charles Waldron. His Sternwood is far too animated and anything but an "old and obvious dying man ... with eyes from which all fire had died long ago...."[28] But the best of the cast remains the two stars whose presence helped make the film so popular.

Marlowe (Bogart) stands helplessly by while Canino (Bob
Steele) prepares to murder Harry Jones.

Lauren Bacall, though not the equal of Claire Trevor,
stands out as one of the best "Marlowe" film women.
Critics, however, generally responded unfavorably to her
performance.   Bosley Crowther remarked that "she hasn't
learned to act."[29]   Manny Farber concurred, claiming
Bacall created "a large empty space in the movie."[30]   The
audience, on the other hand, adored the Bogart/Bacall combination, which clicked in the film's non-Chandler scenes.
A playful call to the police, the race track dialogue scene,
and the argument in Joe Brody's apartment, where the two
are oblivious to Brody's gun, all enlivened the film.

After thirty years, however, Warner Bros.' choice of
Bogart to play Marlowe demonstrates the skill of the studio
system in both fashioning a screen personality and then finding suitable material to maintain the image.   Following, of
course, his deft portrayal of Hammett's Sam Spade in The
Maltese Falcon, Bogart became the ideal Marlowe.   Some
critics, however, felt Bogart was unsuited to the role,
though not because of his acting.   Brian Davis, in his book
on thriller films, commented: "Bogart, although the part

seemed to fit like a glove, is actually miscast as Marlowe.
He is too small, which gives rise to some acid dialogue in
the opening sequences...."31 Here, as before, credit for
parts of the picture mistakenly goes solely to the filmmakers and not to Chandler, where it partially belongs. The
dialogue cited is actually a variation of Chandler's own.
Consider, for example, the narrative which reads "'Tall,
aren't you?' she [Carmen] said. [Marlowe] 'I didn't mean
to be.'"32 The film dialogue runs: "Carmen: 'You're not
very tall, are you?' Marlowe: 'I tried to be.'" Manny
Farber voiced stronger objections to the overall character
of Marlowe.

> 'The Big Sleep' would have been a more effec-
> tive study of nightmarish existence had the detec-
> tive been more complicated and had more curios-
> ity been shown about his sweetheart's relation to
> the crime.... Though Bogart turns in another
> jolting performance as well as some good comedy,
> his detective is a limited dull person, who seems
> to have little sympathy with the sub-rosa world
> with which he must always be associated. 33

Most critics of the film, however, including Chandler
himself, found Bogart and his portrayal perfect. The novel-
ist said in a letter to Hamish Hamilton, his British publisher:

> When and if you see the film of The Big Sleep
> (the first half of it anyhow) you will realize what
> can be done with this sort of story by a director
> with the gift of atmosphere and the requisite touch
> of hidden sadism. Bogart, of course, is so much
> better than any other tough-guy actor. As we say
> here, Bogart can be tough without a gun. Also
> he has a sense of humor that contains that grating
> undertone of contempt.... Bogart is the genuine
> article.... All he has to do to dominate a scene
> is to enter it. 34

Without a doubt, Bogart superbly personifies Marlowe,
and several things contribute to his characterization. The
rapid-fire delivery of his lines makes him the sharpest-
tongued Marlowe. For example, the following exchange
(adapted from the novel) between Marlowe and Mars takes
place as though it was one line of dialogue. Mars: "Is
that any of your business?" Marlowe: "I could make it my

Vivian (Bacall) and Marlowe (Bogart) await the final confrontation with Mars and his men.

---

business." Mars: "I could make your business mine."
Marlowe: "You wouldn't like it. The pay's too small."
For a bit of business, Bogart continually pulls his ear when
he is thinking (much like Powell's sniffing of cigarettes).
But best of all is Bogart's "lived-in" look. His rumpled
appearance, which extends beyond his clothing to his physical features, makes him seem as if he really belongs to the
half-fantasy Chandlerian world Hawks has created. Bogart
so characterizes the role, in fact, that one is apt, as one
critic suggested, to adjust the Marlowe character to fit
Bogart and not the other way around. [35] For this reason,
any arguments that Bogart is not as physically large as
Chandler's detective are inconsequential.

The Big Sleep stands out as the best and most popular
of the Marlowe films staying fresh in people's minds long
after the other Chandler pictures have been forgotten.

Unquestionably, much, but not all, of the credit for this permanence goes to Bogart and Bacall. But the rest of it is due to the faithful Chandler spirit of the picture.

TABLE 4.   PLOT COMPARISON

The Big Sleep

NOVEL	SCRIPT	FILM
1. Marlowe is asked by a dying millionaire, General Sternwood, to investigate the blackmail attempt on his younger daughter, Carmen, by Arthur Geiger. Previously Carmen had been blackmailed by Joe Brody. Sternwood also expresses his regret that a man in his employ and husband of his elder daughter, Vivian, Rusty Regan, left suddenly. On his way out of the Sternwood mansion, Marlowe meets Vivian, who thinks he has been hired to find Regan.	Marlowe is asked by a dying millionaire, General Sternwood, to investigate the blackmail attempt on his younger daughter, Carmen, by Arthur Geiger. Previously Carmen had been blackmailed by Joe Brody. Sternwood also expresses his regret that a man in his employ, Shawn Regan, left suddenly. On his way out of the Sternwood mansion, Marlowe meets Sternwood's elder daughter, Vivian, who thinks he has been hired to find Regan.	Marlowe is asked by a dying millionaire, General Sternwood, to investigate the blackmail attempt on his younger daughter, Carmen, by Arthur Geiger. Previously Carmen had been blackmailed by Joe Brody. Sternwood also expresses his regret that a man in his employ, Shawn Regan, left suddenly. On his way out of the Sternwood mansion, Marlowe meets Sternwood's elder daughter, Vivian, who thinks he has been hired to find Regan.
2. Marlowe goes to Geiger's book store, meets Agnes, the clerk, and learns that Geiger rents pornographic books. He tails Geiger to Geiger's house and waits. Carmen arrives. Marlowe sees a flash of light and hears a scream, gunshots, and someone running away. Breaking in he finds Geiger dead and Carmen naked and drugged. A picture has been taken of Carmen, but it is gone. Marlowe finds a book of Geiger's customers in code and takes	Marlowe goes to Geiger's book store, meets Agnes, the clerk, and learns that the store is not what it seems. He tails Geiger to Geiger's house and waits. Carmen arrives. Marlowe sees a flash of light and hears a scream, gunshots, and someone running away. Breaking in he finds Geiger dead and Carmen drugged. A picture has been taken of Carmen, but it is gone. Marlowe finds a book of Geiger's customers in code	Marlowe goes to Geiger's book store, meets Agnes, the clerk, and learns that the store is not what it seems. He tails Geiger to Geiger's house and waits. Carmen arrives. Marlowe sees a flash of light and hears a scream, gunshots, and someone running away. Breaking in he finds Geiger dead and Carmen drugged. A picture has been taken of Carmen, but it is gone. Marlowe finds a book of Geiger's customers in code and takes Carmen home. When he returns, Geiger's body is gone.

(TABLE 4 cont.)

	Carmen home. When he returns, Geiger's body is gone.	and takes Carmen home. When he returns, Geiger's body is gone.	
3.	Bernie Ohls of Homicide tells Marlowe a car belonging to the Sternwoods has been found in the ocean. Sternwood's chauffer, Owen Taylor, is in the car, dead. It could be suicide or murder. He had once run off with Carmen.	Bernie Ohls of Homicide tells Marlowe a car belonging to the Sternwoods has been found in the ocean. Sternwood's chauffer, Owen Taylor, is in the car, dead. It could be suicide or murder. He had once run off with Carmen.	Bernie Ohls of Homicide tells Marlowe a car belonging to the Sternwoods has been found in the ocean. Sternwood's chauffer, Owen Taylor, is in the car, dead. It could be suicide or murder. He had once run off with Carmen.
4.	Marlowe returns to Geiger's store. Books are being moved out. He follows a truck carrying the books to an apartment building where Joe Brody lives.	Marlowe returns to Geiger's store. Books are being moved out. He follows a truck carrying the books to an apartment building where Joe Brody lives.	Marlowe returns to Geiger's store. Books are being moved out. He follows a truck carrying the books to an apartment building where Joe Brody lives.
5.	Vivian brings Marlowe the nude photo of Carmen and says someone wants $5,000. She says she can borrow the money from Eddie Mars, a gambler whose wife ran off with Regan.	Vivian brings Marlowe the photograph of Carmen and says someone wants $5,000. She says she can borrow the money from Eddie Mars, a gambler whose wife ran off with Regan.	Vivian brings Marlowe the photograph of Carmen and says someone wants $5,000. She says she can borrow the money from Eddie Mars, a gambler whose wife ran off with Regan.
6.	Marlowe goes to Geiger's house. Carmen comes. He questions her and she says Brody killed Geiger. Eddie Mars comes and says he owns the house. Marlowe says someone is taking over Geiger's smut book racket.	Marlowe goes to Geiger's house. Carmen comes. He questions her and she says Brody killed Geiger. Eddie Mars comes and says he owns the house.	Marlowe goes to Geiger's house. Carmen comes. He questions her and she says Brody killed Geiger. Eddie Mars comes and says he owns the house.
7.	Marlowe goes to see Brody. Agnes is there. Marlowe	Marlowe goes to see Brody. Vivian and Agnes are there.	Marlowe goes to see Brody. Vivian and Agnes are there.

explains how Brody is taking over Geiger's racket. Marlowe knows Brody has the photographs. He says Brody can take the rap for Geiger's murder. Carmen comes. Marlowe gets the photos and sends her home. Marlowe explains Taylor killed Geiger because he didn't like what Geiger was doing to Carmen. Taylor stole the photo. Brody followed him and took it from him. Brody answers the door and someone kills him.

Marlowe explains how Brody is taking over Geiger's racket. Marlowe knows Brody has the photographs. He says Brody can take the rap for Geiger's murder. Carmen comes. Marlowe gets the photos and sends her home. Brody says he followed Taylor from Geiger's and stole the photos from him. Taylor killed Geiger. Brody answers the door and someone kills him.

Marlowe explains how Brody is taking over Geiger's racket. Marlowe knows Brody has the photographs. He says Brody can take the rap for Geiger's murder. Carmen comes. Marlowe gets the photos and sends Vivian and Carmen home. Brody says he followed Taylor from Geiger's and stole the photos from him. Taylor killed Geiger. Brody answers the door and someone kills him.

8. Marlowe chases Brody's killer, Carol Lundgren. Marlowe captures him and takes him to Geiger's. Carol and Geiger were homosexuals and Carol shot Brody because he thought Brody killed Geiger. Geiger has been stretched out on a bed. Marlowe calls the police.

Marlowe chases Brody's killer, Carol Lundgren. Marlowe captures him and takes him to Geiger's. Geiger has been stretched out on a bed. Marlowe calls the police.

Marlowe chases Brody's killer, Carol Lundgren. Marlowe captures him and takes him to Geiger's. Geiger has been stretched out on a bed. Marlowe calls the police.

9. The police question Marlowe. Lundgren moved Geiger's body so the police wouldn't discover his relationship with Geiger, but he had second thoughts. Marlowe refuses to tell the police everything.

10.

The police question Marlowe. He says Geiger was running a blackmail racket. Taylor killed Geiger because of what he did

(TABLE 4 cont.)

		to Carmen. Carol killed Brody because Brody was cutting him out of Geiger's business. Brody killed Taylor.
11. Mars invites Marlowe to see him. Marlowe calls the Sternwoods and says he has the pictures. Taylor's death is ruled a suicide. Missing Persons says it looks like Regan ran off with Mars' wife, but that Mars doesn't care.		
12.	Mars invites Marlowe to see him. The police believe Regan ran off with Mars' wife.	
13. Norris, Sternwood's butler, says the case is considered closed and he will pay Marlowe. Marlowe says he will destroy the photos.	Norris, Sternwood's butler, says the case is considered closed and pays Marlowe $500.	Vivian says the case is considered closed and pays Marlowe $500.
14. Marlowe goes to Mars' gambling club. Vivian is there. Marlowe suggests, and discards, the idea that Mars killed Regan. Marlowe says he realizes Sternwood was afraid Regan was behind the blackmail scheme. Vivian wins big at roulette. Someone tries to rob her and Marlowe stops it. He tries to find out what Mars has on Vivian. Marlowe says the winning at roulette and the robbery were staged to convince Marlowe there was	Marlowe goes to Mars' gambling club. Vivian is there. Marlowe suggests, and discards, the idea that Mars killed Regan. Marlowe says he realizes Sternwood was afraid Regan was behind the blackmail scheme. Vivian wins big at roulette. Someone tries to rob her and Marlowe stops it. He tries to find out what Mars has on Vivian. Marlowe says the winning at roulette and the robbery were staged to convince Marlowe	Marlowe goes to Mars' gambling club. Vivian is there. Marlowe suggests, and discards, the idea Mars killed Regan. Marlowe says he realizes Sternwood was afraid Regan was behind the blackmail scheme. Vivian wins big at roulette. Someone tries to rob her and Marlowe stops it. He tries to find out what Mars has on Vivian. Marlowe says the winning at roulette and the robbery were staged to convince Marlowe there was nothing between Vivian and Mars. Vivian refuses to talk.

nothing between Viv-
ian and Mars. Viv-
ian refuses to talk.

there was nothing
between Vivian and
Mars. Vivian re-
fuses to talk.

15. Marlowe returns to
his apartment and
finds Carmen naked
in his bed. He
throws her out.

Marlowe returns to
his apartment and
finds Carmen there.
She makes a play
for him but he
throws her out.

Marlowe returns to his
apartment and finds
Carmen there. She
makes a play for him
but he throws her out.

16.

The police tell Mar-
lowe to lay off the
case. Vivian tells
Marlowe that Regan
has been found in
Mexico and she's go-
ing to join him.
Two men beat up
Marlowe, telling him
to lay off the case.

The police tell Marlowe
to lay off the case.
Vivian tells Marlowe
that Regan has been
found in Mexico and
she's going to join him.
Two men beat up Mar-
lowe, telling him to lay
off the case.

17. Harry Jones, who has
been following Mar-
lowe, says Agnes will
tell Marlowe where
Mars' wife is for
$200. Mars' wife
hid out so the police
would think she and
Regan ran off to-
gether, and not that
Mars killed Regan.
Marlowe agrees and
they set up another
meeting.

Harry Jones, who has
been following Mar-
lowe, says Agnes
will tell Marlowe
where Mars' wife is
for $200. Marlowe
agrees and they set
up another meeting.

Harry Jones, who has
been following Marlowe,
says Agnes will tell
Marlowe where Mars'
wife is for $200. Mar-
lowe agrees and they
set up another meeting.

18. When Marlowe ar-
rives at the meeting
place, Jones and
Canino, one of
Mars' men, are
there. Canino
makes Jones tell
him where Agnes is
and forces him to
drink poison. Mar-
lowe discovers the
address Jones
gave was false.
He meets Agnes
and she tells him
where Mona Mars
is.

When Marlowe ar-
rives at the meeting
place, Jones and
Canino, one of
Mars' men, are
there. Canino
makes Jones tell
him where Agnes is
and forces him to
drink poison. Mar-
lowe discovers the
address Jones gave
was false. He
meets Agnes and
she tells him
where Mona Mars
is.

When Marlowe arrives
at the meeting place,
Jones and Canino, one
of Mars' men, are
there. Canino makes
Jones tell him where
Agnes is and forces him
to drink poison. Mar-
lowe discovers the ad-
dress Jones gave was
false. He meets Agnes
and she tells him where
Mona Mars is.

19. Marlowe goes to find
Mona. He is captured

(TABLE 4 cont.)

by Canino. Mar-
lowe persuades Mona
to cut his ropes,
even though he says
Mars killed Regan.
Canino returns.

20.

Marlowe goes to find
Mona. He is cap-
tured by Canino.
Vivian is there.
Mona says she hid
out so the police
wouldn't think Mars
killed Regan. Mar-
lowe says Mars did
kill Regan and Vivian
never heard from
Regan in Mexico.
Marlowe convinces
Vivian to cut his
ropes. Canino re-
turns.

Marlowe goes to find
Mona. He is captured
by Canino. Vivian is
there. Mona says she
hid out so the police
wouldn't think Mars
killed Regan. Marlowe
says Mars did kill Re-
gan and Vivian never
heard from Regan in
Mexico. Marlowe con-
vinces Vivian to cut his
ropes. Canino returns.

21.

Mona pulls a gun on
Marlowe. Mars and
Canino arrive. Mona
leaves the house and
Mars goes after her.
Marlowe and Canino
fight.

22. Marlowe, with Mona's
help, kills Canino.

Marlowe, with Vivi-
an's help, kills
Canino.

Marlowe, with Vivian's
help, kills Canino.

23. The police question
Marlowe. They have
questioned Mars and
don't think he killed
Regan.

24. Marlowe goes to the
Sternwoods. The
General at first is
angry with Marlowe,
then says he'll pay
Marlowe more money
to find Regan. Mar-
lowe agrees.

Marlowe goes to the
Sternwoods. The
General is angry with
Marlowe, then says
he'll pay Marlowe
more money to find
Regan. Marlowe
agrees.

25.

Marlowe gets a call
from Mars. He sug-
gests Marlowe look
over the books taken
from Geiger's store.

Vivian tells Mar-
lowe she killed Re-
gan by accident and
begs Marlowe to
leave before Mars
kills him.   Marlowe
refuses.

26.

Marlowe and Vivian go
to Geiger's house. He
calls Mars and asks him
to meet him there.
Mars comes and has his
men surround the house.
Mars goes inside and
Marlowe gets the drop
on him.   Marlowe says
Carmen killed Regan
when she was in one of
her spells because Re-
gan liked Mona, not
her.   Mars concurs.
Marlowe then says that's
not true, that Mars
killed Regan.   He forces
Mars out of the house
and Mars is gunned
down by his own men.
Marlowe calls the police
to rescue him and Vivi-
an.

27. Marlowe gives Car-
men back a gun he
had taken from her.
She asks him to teach
her to shoot.   He
agrees and she tries
to kill Marlowe, but
he loaded the gun with
blanks.   Carmen has
an epileptic fit.   Mar-
lowe confronts Vivian.
He explains the case.
Mars was behind
Geiger's blackmailing
Carmen to see if
Sternwood would stand
for blackmail.   If so,
Mars could collect a
lot of money quickly.
If not, Mars would
have to wait until
Vivian inherited the
family fortune.   Geig-
er was killed by Owen
Taylor, who was in
love with Carmen.

(TABLE 4 cont.)

Regan disappeared,
and Mars made it
look like Regan ran
off with Mona so the
police wouldn't find
out the truth about
Regan. Carmen shot
Regan for the same
reason she tried to
kill Marlowe: Regan
rejected her. Vivian
called Mars and
Canino disposed of
Regan's body. Mar-
lowe says he will
not tell the police
if Carmen is sent
to a sanitarium. He
won't tell the Gen-
eral about Regan.

28.

Marlowe goes to Geig-
er's house but he has
been followed by
Mars. Carmen
comes. She makes
another play for Mar-
lowe but he doesn't
respond. Marlowe
gives her back her
gun he had taken
from her. She tries
to kill him saying he
favors Vivian over
her and it was the
same way with Regan.
Marlowe has, how-
ever, filled her gun
with blanks. Vivian
paid Mars to help
cover up the crime
and Carmen says
Marlowe can't do a
thing about it with-
out ruining Vivian and
her father. Marlowe
lets Carmen go and
she is killed by Mars.
Marlowe kills Mars.
Marlowe calls the po-
lice and tells Vivian
about Carmen. He
tells the General that
Carmen was killed in
a car crash and that
Regan's all right.

Chapter 4

THE LADY IN THE LAKE:
LADY IN THE LAKE

By the time of The Lady in the Lake, his fourth novel, Chandler had comfortably settled into novel writing.
Chandler had perfected his method of expanding and combin-
ing earlier short stories in Farewell, My Lovely and carried this method into his latest novel. The characterizations
of The Lady in the Lake also measured up to the author's
high standards, so that while the novel contains no plot or
character irregularities, neither does it offer the reader any
surprises.

The story begins when Derace Kingsley hires Marlowe to find his wife, Crystal, who has been missing for a
month. A telegram states she left Little Fawn Lake to run
off with Chris Lavery. But Marlowe's visit to Lavery nets
only denials that he and Crystal went away together. A Dr.
Almore, however, is upset by Marlowe's presence at Lavery's, as is Degarmo, a Bay City policeman.

Marlowe goes to Little Fawn Lake where he and Bill
Chess find Chess' wife, Muriel, drowned in the lake. Marlowe discovers that a policeman came to the lake looking for
Mildred Haviland, who resembles Muriel. Marlowe proves
Muriel is Mildred. A return visit to Lavery's nets Marlowe
a meeting with Lavery's landlady, Mrs. Fallbrook, and he
discovers Lavery has been murdered.

Kingsley's secretary, once in love with Lavery, informs Marlowe that Almore is a dope doctor and his wife
may have been murdered. Mrs. Almore's parents say Almore murdered their daughter because the doctor was having
an affair with his nurse, Mildred Haviland. Two policemen
sent by Degarmo beat Marlowe up.

Kingsley tells Marlowe that he, Kingsley, has been in
touch with his wife. She wants money and Marlowe agrees

to take it to her. Marlowe meets her, realizes she killed
Lavery, and is knocked out. He awakes to find Crystal
murdered. Marlowe says it was Mildred who murdered
Mrs. Almore and Degarmo covered up for her. Marlowe
reveals that Crystal, not Mildred, was the one that
drowned. She murdered Crystal for her money and identity.
Degarmo murdered her. Degarmo dies while trying to escape.

Following the practice he had established in writing
his first two novels, Chandler constructed The Lady in the
Lake, published in 1943, out of several short stories. The
novel was, in fact, the last he would write in this manner.
"Bay City Blues" (Dime Detective Magazine, November,
1937), "The Lady in the Lake" (Dime Detective Magazine,
January, 1939), and "No Crime in the Mountains" (Detective
Story Magazine, September, 1941) formed the core of the
narrative. [1] (For an example of one method Chandler used
to expand portions of his short stories, see page 40.) From
"Bay City Blues" came material for chapters 3, 32, 33,
and 34. "The Lady in the Lake" supplied all or part of
chapters 1, 2, 5-13, and 17. And "No Crime in the Mountains"
provided most of chapters 7, 8, and 9. "Bay City Blues" furnished the Dr. Almore subplot, while the latter two stories provided the lady in the lake plot, with a few variations. Most of
the other twenty-five chapters were new material.

The bulk of the novel's characters came from "The
Lady in the Lake," which provided all of Adrienne From-
sett, Bill Chess, Chris Lavery, Crystal Kingsley, and Derace
Kingsley, and part of Mildred Haviland and Jim Patton.
From "Bay City Blues" came all of Mrs. Almore, Dr. Al-
more, Degarmo, and Shorty, and part of George Talley,
Mildred Haviland, and Captain Webber. "No Crime in the
Mountains" provided part of Jim Patton and his assistant, Andy.
Other parts not accounted for were largely new material.

Critical reaction to The Lady in the Lake was quite
favorable, although Chandler's new-found fascination with
Hollywood was more important to him at the moment. [2]
Reviewers stated that the author had achieved "spectacular
results" with a "beautifully organized ... A-1 job."[3] Despite such ecstatic praise, The Lady in the Lake rarely
rises above any other well-written routine detective story.
The plot is relatively simple, for Chandler, at any rate,
and the climatic revelation that Crystal Kingsley is dead is
strongly hinted at in the fifth chapter, when Bill Chess says
his wife was physically like Crystal. The characters, while
carefully drawn, are perhaps not as memorable as some of
Chandler's other creations--Orfamay Quest or Terry Len-

TABLE 5.   LADY IN THE LAKE

Cast

Phillip Marlowe	Robert Montgomery
Adrienne Fromsett	Audrey Totter
Lieut. DeGarmot	Lloyd Nolan
Captain Kane	Tom Tully
Derace Kingsby	Leon Ames
Mildred Haviland	Jayne Meadows
Chris Lavery	Dick Simmons
Eugene Grayson	Morris Ankrum
Receptionist	Lila Leeds
Artist	William Roberts
Mrs. Grayson	Kathleen Lockhart
Chrystal Kingsby	Ellay Mort

A Metro-Goldwyn-Mayer picture

Running time: 105 minutes

Release date: January, 1947

Credits

Produced by	George Haight
Directed by	Robert Montgomery
Screenplay by	Steve Fisher
Based on novel by	Raymond Chandler
Special Effects by	Arnold Gillespie
Dir. of Photog.	Paul C. Vogel, A.S.C.
Art Directors	Cedric Gibbons
	Preston Ames
Set Decorations	Edwin P. Willis
	Thomas Theuerkauf (Assoc.)
Recorded by	Douglas Shearer
Music by	David Snell
Choral Direction	Maurice Goldman
Costume Supervision	Irene
Edited by	Gene Ruggiero
Hair Designs, Miss Totter	Sydney Guilaroff
Make-up Created by	Jack Dawn

nox, for instance.   What is most notable, however, is that
The Lady in the Lake is structurally superior to some of
Chandler's other novels (The Big Sleep or The Little Sister,
for instance) in that the author provides a better balance between
plot and characterizations.   The plot is well developed, containing no errors, and the character relationships are fully explained.

Chandler had been in Hollywood for several years
when he was called upon to script The Lady in the Lake.
(MGM had purchased the novel in February, 1945, for
$35,000.[4])   It remains the only time Chandler adapted one
of his own novels.   But the resulting 175-page screenplay
was too loosely organized and fifty pages too long for producer George Haight to use.   Haight called in his own
screenwriter, Steve Fisher, to redo the script.   Fisher, a
prolific and experienced screenwriter and Black Mask alum-
nus, retained as much of Chandler's dialogue as possible,
along with a few necessary scenes.   In the process of producing the script, Fisher tightened the story and gave it
greater continuity.[5]   The plots are compared in Table 6.

The two plots bear much resemblance.   Nearly all of
the intrigue in Chandler's novel was retained, although the
Dr. Almore subplot has been considerably shortened in the
script.   The film unfortunately eliminates the sequences at
Little Fawn Lake; these are only mentioned in dialogue or
narration.   These passages are among the best in the novel,
but were eliminated to shorten the picture.   And, of course,
plot elements have been rearranged to better suit film form.
The script only falters slightly at the end, when Marlowe
intuitively guesses that Crystal is really Mildred.   But then,
that is how the book Marlowe arrives at the same conclusion.

Marlowe (Robert Montgomery) has just had a story accepted by Kingsby Publications, whom he prepares to visit. (Note the extra "l.") All photos in this chapter are from <u>Lady in the Lake</u> (MGM, 1946).

The completed script went into the hands of Robert Montgomery, who had just returned to MGM after a five-year absence. Montgomery's initial reaction was that the script seemed to him just another routine private eye adventure. He changed his mind, however, when he felt the studio might give him permission not only to direct and star in the movie, but also to experiment with the film's point of view. The audience would view events as Marlowe saw them. [6] The idea of a subjective camera, one in which the camera takes the place of a character (you see what the character sees, the way he sees it), was not of course new. Many films had used this technique for short scenes; for instance, to show what it's like to be drunk in <u>The Last Laugh.</u> But no previous American film had attempted to tell

its story almost exclusively from the point of view of the
camera. (A few European films had used this technique. 7)
Since 1938 Montgomery wanted to do a film in this manner;
Lady in the Lake gave him his chance.

Montgomery, Fisher, and Haight met with a top-level
executive producer at MGM (who shall remain nameless),
explained the idea, and got the go-ahead. Fisher rewrote
the screenplay so Montgomery was visible only in four narration scenes (when he appeared to explain material that had
been cut), when he was reflected in a mirror, and at the
very end, when Montgomery kisses Totter (the only time
Montgomery and another character are viewed with a third-
person camera. Miss Totter explained that this scene was
included because the film was previewed three times and
each time the audience's review cards came back saying the
viewers missed seeing Montgomery and Totter kiss. So this
last scene was shot and added to the final print of the film. 8)
But MGM had second thoughts about the project and gave the
signal to shoot only the first reel. The final go-ahead
would be based on that test footage. So the studio executive
joined Montgomery, Fisher, and Haight in the projection
room. As Fisher recalls, "He [the executive] saw the reel,
then turned to us (we almost fainted) and said 'It's fine, just
fine, but where's Bob Montgomery?'"9 Although the executive never did understand what the filmmakers were doing,
he told them to go ahead. 10

When the final shooting script was ready, George
Haight suggested Fisher take a copy over to Chandler, who
was then living on Third Street in Los Angeles. Fisher's
greeting to the author when Chandler answered the doorbell,
"Philip Marlowe, I presume?"11 received only a scowl in
return, and Fisher was left standing at the door. The next
day Chandler called Haight and expressed his feeling that
the subjective camera wouldn't work, leaving Haight and
Fisher with the impression Chandler didn't like the script.
In 1949 Chandler wrote:

> The camera eye technique of Lady in the Lake
> is old stuff in Hollywood. Every young writer or
> director has wanted to try it. 'Let's make the
> camera a character'; it's been said at every lunch
> table in Hollywood one time or another. I knew
> one fellow who wanted to make the camera the
> murderer; which wouldn't work without an awful lot
> of fraud. The camera is too honest. 12

(Top) Marlowe's (R. Montgomery) first meeting with Adrienne Fromsett (Audrey Totter) in the offices of Kingsby Publications. Except for narration sequences, Marlowe is seen only mirrored in this film. (Bottom) Marlowe (on a later visit to Adrienne): "It's an old sickness: re-occurring black eyes."

Marlowe (R. Montgomery) makes a late night visit to Adrienne's (Totter) apartment.

But probably what upset Chandler most was that his script had been rewritten, for he loathed the Hollywood system that allowed tampering with a scriptwriter's work. Before Lady in the Lake's release, MGM wanted Fisher to share scripting credit with Chandler. Fisher objected to this, but before any action was taken, Chandler refused any credit for the screenplay. [13]

The subjective camera, of course, required special filming techniques. Special camera harnesses had to be developed to facilitate the filming. In addition, every set had to be constructed in a "breakaway" fashion to allow the camera and necessary equipment complete freedom of movement. For example: "As the hero (camera) gets into his auto and looks around, the car is broken away to permit the camera to circle in the same way."[14] Even something as simple as lighting a cigarette required one man for the right hand, one for the left, and a third lying on his stomach under the camera blowing smoke under the lens. Montgomery conceded that he spent three-quarters of Lady in the Lake's shooting time on his stomach. [15]

The one million dollar picture was released in January, 1947. (Apparently the time of the story in the novel, July, was changed to Christmas to coincide with the season of the film's release.) It met with favorable audience response (Fisher states it earned four million dollars in the first month [16]), and generally favorable critical reviews. The plot generated little debate, with critics about evenly divided on its quality. Most reviewers praised Montgomery's attempt to do something different and then went on to divide themselves into three groups. Those who enjoyed Lady in the Lake singled out the subjective camera idea and thought it worked well in the film. For instance, Time magazine felt the subjective camera was "particularly well-suited to an action-crammed thriller," [17] and Newsweek called it a "fascinating experiment in movie making." [18] The second group was more critical. Thomas M. Pryor stated: "The picture is different and ... fresh ... [but] Mr. Montgomery has ... failed to exploit the full possibilities suggested by this unusual technique." [19] The last group found little to like in Montgomery's use of the camera. Bosley Crowther thought the story "might just as well--if not better-- be told in an objective way." [20] He claimed that to be truly subjective the camera character should not speak at all, for when he does it mixes a third-person voice with a first-person image. [21]

Central to a critical examination of the picture is a discussion of the subjective camera technique used in the film. Because the camera, in effect, "substituted" for Marlowe, a treatment of this aspect of the movie is left until a discussion of the Marlowe character.

The major differences between the novel and film occur in the characterizations. The characters at Little Fawn Lake have been left out, as well as the lake setting, of course, and two characters have undergone radical alterations. Derace Kingsley has suffered a major personality change from a strong character in the novel to Derace Kingsby, a weak ineffectual character who seems scarcely capable of turning the page of one of his own pulp publications without help. Adrienne Fromsett, on the other hand, has been blown up from a moderately important character in the book, to a force to be reckoned with in the film. She has received the strength of character taken from Kingsley.

This has been done, of course, to provide a love interest
for Marlowe, which filmmakers felt was an absolute must
for the filmic version of the sleuth (until The Long Goodbye).   Like, Murder, My Sweet and The Big Sleep, this
love interest is produced by altering a character from the
novel.

The film is generally well acted, but Audrey Totter
leaves something to be desired in this picture that is essentially one big screen test (because the actors must continually play directly into the camera).   Miss Totter, who went
on to play in other films and television series (she is cur-
rently [1975] a semi-regular on the television show "Medical
Center"), often appears to be over acting, either because of
her interpretation of the role or, more probably, because
of Robert Montgomery's direction.   This is especially true
in many of the close-ups, in which her facial expressions
often seem needlessly exaggerated.   This is not the case,
however, with Lloyd Nolan and Jayne Meadows.   Nolan
plays the perfect Degarmo; Chandler's character to the hilt.
His deft portrayal of the only crooked cop in the Marlowe
films accurately reflects the hardness and cynicism of
Chandler's policemen, who must deal with private detectives
that often cause them more trouble than some criminals.   And
Jayne Meadows' interpretation of Mildred as criminally insane and her Fallbrook characterization are two good bits
in the picture.   She has only these short sequences to put
across the personality of Mildred, and she makes the most
of the opportunities, primarily by very rapid dialogue and
quick, nervous hand movements.

In closing out the character discussion, a look at the
cast list (Table 5) provides some interesting bits of trivia.
First off, Marlowe has gained an "l" in his first name: it
has gone from Philip to Phillip.   This extra "l" appears
not only on the cast list but also on Marlowe's office window
and on his wallet identification.   The advantage or signifi-
cance of this change remains unclear, but it does provide
two legitimate spellings of "Philip" for crossword puzzle use.
Secondly, Degarmo has been given some French flavor, with
his name being altered to DeGarmot.   Fisher states that
these and other spelling changes were "instigated by a nervous legal department at MGM, always afraid of being
sued."22   But Montgomery's clincher is a joke he played on
the audience, which, incidently, if interpreted correctly by
an alert viewer, would give the whole plot away before the
first scene.   In both the film and the novel, Crystal

Kingsley dies before the story opens. And yet she appears
in the film's credits as being played by someone called Ellay Mort. Ellay Mort, in phonetic French, means "She is
dead." So much for Montgomery's sense of black humor.

The main concern of this study is, of course, the
portrayal of Marlowe, and it becomes difficult to separate
Montgomery's performance from the subjective camera technique. As Marlowe says, "You'll see it just as I saw it.
You'll meet the people; you'll find the clues. And maybe
you'll solve it quick and maybe you won't." But does this
technique work? Is the viewer made to feel he has taken
the place of Marlowe? The answer is that although the
technique is often effective, it does not make the viewer
feel he is actually Marlowe.

The subjective camera does not make or break the
film. Any film, no matter how it is photographed, must
have a good script to be a good movie. It is nearly impossible to produce a good film from a bad script. Given,
then, that Lady in the Lake has a good script (and it does,
for the script is deft blend of the novel's major elements
and the special requirements of the subjective filmmaker)
then almost any method of photography should result in at
least a watchable film. Montgomery's approach is an interesting one that works throughout most of the film, particularly in the action sequences. The scene where Montgomery gets into his car and is followed by DeGarmot, for
instance, is quite effective. The technique falters mainly
in the long dialogue scenes; these put the viewer somewhat
ill at ease because they are so static. Then, too, the
camera cannot possibly accurately mimic the movements of
a person's eyes and head. In conversations, people rarely
stare into the face across from them for any great length
of time. But in the film, the camera stares right at Adrienne, for instance, through numerous long scenes. Although
the subjective camera is effective, it does not involve the
audience more than some other filming method. The viewer
still remains aware that this is a film, and not that he has
become Marlowe.

Facing page: (top) publicity still (not a scene from film)
showing Bay City Police Captain Kane (Tom Tully, left),
Lieut. DeGarmot (Lloyd Nolan), and Marlowe (R. Montgom-
ery). (Bottom) Marlowe interrupts the Kingsby Publications
Christmas office party; Derace Kingsby (Leon Ames) and
Adrienne (Totter) are in front.

The subjective camera aside, what of Marlowe?
Robert Montgomery began in films in 1929.   Like Powell,
he began to be dissatisfied with his roles (he played juvenile
leads) but it was not until 1939 that he broke out of this
stereotyping.   Montgomery, who was instrumental in setting
up the Screen Actors Guild, enlisted in the American Field
Service in London in 1940.   He drove an ambulance in
France until Dunkirk and then made several pictures in 1941
while waiting for his Navy commission.   He served on de-
stroyers and commanded PT boats, seeing action in the
Pacific and the invasion of Normandy.   His involvement in
a film about PT boats, They Were Expendable (1945), led
him into direction.   The director of They Were Expendable,
John Ford, became ill during the last three weeks of filming and Montgomery directed the last portion of the film.
Ford later remarked that he couldn't tell where he left off
and Montgomery began and the picture served as a spring-
board for Montgomery's participation in Lady in the Lake. [23]

Most statements about Montgomery's Marlowe must
be made on the basis of his dialogue.   This is fortunate,
for Montgomery turns in a very routine performance.   He
is the most down-and-out Marlowe, surpassing even Elliot
Gould.   He works for only ten dollars a day (versus twenty-
five a day and eight cents a mile in the novel). [24]   He
doesn't even have an apartment, but lives in a run-down
Hotel Del Vista.   And he is even ready to give up sleuthing
for a detective story writing career, à la Dashiell Hammett.   (Interestingly enough, the Kingsby Publication writers
get a penny a word, the same price Chandler got for his
first short story.)   Throughout the film, in fact, constant
reference is made to how bad the detective business is.
(When Marlowe gives Lavery one of his cards, Lavery in
his faked Southern accent remarks, "Well I declare, you
fellows going from door to door now?   Shame business is
so bad."   And later when DeGarmot learns of Marlowe's
story writing he says, "The detective business must be on
the skids."   Also mentioned is Marlowe's lack of money.
This, of course, goes back to Chandler's concept of his
hero: society considers Marlowe a failure because he doesn't
have any money.   Marlowe's frustration shows itself in the
dialogue; he cracks wise, but many of these remarks border
on rudeness, something no other film Marlowe approaches.
For example, Marlowe says Adrienne's lipstick is on
crooked and when she checks it in the mirror, he remarks,
"Vain female, aren't you?"   And Marlowe constantly quits
the case, fed up with all the trouble it's brought him.

Adrienne (Totter) comes to Marlowe's (R. Montgomery) hotel
room to make up after a fight.

The Marlowe of Lady in the Lake differs from the
one in the novel. He is more tired, more cynical, more
conscious of the pleasure he misses by not possessing
money. As Fisher explains it: "If Montgomery's Marlowe's sarcasm came out pessimistic, it wasn't intended,
instead: bitterness at being broke, shoved around, etc.
laced with a sort of acid humor, which in any case was
always Robert Montgomery's bag."[25] But, at heart, he remains Chandler's Marlowe, carrying on when the chips are
against him, defying the police, and struggling to see justice
done.

Lady in the Lake emerges as not the best, nor the
worst, of the "Marlowe" pictures. It represents an interesting and novel approach to Chandler's world that succeeds
most of the time.

TABLE 6.   PLOT COMPARISON

The Lady in the Lake / Lady in the Lake

NOVEL   FILM

1.   Marlowe visits the office
      of Derace Kingsley, of the
      Gillerlain Cosmetic Com-
      pany.   He meets Kingsley's
      secretary, Adrienne From-
      sett.   Kingsley wants Mar-
      lowe to find his wife,
      Crystal, who has been
      missing for a month.   A
      telegram states Crystal
      left Little Fawn Lake to
      run off with Chris Lavery.
      But Kingsley has just talked
      to Lavery and he denies
      having gone off with Cry-
      stal.   Marlowe takes the
      case.

                                          Marlowe, fed up with detective
                                          work, has submitted a story
                                          to Kingsby Publications, a pulp
                                          magazine publisher.   Marlowe
                                          has been asked to see A.
                                          Fromsett.   When he goes to
                                          Kingsby Publications, Marlowe
                                          learns Adrienne Fromsett
                                          doesn't really want his story.
                                          She needs a detective to find
                                          Chrystal Kingsby, her boss'
                                          wife, without Derace Kingsby
                                          knowing about it.   Adrienne
                                          says it's so Chrystal can be
                                          served with divorce papers.
                                          Marlowe is interested enough
                                          to go with Adrienne to her
                                          apartment.   At the apartment,
                                          Marlowe spots a telegram from
                                          Chrystal saying she is going
                                          away with Chris Lavery.   But
                                          Adrienne has seen Lavery and
                                          he denies having gone off with
                                          Chrystal.   Marlowe asks

(TABLE 6 cont.)

Adrienne about her involvement
with Lavery and she becomes
angry. Marlowe says Lavery
jilted Adrienne and now she
wants to marry Kingsby. Marlowe agrees to see Lavery.

3.   Marlowe visits Lavery,   Marlowe visits Lavery, but
     but Lavery denies having   Lavery denies having seen
     seen Crystal.   Chrystal.

4.   Marlowe leaves, but waits
     outside the house. Lav-
     ery's neighbor, Dr. Al-
     more, becomes so upset
     at Marlowe's presence
     that he summons a Bay
     City policeman, Degar-
     mo, to check Marlowe
     out. Almore's wife had
     committed suicide.

5.   Lavery punches Marlowe un-
                                      conscious and he wakes up in
                                      Bay City jail. Lieutenant De-
                                      Garmot and Captain Kane say
                                      Marlowe was picked up for
                                      drunk driving, but Marlowe
                                      says Lavery rigged it to look
                                      that way. The police release
                                      Marlowe.

6.   Marlowe goes to Kings-
     ley's cabin at Little Fawn
     Lake and meets Kingsley's
     caretaker, Bill Chess.
     Bill says his wife, Muriel,
     left him the same day
     Crystal left the lake.
     Marlowe searches the
     cabin and finds nothing.
     Marlowe and Chess dis-
     cover a body in the lake
     a month old. Bill says
     it's Muriel. Bill is ar-
     rested for murder.

7.   Marlowe goes to see Adrienne.
                                      She says Chrystal was last
                                      seen at Little Fawn Lake.
                                      Marlowe refuses to go, but he

overhears a man tell Derace that Kingsby's caretaker's wife, Muriel Chess, has been found drowned in the lake and her husband, Bill, arrested. Adrienne thinks Chrystal may have murdered Muriel because Chrystal hated Muriel. Marlowe agrees to go.

8. Marlowe learns that a policeman came to the lake looking for someone called Mildred Haviland, but who looked like Muriel Chess. Marlowe calls Kingsley.

9. Marlowe finds an anklet in Bill Chess' cabin proving Muriel Chess is really Mildred Haviland. Marlowe thinks she may have been murdered by someone from her past.

10.

Marlowe returns from the lake and goes to see Adrienne. Marlowe has learned that Muriel Chess was really Mildred Haviland and that she married Bill Chess because she wanted some place to hide from the policeman that was after her. She and Muriel had fought over Chris Lavery. Marlowe finds an anklet that links Mildred to Lavery. Marlowe threatens to quit, but doesn't. Adrienne tells Marlowe to stay away from Lavery.

11. Marlowe goes to San Bernardino, where Crystal's car had been left. He learns Crystal was unhappy to see Lavery. Marlowe returns to his apartment and is visited by the L. A. police, who question him about the events at the lake. Marlowe calls Kingsley.

(TABLE 6 cont.)

12. Marlowe goes to Lavery's and finds the landlady, Mrs. Fallbrook, there. She says she came for her rent, but can't find Lavery. She hands Marlowe an empty gun she says she found on the stairs and leaves. Marlowe finds Lavery shot to death in the bathroom and a handkerchief with Adrienne Fromsett's initials on it.

Marlowe goes to Lavery's and finds the landlady, Mrs. Fallbrook, there. She says she came for her rent, but can't find Lavery. She hands Marlowe an empty gun she says she found on the stairs and leaves. Marlowe finds Lavery shot to death in the bathroom and a handkerchief with Adrienne Fromsett's initials on it.

13. Marlowe goes to see Kingsley. He shows Kingsley the gun and says it looks like Crystal killed Lavery. Kingsley offers Marlowe money to cover up the murder. Marlowe refuses. Kingsley says Adrienne was in love with Lavery and knew Dr. Almore's wife. Kingsley offers Marlowe $500 if he proves Crystal innocent.

14.

Marlowe goes to see Adrienne. He shows her the gun and the handkerchief and suggests she killed Lavery. Kingsby enters and is angry when Adrienne tells him she hired Marlowe. Marlowe suggests Kingsby killed Lavery because of his involvement with Chrystal. Kingsby tries to buy Marlowe off. Marlowe refuses. Kingsby denies any romantic interest in Adrienne. Adrienne throws Marlowe out because he ruined her chances with Kingsby.

15.

Kingsby hires Marlowe to find Chrystal and tries to put the suspicion for Lavery's murder on Adrienne.

16. Marlowe goes to see Adrienne. She says she knew Mrs. Almore and that Crystal did too. She says Almore earns his living by giving dope to rich clients. Mrs. Almore had been drugged the night she was supposed to have committed suicide. It was Lavery who found the body. Perhaps Almore killed her and had the whole thing hushed up. Mrs. Almore's parents, the Graysons, hired a private detective to investigate but he was intimidated off the case. Marlowe shows Adrienne the handkerchief. She says she didn't kill Lavery and Marlowe believes her.

17. Marlowe returns to Lavery's and calls the police. Degarmo and Captain Webber investigate. Marlowe tells them that Crystal may have been in the house and what happened at Little Fawn Lake. Marlowe mentions to Degarmo that perhaps Lavery was blackmailing Almore and that the police covered up Mrs. Almore's murder. Degarmo hits Marlowe.

Marlowe returns to Lavery's and calls the police. DeGarmot and Captain Kane investigate. Marlowe tells them what happened at Little Fawn Lake. He says DeGarmot went up there looking for Mildred. DeGarmot slaps Marlowe around and Marlowe hits him.

18.

The police bring Marlowe in. He tells Kane that DeGarmot knew Mildred and Lavery. Kane lets Marlowe go.

19.

Marlowe goes to his hotel room. Adrienne comes. Marlowe still thinks she may have killed Lavery. Marlowe learns that Mildred was a nurse for a Bay City doctor named Almore. One night his wife was found dead. DeGarmot investigated

(TABLE 6 cont.)

and the death was ruled a suicide. But Mrs. Almore's
parents, the Graysons, thought
different. Mildred disappeared.

20. Marlowe visits Mrs. Almore's parents, the
Graysons. They say Al-
more dispenses dope
and that he murdered
their daughter because
he was having an affair
with his office nurse and
couldn't afford a scandal.
The nurse's name was
Mildred Haviland.

21.

Marlowe goes to see the Graysons. They are frightened and
won't talk. Marlowe says
Mrs. Almore was murdered and
a cop covered it up.

22.

Marlowe is followed when he
leaves the Graysons. Marlowe
tries to escape but the pursuer
forces Marlowe's car to tip
over. The pursuer, DeGarmot,
pours whiskey over Marlowe
and calls the police to report
a drunk driver. Marlowe
knocks out a drunk, places his
wallet in the drunk's shirt, and
escapes just as the police
come. He calls Adrienne for
help and passes out.

23. Marlowe visits Mrs. Talley, the wife of the de-
tective the Graysons had
hired. She is frightened
and refuses to tell Mar-
lowe where her husband
is. Marlowe is followed
from her house by two
Bay City policemen,
Cooney and Dobbs, who
beat Marlowe up and ar-
rest him. Marlowe sees
Captain Webber and De-
garmo. Degarmo says he

sent Cooney and Cobbs to
Talley's house. Webber
says Talley once had a
piece of evidence from the
Almore case and that De-
garmo was once married
to Mildred Haviland.
Marlowe returns to his
apartment and Kingsley
calls. Kingsley has heard
from Crystal.

24.   Marlowe comes to in Adrienne's
                                       apartment. She is in love with
                                       Marlowe and wants him to quit
                                       the case. Marlowe says he
                                       can't because DeGarmot is af-
                                       ter him. She says Marlowe
                                       is in love with her and they
                                       could become writing partners.
                                       Kingsby comes looking for
                                       Marlowe.

25.   Kingsley tells Marlowe   Kingsby tells Marlowe that
       Crystal wants money.   Chrystal wants money. Mar-
       Marlowe agrees to take   lowe agrees to take it to her.
       it to her.

26.   Marlowe says he will leave a
                                       trail of rice so Adrienne can
                                       follow him with the police.

27.   Marlowe meets Crystal
       but refuses to give her
       the money until they talk.
       They go to her hotel
       room. Marlowe realizes
       she was Mrs. Fallbrook
       and she admits she shot
       Lavery. She pulls a gun
       on Marlowe. He tries
       to take it away from her
       when someone knocks
       him out.

28.   Marlowe meets Chrystal but re-
                                       fuses to give her the money
                                       until they talk. They go to her
                                       hotel room, with Marlowe leav-
                                       ing a trail of rice. She pulls
                                       a gun on Marlowe. She was
                                       Mrs. Fallbrook and she killed
                                       Lavery.

(TABLE 6 cont.)

29.   Marlowe awakes to find
      himself soaked in gin and
      Crystal naked on the bed,
      strangled. Marlowe es-
      capes from the room just
      ahead of the police, but
      he is captured by Degar-
      mo. Marlowe tells De-
      garmo what happened,
      but leads Degarmo to be-
      lieve Kingsley killed
      Crystal. Marlowe and
      Degarmo drive to Little
      Fawn Lake to question
      Kingsley. On the way,
      Marlowe says Degarmo's
      wife, Mildred, killed
      Mrs. Almore because
      she was having an affair
      with Dr. Almore and
      Degarmo covered up the
      crime. Mildred went to
      the lake and Degarmo
      went looking for her.

30.   Marlowe has guessed that Chry-
                                      stal is really Mildred and Chry-
                                      stal is the one drowned in the
                                      lake. Lavery met Mildred in
                                      El Paso and was the only one
                                      who knew who she really was.
                                      Marlowe takes Mildred's gun
                                      but DeGarmot comes in. Mar-
                                      lowe thinks Adrienne has
                                      double crossed him. DeGarmot
                                      is surprised to find Mildred
                                      alive and shoots her because
                                      she played him for a sucker.
                                      He plans to kill Marlowe but
                                      the police come and kill him.
                                      Kane says DeGarmot messed
                                      up the rice trail. Marlowe
                                      and Adrienne go away together.

31.   Marlowe, Degarmo, and
      Jim Patton go to Kings-
      ley's cabin and find him
      drunk. They discuss the
      case. Marlowe says it
      was really Crystal who
      was drowned in the lake.

Mildred killed Crystal because she didn't like
Crystal and wanted her
money.   Mildred went to
San Bernardino as Crystal
and met Lavery by acci-
dent.   Lavery knew her
but not that she had traded
places with Crystal.
Mildred killed Lavery be-
fore someone found out
the truth.   Degarmo killed
Mildred because he hated
her.   Degarmo is killed
by Army guards while try-
ing to get away.

Chapter 5

THE HIGH WINDOW:
THE BRASHER DOUBLOON

The High Window, Chandler's third novel, ranks as
one of the author's structurally superior efforts.   The plot,
like Farewell, My Lovely before it and The Lady in the
Lake after it, was carefully constructed to avoid the loop-
holes of The Big Sleep.   The High Window, however, falters
slightly in characterization.   While the novel contains many
of Chandler's classic characters, a few of the minor characterizations are not up to his best.   Overall, then, the
plot is slightly superior to the characterizations.

Chandler began planning his third novel in 1939.   He
labeled it "A Burlesque on the Pulp Novelette...."[1]   By
1942 the book was complete, except for the now-customary
titling problems.   Chandler wrote his publisher:

> As to the title, let me say at once that what-
> ever I might think or like or not like I am not
> going to set my opinion against yours. The title,
> Brasher or Brasher Doubloon, was the origin of
> the story, but that's not important.   I never
> thought of your idea that booksellers might pro-
> nounce Brasher as brassiere.   I can see the point
> now.
> Brasher, more commonly Brashear, is an actu-
> al name.   There was an Ephraim Brashear or
> Brasher, and he actually did make a coin for the
> State of New York in 1787.   It is not the most
> valuable American coin, but except possibly the
> 1822 five-dollar gold piece it is the only one exist-
> ing in sufficient numbers, and being of sufficient
> value, to be of any use for my purpose.   There
> are a couple of small towns named Brashear and
> also a Brasher Falls.   However, all this, which
> gives the title a hard reality to me, is nothing to
> the bookseller.

I have not the ingenuity to devise the sort of
intricate and recondite puzzle the purest aficionados go for.   The title might lead them to expect
a type of story they are not getting.   But that
again is really your problem. ...   All I can think
of along this line at the moment is The Lost
Doubloon, The Lost Doubloon Mystery, The Stolen
Coin Mystery, The Rare Coin Mystery.   All rather
pedestrian.   I'd like something with a bit more
oomph. 2

Chandler finally elected to call the book The High
Window, because it was "simple, suggestive and [points]
to the ultimate essential clue."3

Marlowe's third adventure starts when the detective
is hired by Mrs. Elizabeth Murdock to recover the Brasher
Doubloon, a valuable coin that has been stolen from her.   A
coin dealer, Elisha Morningstar, called her about it and
Mrs. Murdock believes her son Leslie's wife, Linda, took
the coin.   Marlowe also notices that Mrs. Murdock's secretary, Merle Davis, is very afraid of men.

Marlowe visits Linda's friend, Lois, the wife of a
gambler named Alex Morny.   She is with a man named
Vannier.   Marlowe confronts the man who has been following him, George Phillips, who says he is working for Linda.
Marlowe visits Morningstar who says he will have the coin
the next day when Marlowe can buy it back.   Marlowe discovers a connection between Morningstar and Phillips.

Marlowe finds Phillips murdered.   A package con-
taining the doubloon is delivered to Marlowe.   Marlowe calls
Mrs. Murdock, but she says the coin has been returned.
A second visit to Morningstar reveals he too is dead.

Marlowe visits Morny, who wants him to investigate
Vannier.   Marlowe talks to Linda and she says she didn't
take the coin.   Marlowe returns to Mrs. Murdock's.   Leslie says he stole the coin but had to return it.   Marlowe
learns Merle was Mrs. Murdock's first husband's secretary
when he fell out of a window.

Merle comes hysterically to Marlowe's apartment.
Mrs. Murdock has been paying Vannier blackmail money for
the past eight years.   Merle says she shot Vannier, but
Marlowe doesn't believe her.   Marlowe goes to Vannier's

TABLE 7.   THE BRASHER DOUBLOON

Cast

Philip Marlowe	George Montgomery
Merle Davis	Nancy Guild
Leslie Murdock	Conrad Janis
Lieut. Breeze	Roy Roberts
Vannier	Fritz Kortner
Mrs. Murdock	Florence Bates
Blair	Marvin Miller
Morningstar	Houseley Stevenson
Sergeant Spangler	Bob Adler
George Anson	Jack Conrad
Eddie Prue	Alfred Linder
Manager	Jack Overman
Mike	Jack Stoney
Figaro	Ray Spiker
Coroner	Paul Maxey
Attendant	Joe Palma
Baggage Rm. At- tendant	Al Eben

A Twentieth Century-Fox film

Running time: 72 minutes

Release date: May 21, 1947

Credits

Produced by	Robert Brassler
Directed by	John Brahm
Screenplay by	Dorothy Hannah
Adaption by	Leonard Praskins
Based on novel by	Raymond Chandler
Dir. of Photog.	Lloyd Ahern, A. S. C.
Special Effects by	Fred Sersen
Art Directors	James Basevi
	Richard Irvine
Set Decorations	Thomas Little
Sound	Eugene Grossman
	Harvey M. Leonard
Music by	David Buttolph
Musical Direction	Alfred Newman
Orchestral Arrange- ments	Maurice de Packh
Costumes	Eleanor Behm
Edited by	Harry Reynolds
Associate	Frank E. Hughes
Make-up by	Ben Nye

and finds him dead.   He also finds a photograph of Mrs.
Murdock's first husband falling out of a window.

Marlowe solves the case: Leslie gave the doubloon
to Vannier, who counterfeited it.   Vannier hired Phillips
to take the counterfeit to Morningstar to see if it would
pass as genuine.   Vannier killed Phillips and Morningstar,
and Leslie killed Vannier.   Mrs. Murdock, not Merle,
pushed her husband out of the window and the photograph
Vannier had proves it.

The High Window, published in 1942, was Chandler's
first "original" one.   Whereas The Big Sleep and Farewell,
My Lovely had been created largely out of the author's previous short stories, virtually all the material for The High
Window was newly written.   (The novel did, however, use a
small bit from "The King in Yellow," published in Dime
Detective Magazine, March, 1937. [4])   The novel demonstrated
that Chandler was as adept at writing an original novel as
he was at creating books out of his old short stories.

Reviewers expressed general enthusiasm for Chandler's latest work.   They now had begun to look to Chandler
for a relief from the run-of-the-mill detective story. [5]
Chandler had become, as one critic put it, "the pick of the

Mrs. Murdock (Florence Bates), assisted by Merle Davis
(Nancy Guild), hires Marlowe (George Montgomery) to find
the purloined coin. All photos in this chapter are from
The Brasher Doubloon (20th-C. Fox, 1947).

---

hard-boiled mystery scribblers."[6] Marlowe also drew
praise as "a detective who is hard-boiled enough to be con-
vincing without being disgustingly tough...."[7] Surprisingly,
the chief criticism of the novel came from Chandler himself.
He expressed his displeasure by writing that The High Window had "No action, no likable characters, no nothing. The
detective does nothing."[8]

     Although Chandler was too hard on himself, his com-
ment about the novel's characters deserves examination.
Chandler's novels usually are similar to a well-cast film:
the audience not only can appreciate the major characters,
but also delight in the minor ones as well. But in The High
Window, several of the minor characters display all the attributes of film stereotypes. For example, the old Jew who
runs the pawn shop comes complete with a black skull cap
and cut out glasses. And he talks stereotyped Jewish-style
English in lines like, "So ten dollars you are wanting?"[9]
An Italian named Palermo, affectionately called a "wop" in
the novel, displays similar characteristics. He is a vaguely
sinister man who runs a funeral parlor and wields a good
deal of power in the city. He, too, has his own brand of
speech, evident in such lines as "Is stair from second floor

also. "10 (Unfortunately, he and the pawnbroker never meet
in the novel; a conversation between them would be a notable
exercise in grammatical aberration.   This is not to suggest authors should not use vernacular speech.   These two
individuals merely illustrate Chandler's use of stereotypes
in this instance.   The fault, then, lies not so much in
whether or not the characters are likable as in the way
Chandler drew them.)

It should be noted that the link between Chandler's
third novel and Hollywood is much stronger than a sharing
of stereotyped characters.   Although Chandler did not go to
Hollywood until after he wrote the book, he seems to have
had the movie capital at least partly on his mind.   Much of
the Idle Valley Club came directly from traditional film
lore.   Its owner, Alex Morny, had been an actor ten years
previously and apparently carried over his screen image of
a "heavy" into his personal life.   Morny even thinks in
filmic terms, calling the act put on by his wife Lois in
Vannier's house "Early Lillian Gish."11   From the first we
see the Idle Valley Club as a movie set: Marlowe describes
the lobby as looking "like a high-budget musical."12   And
the club itself had "A lot of light and glitter, a lot of
scenery, a lot of clothes, a lot of sound, an all-star cast,
and a plot with all the originality and drive of a split finger-
nail."13   When Marlowe is ready to leave, his statements
make the reader feel like he is walking away from a private
eye film in the midst of production:

> What I like about this place is everything runs
> so true to type....   The cop at the gate, the
> shine on the door, the cigarette and check girls,
> the fat greasy sensual man with the tall stately
> bored showgirl, the well-dressed, drunk and hor-
> ribly rude director cursing the barman, the silent
> guy with the gun, the night club owner with the
> soft gray hair and the B-picture mannerisms, and
> now you--the tall dark torcher with the negligent
> sneer, the husky voice, the hard-boiled vocabu-
> lary.14

These references to Hollywood foreshadowed The Little Sister in which Chandler took on the agents, actors, and studios
with his unflattering pen.

Twentieth Century-Fox had purchased Chandler's novel
for $2000 in 1941 (see p. ix) and elected to remake it.15

Sgt. Spangler (Bob Adler), Marlowe (G. Montgomery), and Lt. Breeze (Roy Roberts) listen while the coroner (Paul Maxey) reports the cause of Anson's death: "Shot in the chest with a very small calibre gun with soft-nosed bullets. Been dead about two hours...."

Leonard Praskins adapted The High Window for the screen and Dorothy Hannah wrote the screenplay. The initial reworking of the novel resulted in a modified, although reasonably faithful, plot line. But when the film went into production, this written blueprint underwent modification. (Table 8 compares the novel, script, and film plots.) The effect of this modification was to shorten the story, presumably to conserve filming time and save production costs. Thus, while the initial story adaption accurately reflects the book, the final film does not, particularly in the area of characterizations (as discussed later). In both the script and the film, the importance of the stolen doubloon has been increased and the counterfeiting scheme dropped. Both the script and the film suffer from a basic plot flaw, namely that no explanation is given about how Anson happened to have the doubloon. Since the novel suffers no plot irregularities, The Brasher Doubloon stands as the only Marlowe film with a more confused plot than its source novel.

Twentieth Century-Fox assigned John Brahm the directorial chores for the film, which was released in early
1947 (a few months after Lady in the Lake).   Brahm, a
German, had worked in the theatre and had been brought to
Hollywood by Myron Selznick in 1937.   He became established as a "B" picture director and had most of his film
successes in the late forties.   He went into television directing in 1955. [16]

The critics greeted The Brasher Doubloon without
serious debate.   A few reviewers liked the picture, but
most felt it a rather boring affair.   The New York Times
called it "the least of his [Marlowe's] exploits to date ...
due to a pedestrian adaption ... plodding and conventional
direction ... and to the lack of conviction in George Montgomery's interpretation of Marlowe."[17] The critics leveled most of
their unfaborable comments at Montgomery's performance.

The Brasher Doubloon reflects Brahm's German origins and the film even contains an "in" joke dealing with
Brahm's past.   (The character of Vannier is patterned after
Brahm; Vannier is German and came to Hollywood in 1937
to work in the film industry.)   Early in the film, a sinister
mood strongly reminiscent of the German cinema in the
1920's is established through combination of set design and
lighting.   The chief result is irregular shadows that typify
many German silent films.   Especially interesting are the
moving shadows of wind-blown ferns projected on the characters inside the Murdock Mansion.

Unfortunately, the mood Brahm creates in the opening
sequences of the film is wasted, since the picture quickly
becomes loaded with gimmicky techniques.   The wind that
was so effective in the opening continues to blow throughout
the film with no meaningful purpose.   In contrast, Chandler
begins the novel with no wind at all; not until the story is
well advanced does the wind rise.   The Brasher Doubloon
also tries unsuccessfully to borrow techniques and material
from previous popular films.   The picture uses narration in
a manner similar to Murder, My Sweet, but this narration
lacks the wit and Chandler-type characteristics of that ear-

Facing page: (left) a desperate Rudolph Vannier (Fritz Kort-
ner) comes to Marlowe's office to get the doubloon.   (Right)
After trying Vannier's method to obtain the coin, Merle
(Guilt) has little luck (it's in Marlowe's [G. Montgomery]
tobacco pouch).

lier film.   The movie also tries to borrow from The
Maltese Falcon, which incorporates a valuable object with a
long and violent past.   Similarly, The Brasher Doubloon
supplies a violent history for the title coin which the novel
does not have.   As Morningstar tells Marlowe: "The man
who coined it was murdered and robbed through the treachery of a female.   Since then, at least seven other owners
of the coin have come to abrupt unhappy ends."   While the
coin is used as a foreshadowing device (the Murdock family
does come to an unhappy end), very little use of the coin's
violent history is made.   Even at the end of the picture,
the audience is not reminded that the coin caused the Murdocks' downfall.   The opportunity exists, for Marlowe produces the doubloon to give to Mrs. Murdock.   But the chance
to stress the doubloon's history is lost.

     For all its low-budget characteristics, The Brasher
Doubloon gained a fair amount of attention, even opening at
New York's prestigious Roxy theatre, accompanied by a
stage show featuring Jack Benny, his radio troupe, and a
special appearance by Fred Allen.   (One critic likened this
event to a contemporary premiere of an American International horror film at Radio City Music Hall with the cast of
"All in the Family" on stage. 18)   The opening was a success, but only due to the appearance of Mr. Benny.

     More than any other Marlowe film, The Brasher
Doubloon most completely violates the spirit of Chandler,
especially in the area of characterizations.   This becomes
particularly apparent in the case of Merle Davis.   While
the script left Merle essentially as Chandler depicted her
(until the end, at least), the character (played by Nancy
Guild) underwent restructuring during filming.   This change
points out the problem the first five Marlowe films felt it
necessary to solve: providing Marlowe with a love interest.
The Brasher Doubloon tried to accomplish this by making
Merle the love interest.   At the same time, however, the
filmmakers also tried to retain Chandler's conception of her.
The result was the most un-Chandler-like female in any
Marlowe film.

     The basic problem is that the reconstructed Merle
simply cannot make up her filmic mind whether she has
stayed the meek girl of Chandler's novel who fears men, or
developed into a sexual bombshell on the order of Lauren
Bacall.   This uncertainty sometimes manifests itself in al-
ternating lines of dialogue.   In a conversation with Marlowe

Vannier's newsreel footage. (Marlowe says: "Here we have Mrs. Murdock in the very act of giving her husband the old heave-ho.")

---

she says: "It's just that I don't like to have men touch me." Marlowe comments on her sexy appearance. She says: "I should have said I wasn't used to being touched. It's a phobia, I guess." Marlowe expresses his sympathy and she quickly replies, "But that doesn't mean I wouldn't like to get over it." Marlowe has her character pinpointed when he tells her, "You just can't seem to make up your mind, can you Miss Davis?" And later he comments that "the girl [Merle] was what bothered me most. I couldn't figure the switches she pulled."

The defects in characterization extend beyond Merle

to some of the lesser characters, particularly Blair, Prue,
and Vannier. Blair and Prue are certainly not the gangsters of Chandler's world. Chandler's racketeers are high-
class mobsters who frequent only the plushest clubs. And
even their henchmen have a certain kind of style about
them, such as Mars' right hand man, Canino. But Blair
and Prue are petty hoods who do not fit in, and Blair's
Lucky Club belongs more to a 1930's gangster picture than
it does to a Marlowe film. Vannier, too, does not reflect
the character in The High Window. This Vannier is prac-
tically scared of his own shadow, while Chandler's better
one reflects the blackmailing type.

Not all the film's characters violate the spirit of
Chandler, however. Florence Bates gives an excellent performance as Mrs. Murdock. Her Murdock has all the pent-
up hatred and total disregard for everyone but her son
Chandler instilled in the character. She stands out as the
perfect Chandler villainess: an over-possessive rich woman
far more evil than the blackmailer with whom she deals.

Finally, we turn our attention to George Montgomery.
A former boxer and stuntman, Montgomery, primarily a
"B" film actor, is known less for his acting ability than for
being the husband of Dinah Shore, an amateur furniture
maker, and a salesman for Johnson's Wax. Montgomery,
whose acting is as wooden as his furniture, portrays a
somewhat different Marlowe than the previous ones. He is
still a wise-cracking cynic, but his delivery of these wise
cracks is flat and without enthusiasm. (In this respect, he
matches the level of his material, for the film contains
some of the worst quips of any Marlowe picture. For example, in dialogue not from the book, Montgomery says, "I
got into this thing on account of a pretty face. The ancient
Trojans were sucked into a ten-year war for the same reason, but they didn't regret it any more than I did.") His
worst characteristic, both in the way the role is written and
the way Montgomery plays it, is that, unlike the other film
Marlowes, he isn't really concerned with seeing justice done.
He knows that if he solves the case, Merle's fear of men
will be removed and she will be open for sexual conquest,
and this is his major reason for staying on the case. He
is the only Marlowe to sport a mustache, although this addition does nothing for the hero's character. Montgomery's
Marlowe also remains the only one who plays golf. Perhaps
he doesn't get enough exercise on his cases. And finally,
he is the first of the two cinematic Marlowes to smoke a
pipe (James Garner is the other).

One can summarize The Brasher Doubloon by saying it stands out as the poorest Marlowe film and scarcely deserves the critical comments made about it in a Films in Review article on John Brahm, which characterized the picture as the "least violent, moodiest, and perhaps finest, U.S. private-eye film."[19]

TABLE 8.   PLOT COMPARISON

The High Window / The Brasher Doubloon

	NOVEL	SCRIPT	FILM
1.	Marlowe is called to the home of Mrs. Elizabeth Bright Murdock. He meets Merle Davis, Mrs. Murdock's secretary.	Marlowe is called to the home of Mrs. Elizabeth Bright Murdock. He meets Merle Davis, Mrs. Murdock's secretary.	Marlowe is called to the home of Mrs. Elizabeth Bright Murdock. He meets Merle Davis, Mrs. Murdock's secretary.
2.		Marlowe meets a young loudly dressed man leaving the house.	
3.		Marlowe meets Mrs. Murdock's son, Leslie, who tells him his mother doesn't need him.	Marlowe meets Mrs. Murdock's son, Leslie, who tells him his mother doesn't need him.
4.	Mrs. Murdock wants Marlowe to recover a rare coin, the Brasher Doubloon, that has been stolen from her late husband's collection.	Mrs. Murdock wants Marlowe to recover a rare coin, the Brasher Doubloon, that has been stolen from her late husband's collection.	Mrs. Murdock wants Marlowe to recover a rare coin, the Brasher Doubloon, that has been stolen from her late husband's collection.
5.		Mrs. Murdock says she knows who took the coin, but she won't tell Marlowe. She says that the only two people besides herself with the combination to the safe where the coin was kept are Leslie and Merle.	Mrs. Murdock says she knows who took the coin, but she won't tell Marlowe. She says that the only two people besides herself with the combination to the safe where the coin was kept are Leslie and Merle.
6.	A coin dealer, Elisha Morningstar, called about the coin and that's how Mrs. Murdock discovered it was missing.	A coin dealer, Elisha Morningstar, called about the coin and that's how Mrs. Murdock discovered it was missing.	A coin dealer, Elisha Morningstar, called about the coin and that's how Mrs. Murdock discovered it was missing.

7. Mrs. Murdock believes
    her son's wife, Linda
    Conquest, took the coin
    before she ran off.
    Mrs. Murdock wants
    an uncontested divorce
    for her son and the
    coin recovered.   Mar-
    lowe agrees to take
    the case on the condi-
    tion he is not being
    hired to frame Linda,
    who used to work at
    the Idle Valley Club.

8.   Because Mrs. Mur-   Because Mrs. Murdock
                                  dock won't tell him   won't tell him everything,
                                  everything, Marlowe   Marlowe decides not to
                                  decides not to take   take the case. He goes
                                  the case. He goes   to Merle to return the
                                  to Merle to return   retainer check Mrs. Mur-
                                  the retainer check   dock gave him. Merle
                                  Mrs. Murdock gave   is not only afraid of Mrs.
                                  him. Merle is not   Murdock, but also afraid
                                  only afraid of Mrs.   to have men touch her.
                                  Murdock, but also   She pleads with Marlowe
                                  afraid to have men   to take the case. He
                                  touch her. She   finds a revolver in her
                                  pleads with Marlowe   desk.
                                  to take the case.
                                  He finds a revolver
                                  in her desk.

9.   Marlowe returns to
                                  Mrs. Murdock and
                                  says he'll take the
                                  case. He refuses to
                                  tell her why.

10.   Marlowe says he'll take
                                                             both cases; Mrs. Mur-
                                                             dock's and Merle's.

11. Marlowe tries to
    comfort Merle, who
    is crying. Not only
    is she afraid of Mrs.
    Murdock, but she
    doesn't like men to
    touch her. She says
    Linda's roommate,
    Lois Magic, had
    once come to the
    house with a man
    named Vannier.
    Marlowe is followed
    when he leaves the
    house.

(TABLE 8 cont.)

12.	The man Marlowe saw when he went into the house is waiting in a car. Marlowe fails to see Merle leave the house as he drives away.	
13. Marlowe goes to his office. Mrs. Murdock's son, Leslie, comes. He tries to find out why his mother wants Linda found but Marlowe refuses to tell him. Leslie says he owes Alex Morny $12,000. Linda used to work for him. Leslie says his father, Horace Bright, jumped out of his office window when he lost all his money in the crash.		
14.	Marlowe goes to his office. Eddie Prue comes. He says he represents a night club owner named Blair. He tries to buy Marlowe off the Murdock case. Marlowe refuses the money. Prue pulls a gun and wants Marlowe to come and see Blair. Marlowe takes the gun away from him.	Marlowe goes to his office. Eddie Prue comes. He says he represents Vince Blair, owner of the Lucky Club. He tries to buy Marlowe off the Murdock case. Marlowe refuses the money. Prue wants Marlowe to meet Blair. Marlowe refuses and Prue pulls a gun. Marlowe takes the gun away from him.
15. Marlowe learns Morny owns the Idle Valley Club. Marlowe leaves his office and is followed. Morny is married to Lois Magic and Marlowe goes to see her. She is with Vannier and doesn't tell Marlowe anything.		

16. Marlowe is followed
     again and he confronts
     his pursuer. The
     man, George Anson
     Phillips, says he is
     a detective working
     for Linda. Someone
     is following him and
     he wants Marlowe's
     help. He arranges
     to meet Marlowe at
     Phillips' apartment.

17.   Marlowe is followed
                             by the man that was
                             at Mrs. Murdock's.
                             Marlowe confronts
                             him. He says his
                             name is Anson. He
                             is a detective and
                             wants Marlowe's
                             help. His apart-
                             ment has been
                             searched and he
                             was shot at by a
                             man that looked like
                             Prue. He hints
                             that he may have
                             the doubloon and ar-
                             ranges to meet Mar-
                             lowe in Anson's
                             apartment.

18. Marlowe goes to see   Marlowe goes to see   Marlowe goes to see
     Morningstar, who tells   Morningstar, who   Morningstar, who tells
     him the history of the   tells him the history   him the history of the
     Brasher Doubloon.   of the Brasher Doub-   Brasher Doubloon. Mar-
     Marlowe says someone   loon. Marlowe says   lowe says someone tried
     tried to sell the coin   someone tried to   to sell the coin to Morn-
     to Morningstar.   sell the coin to   ingstar.
                              Morningstar.

19. Marlowe offers to
     buy the coin and
     Morningstar says
     he will have it the
     next day.

20.   Marlowe threatens   Marlowe threatens Morn-
                             Morningstar with the   ingstar with the police,
                             police, but he will   but he will not tell Mar-
                             not tell Marlowe who   lowe who offered him the
                             offered him the coin.   coin.

21. Marlowe pretends to   Marlowe pretends to   Marlowe pretends to leave
     leave and hears   leave and hears   and hears Morningstar
     Morningstar call a   Morningstar call   call Anson.

(TABLE 8 cont.)

Mr. Anson, who Marlowe realizes is Phillips.	Anson.	

22. Marlowe goes to Phillips' apartment and finds Phillips shot to death. Marlowe goes to the manager, who says a Mr. Palermo owns the building and most of the district. Marlowe and the manager go up to Phillips' room but before they go in, there is trouble with a man named Hench in the room across the hall. Hench pulls a gun but says it isn't his. Marlowe takes the gun and notices it has been fired. The police are called and Lt. Jessie Breeze investigates. Hench denies shooting Phillips. Breeze suggests the killer switched guns with Hench. Breeze questions Marlowe, who tells him about Phillips.

23.   Marlowe goes to see Anson. He searches the apartment and finds Anson murdered. Marlowe searches the body and finds a baggage claim check. The police are called and Breeze and Spangler investigate. They search Marlowe and he lies about the claim check.

Marlowe goes to see Anson. He searches the apartment and finds Anson murdered. Marlowe searches the body and finds a baggage claim check. The police are called and Breeze and Spangler investigate. They search Marlowe and he lies about the claim check.

24. Marlowe returns to his office. A package comes. It is the Brasher Doubloon.

Marlowe gets a cryptic
telephone warning.

25.

Marlowe redeems
the claim check and
receives the Brash-
er Doubloon.

Marlowe redeems the
claim check and receives
the Brasher Doubloon.

26. Marlowe calls Mrs.
Murdock. She doesn't
know Phillips and
says the Doubloon
has been returned.
Marlowe pawns his
coin.

27. Marlowe goes to see
Morningstar and finds
he has been mur-
dered.

Marlowe goes to
see Morningstar and
finds he has been
murdered.

Marlowe goes to see
Morningstar and finds he
has been murdered.

28. Marlowe notices that
H. R. Teager Dental
Laboratories has an
office in Morning-
star's building.

29.

Marlowe finds what
looks like Merle's
gun next to Morning-
star's body. He
goes to Mrs. Mur-
dock's to check it
out. It is Merle's
gun, but she denies
knowing anything
about how it got
where it did.
Merle says she
sent Marlowe a
telegram saying
the coin had been
recovered. Leslie
comes and Marlowe
mentions that two
men have been
murdered. Leslie
says he took the
coin to pay a
gambling debt. His
mother threatened
to disinherit him,
so he got the doub-
loon back. Mar-
lowe doesn't believe
his story. Mrs.
Murdock hints Merle

Marlowe finds what looks
like Merle's gun next to
Morningstar's body. He
goes to Mrs. Murdock's
to check it out. It is
Merle's gun, but she
denies knowing anything
about how it got where it
did. Merle says she
sent Marlowe a telegram
saying the coin had been
recovered. Leslie comes
and Marlowe mentions
that two men have been
murdered. Leslie says
he took the coin to pay a
gambling debt. His
mother threatened to dis-
inherit him, so he got the
doubloon back. Marlowe
doesn't believe his story.
Mrs. Murdock hints
Merle is insane and says
Merle has been with her
since her husband fell
to his death seven years
ago. Marlowe accuses
them all of lying and
shocks them by showing
them the doubloon.

(TABLE 8 cont.)

is insane and says
Merle has been with
her since her hus-
band fell to his death
seven years ago.
Marlowe accuses
them all of lying
and shocks them by
showing them the
doubloon.

30. Breeze and Lt.
Spangler come to
question Marlowe
about Phillips.
Breeze doesn't think
Hench shot Phillips.
They give Marlowe
12 hours by which
time he must tell
them everything.
They say Palermo
saw a blonde com-
ing out of Phillips'
building.   Marlowe
gets a call from
Eddie Prue to see
Morny at the Idle
Valley Club.

31. Marlowe goes to the
Idle Valley Club.
He learns Linda is
there and meets Ed-
die Prue, who takes
him to see Morny.
Marlowe tells Morny
about Phillips and
Morny says he wants
Marlowe to investi-
gate Vannier. Morny
shows Marlowe a
bill for dental sup-
plies made out to
H. R. Teager and
signed by Vannier.
Marlowe says Prue
was the one follow-
ing Phillips and
learns Leslie has
been out to the club.
He told Linda about
Marlowe.   Linda
enters.   Marlowe
tells her Mrs. Mur-
dock wants the coin

back, but Linda
denies taking it.
Linda says Vannier
knows Mrs. Mur-
dock very well.

32. Marlowe goes to see
    Mrs. Murdock. He
    tells her about the
    murders of Phillips
    and Morningstar,
    but she isn't con-
    cerned that Marlowe
    is in trouble with
    the police. She
    says her son stole
    the coin and gave it
    to Morny as secur-
    ity for his gambling
    debt. He knew
    where Linda was
    all along. When he
    told Morny the po-
    lice might come
    after him, Morny
    gave back the coin.
    Marlowe doesn't be-
    lieve the story.
    Marlowe thinks Linda
    might have stolen
    the coin and Leslie
    is trying to protect
    her. Mrs. Mur-
    dock becomes angry.

33. Merle asks Marlowe
    to keep helping Mrs.
    Murdock. Merle
    says the man that
    scared her fell out
    of a window. Merle
    was the man's secre-
    tary and the man
    was Mrs. Murdock's
    first husband. Mar-
    lowe decides to in-
    vestigate Merle's
    problem.

34.   Merle goes after
                               Marlowe and says
                               he must give her
                               the coin. She will
                               be in trouble if she
                               doesn't get it. She
                               admits the gun is
                               hers, but says she
                               didn't shoot anyone.

(TABLE 8 cont.)

35.		Mrs. Murdock tells Merle to get the coin or her responsibility for Merle will end.
36.	Marlowe goes to see Breeze and Spangler. Breeze says Hench asked to see Palermo and then confessed to the murder of Phillips.	
37.		Marlowe wants to help Merle so he sees his office neighbor, Carl Moss, a psychiatrist. Moss says if Merle is a homocidal maniac she should be locked up before she can murder someone else.
38.		Marlowe goes to his office to find a Rudolph Vannier there. Vannier wants the doubloon in exchange for something else. He pulls a gun on Marlowe and says he will die if he doesn't get the coin. Marlowe takes the gun away from him and discovers Vannier is a newsreel cameraman. Vannier refuses to tell Marlowe anything.	Marlowe goes to his office to find a Rudolph Vannier there and Merle's telegram. Vannier wants the doubloon in exchange for something else. He pulls a gun on Marlowe. Marlowe takes it away from him and Vannier says he will die if he doesn't get the coin. Marlowe discovers Vannier was a freelance newsreel cameraman and reasons Vannier is using newsreel footage for blackmail. Vannier refuses to tell him what the film shows.
39.	Marlowe goes to see Palermo. Marlowe says Hench didn't kill Phillips. Palermo says he got Hench to confess to protect one of his brothers.	
40.	Marlowe goes to Teager's office. No	

one is there. He
searches the office
and decides Teager
has left town. A
visit to Teager's
house confirms this.

41. Marlowe gets a call
     from his apartment
     manager that Merle
     wants to be let into
     Marlowe's apartment
     and is hysterical.
     Marlowe goes to his
     apartment. Merle
     says she just came
     from Vannier's.
     For the past eight
     years she has taken
     Vannier money at
     intervals. She says
     she shot Vannier.
     Marlowe checks her
     gun and finds it has
     been fixed so it won't
     fire. Merle faints
     and Marlowe calls
     Dr. Carl Moss.
     The doctor says
     Merle suffers from
     regressive emotional
     shock and calls a
     nurse to stay with
     Merle.

42.   Marlowe goes to his
                             apartment. Merle is
                             there and she pulls a
                             gun on him. She
                             searches Marlowe
                             but doesn't find the
                             coin, which Marlowe
                             has hidden in his
                             tobacco pouch. She
                             starts to tell Mar-
                             lowe about the day
                             Mr. Murdock died
                             when she notices the
                             pouch. Marlowe
                             gives it to her and
                             Breeze and Spangler
                             come. He says
                             Merle is Miss Jones
                             and they were going
                             out. Breeze, who
                             knows Marlowe was
                             in Morningstar's office
                             after he was

(TABLE 8 cont.)

murdered, says he
will have to go with
them. Marlowe
starts to light his
pipe and asks Merle
for the pouch. She
has to give it to him.

43.   Marlowe goes to his
                                            apartment house and the
                                            manager says a Miss
                                            Jones is in his apart-
                                            ment. It is Merle. She
                                            tells Marlowe she didn't
                                            like Mr. Murdock's
                                            touching her when she
                                            was his secretary. They
                                            were watching the Tourna-
                                            ment of Roses Parade,
                                            he grabbed her, and he
                                            fell. She says she wanted
                                            Marlowe to find out who
                                            took the coin to prove
                                            her innocence. She pulls
                                            a gun on Marlowe. She
                                            searches Marlowe but
                                            can't find the coin. She
                                            says she wants to give
                                            the doubloon to Vannier
                                            to suppress his film; that
                                            he would give up the
                                            film for the coin.

44.   Marlowe takes
           Breeze to a coffee
           shop and convinces
           him he can deliver
           the murderer in 24
           hours. Pretending
           to be broke, Mar-
           lowe leaves the
           doubloon with the
           shop's proprietor
           saying he'll pick
           it up the next day
           when he pays the
           bill.

45.   Marlowe returns to
           his apartment to
           find it searched
           and Merle tied up
           in a closet. She
           says she wanted
           the doubloon to
           give to Vannier.

Mrs. Murdock paid
Vannier to suppress
the film. Merle
faints and Marlowe
calls Dr. Moss.
Moss says Merle
has a guilt com-
plex but isn't really
crazy. Moss says
he'll call a nurse
to stay with Merle.

46.

Marlowe leaves his
apartment and is
knocked uncon-
scious and taken to
Blair at the Lucky
Club. Leslie is
there.

Marlowe leaves his apart-
ment and is knocked un-
conscious and taken to
Blair at the Lucky Club.
Leslie is there.

47.

Blair offers Mar-
lowe $5000 for the
coin. Marlowe men-
tions Vannier and
Leslie becomes
hysterical. Marlowe
says the Murdocks
have the coin and
shows them Merle's
telegram. Marlowe
says Leslie hired
him to pin the two
murders on Prue
and Blair. Spang-
ler, who has fol-
lowed Marlowe,
comes and asks
Marlowe if he
wants to leave.

48.

Marlowe refuses to give
Blair the coin and
Blair's men beat him up.
Marlowe mentions Vannier
and Leslie says maybe
Marlowe wants the film
so he can blackmail
Mrs. Murdock. Marlowe
shows them Merle's tele-
gram. Leslie and Prue
fight, and Marlowe es-
capes.

49.

Marlowe recovers
the doubloon from
the coffee shop.

50.

Dr. Moss calls

(TABLE 8 cont.)

	Marlowe at his office and says Merle is gone. Marlowe calls the Murdocks and Leslie says Merle isn't there.	
51.	Merle calls Marlowe and tells him to come to Vannier's.	Merle calls Marlowe and tells him to come to Vannier's.
52. Marlowe goes to Vannier's and finds him dead, shot in the head. Marlowe finds a photograph that shows Horace Bright falling out a window. Morny and Lois come. Marlowe hides. Morny says he had Prue follow Lois. Morny tries to make it look like Lois shot Vannier and says he is going to turn Lois in. They leave. Marlowe rearranges the evidence to make it look like suicide.		
53.	Marlowe goes to Vannier's. Vannier is dead. Marlowe and Merle search the house for the film. She says she pushed Murdock when he tried to embrace her and he fell. She fainted when Murdock fell. Mrs. Murdock and Leslie said they would protect her. Marlowe tells Merle that Leslie killed Anson and Morningstar. Marlowe and Merle find the film. She tries to burn it but Leslie steps out of hiding with gun drawn and	

grabs it. Marlowe
gets the gun and
calls the police.
He tells them to
pick up Blair and
Prue. He calls
Mrs. Murdock and
tells her she can
get the doubloon at
his apartment that
evening.

54.   Marlowe goes to Vanni-
                                    er's. He is dead and
                                    the evidence points to a
                                    woman, but Merle says
                                    she didn't kill him.
                                    Marlowe and Merle
                                    search the house for the
                                    film. Merle says Mrs.
                                    Murdock paid Vannier to
                                    avoid a scandal. They
                                    find the film and Merle
                                    tries to burn it. Leslie
                                    enters, gun drawn, and
                                    retrieves the film. Mar-
                                    lowe gets the gun and
                                    calls the police. He
                                    tells them to pick up
                                    Blair and Prue.

55. Marlowe meets Prue
     and tells Prue he
     has learned what
     the dental supplies
     on Vannier's bill
     were used for.
     Marlowe goes to
     his apartment.
     Merle says she
     didn't shoot Vanni-
     er. Marlowe re-
     deems his doubloon
     from the pawnshop.

56. Marlowe goes to
     see Mrs. Murdock
     and tells her what
     happened to Merle.
     He says Horace
     Bright made a pass
     at Merle and she
     pushed him out the
     window. Vannier
     knew about it and
     blackmailed Mrs.
     Murdock. Mar-
     lowe tells Mrs.

(TABLE 8 cont.)

Murdock about Merle
and Vannier.

57.   Marlowe has sum-
                               moned everyone to
                               his apartment. He
                               says the doubloon
                               was never anything
                               more than a medium
                               of exchange; the
                               only thing that
                               could get the film
                               away from Vanni-
                               er. Leslie wanted
                               the film to give to
                               Blair and Prue to
                               pay his gambling
                               debt. They were
                               going to use the
                               film to blackmail
                               Mrs. Murdock.
                               Anson had refused
                               to give the films
                               to Leslie, so Les-
                               lie killed him and
                               then killed Morning-
                               star and threatened
                               Vannier.

58. Marlowe meets Les-
     lie. He says Les-
     lie was at Vanni-
     er's. Marlowe says
     Phillips sent him the
     doubloon. Vannier
     and Teager decided
     to counterfeit the
     coin, using dental
     materials. Leslie
     gave Vannier the
     doubloon. Vannier
     and Teager wanted
     to see if the counter-
     feit coin appeared
     genuine, so they
     hired Phillips to try
     to sell the coin to
     Morningstar. Lois
     Morny was to go-
     between for Vannier
     and Phillips. Phil-
     lips was scared and
     told Vannier he was
     going to the police,
     so Vannier shot him.
     But Vannier couldn't

find the coin, be-
cause Phillips had
sent it to Marlowe,
so he went to see
Morningstar.
Morningstar didn't
have it and Van-
nier killed him.
Marlowe says Les-
lie killed Vannier.
Leslie says it was
an accident.   Mar-
lowe leaves.

59.

Marlowe has summoned
everyone to his office.
He gives Breeze Leslie's
confession of Anson and
Morningstar's murders.
Marlowe says the doubloon
was never anything more
than a medium of ex-
change; the only thing
that could get the film
away from Vannier.   Leslie wanted the film to
give to Blair and Prue
to pay his gambling debt.
They were going to use
the film to blackmail
Mrs. Murdock.

60.

Marlowe shows Van-
nier's film, which
shows Mr. Murdock
falling from a win-
dow ledge.   Marlowe
then shows an en-
larged version in
which clearly shows
Mrs. Murdock push-
ing her husband out
of the window.   Mar-
lowe says Mrs. Mur-
dock killed Vannier
because he told her
about Leslie being
in a plot to black-
mail her.

61. Marlowe has offered
to take Merle to her
parents.   He tells
her Vannier com-
mitted suicide and
says she didn't push
Horace Bright out
of the window.

Vannier's photograph
proves Mrs. Mur-
dock killed her hus-
band, but Merle re-
fuses to believe it.
Marlowe takes her
home.   The police
believe Vannier
committed suicide
and prove he shot
Phillips.

62.

Mrs. Murdock says Les-
lie confessed to the mur-
ders to protect Merle,
but Marlowe doesn't buy
it. He runs Vannier's
film, which shows Mr.
Murdock falling from a
window ledge. An en-
larged version clearly
shows Mrs. Murdock
pushing her husband out
of the window.   Mrs.
Murdock tries to draw a
gun, but Marlowe stops
her. She killed Vannier
because he told her about
Leslie being in a plot to
blackmail her.

Chapter 6

THE LITTLE SISTER:
MARLOWE

With the publication of The Little Sister, Chandler had his first completed novel in six years. Unfortunately the long wait for the reader was not justified, for Chandler's fifth book came as a disappointment after the near-perfect previous three novels. The same problems that plagued The Big Sleep returned to haunt The Little Sister: trivial writing errors and major plot weaknesses. Then, too, for the first time a change in Marlowe can be detected, for he has grown disenchanted with the city he loved.

For Chandler, his sixth novel, The Little Sister, was the most difficult to write. He began work on the book in 1944 and by October was halfway through it. In early 1946 he stated the as yet untitled novel "should be done not later than June, unless I get mad and throw it away."[1] By October, 1946 the author had selected the tentative title of The Little Sister but had not progressed further on the book. In March, 1947, Chandler wrote: "I am working, or was, on another Marlowe, because for business and professional reasons I think the guy is too valuable to let die out."[2] Over a year later the writer was halfway through his latest Marlowe adventure. He wrote:

> I am desperately trying to finish The Little Sister and should have a rough draft done almost any day I get up enough steam. The fact is, however, there is nothing in it but style and dialogue and characters. The plot creaks like a broken shutter in an October wind.[3]

The book commences when Orfamay Quest engages Marlowe to locate his missing brother, Orrin. The quest takes Marlowe to a Bay City hotel where he encounters the manager, Clausen, soon murdered with an ice pick, and a man named Hicks. Clausen had pointed the way to a doctor

115

TABLE 9. MARLOWE

Cast		Credits	
Philip Marlowe	James Garner	Produced by	Gabriel Katzka
Mavis Wald	Gayle Hunnicutt		Sidney Beckerman
Lt. Christy French	Carroll O'Connor	Directed by	Paul Bogart
Dolores Gonzales	Rita Moreno	Screenplay by	Stirling Silliphant
Orfamay Quest	Sharon Farrell	Based on novel by	Raymond Chandler
Mr. Crowell	William Daniels	Dir. of Photog.	William H. Daniels,
Sonny Steelgrave	H. M. Wynant		A.S.C.
Grant W. Hicks	Jackie Coogan	Special Effects by	J. McMillan Johnson
Sergeant Fred	Kenneth Tobey		Carroll L. Shepphird
Beifus		Art Directors	George W. Davis
Winslow Wong	Bruce Lee		Addison Hehr
Chuck	Christopher Cary	Set Decorations	Henry Grace
Oliver Hady	George Tyne		Hugh Hunt
Julie	Corinne Camacho	Recorded by	Franklin Milton
Dr. Vincent La-	Paul Stevens	Music by	Peter Matz
gardie		Song: "Little Sister"	
Orrin Quest	Roger Newman	Words by	Norman Gimbel
Gumpshaw	Read Morgan	Music by	Peter Matz
Haven Clausen	Warren Finnerty	Sung by	Orpheus
		Miss Hunnicutt's	Jean Louis
		gowns and furs by	

Filmed in Metrocolor; presented by
  Metro-Goldwyn-Mayer.
Running time: 95 minutes
Release date: October, 1969
Rated M (suggested for Mature audiences)
Produced by Katzka-Berne Productions,
  Inc. and Cherokee Productions, a
  joint venture in association with Beck-
  erman Productions, Inc.

Edited by	Gene Ruggiero
Asst. Director	Bud Grace
Make-up by	William Tuttle
Hair Styles by	Sidney Guilaroff
United Production	Sergei Petschnikoff
Mgr.	

named Lagardie, and Marlowe calls him using Hicks'
name.

A call for help takes Marlowe to the Van Nuys
Hotel, where Marlowe finds the caller, Hicks, murdered
with an ice pick. A woman in Hicks' room slugs Marlowe
and escapes. The ice pick was a trademark of Sunny Moe
Stein's mob, and Stein has recently been murdered, perhaps
by Weeper Moyer, alias Steelgrave. Marlowe locates the
woman in Hicks' apartment, Mavis Weld, and meets Mavis'
friend, Dolores Gonzales. Mavis throws Marlowe out when
he offers help and he meets Steelgrave going in to see
Mavis.

Marlowe recovers some photographs that were once
in Hicks' possession. They show Mavis and Steelgrave together on the day Stein was killed. Thus the picture could
not only destroy Mavis' movie career, but also disprove
Steelgrave's alibi that he was in jail when Stein died. Marlowe reasons the photographs were taken by Orrin Quest.

Marlowe deduces Orrin is Mavis' brother and goes to

see Lagardie. Marlowe says Lagardie got Orrin to take the
pictures for revenge against Steelgrave, and then passes
out from a doped cigarette. Marlowe regains conscious-
ness to find Orrin dying, an ice pick in his hand. Dolores,
who used to be Steelgrave's girl, tries to get Marlowe to
blackmail Steelgrave. She takes Marlowe to Steelgrave's
house, where he finds Mavis and Steelgrave, who is dead.
Marlowe discovers Orfamay was Orrin's partner in the attempt to blackmail Mavis.

Marlowe visits Dolores and sorts the whole thing out.
Dolores, Lagardie's ex-wife, got Orrin to take the photographs and killed Stein to strengthen the blackmail scheme
against Steelgrave. She killed Orrin and then Steelgrave.
She didn't like Mavis' being Steelgrave's girl.

The Little Sister, published in 1949, became Chandler's second "original" novel and was, in fact, the only one
of his books in which not even a small part came from previous material. It also remains the first Marlowe adventure to be written after the detective had appeared on the
screen. The effect of these screen Marlowes on Chandler's
concept of his hero, however, appears to have been in-
significant. Chandler did not have Marlowe being beaten
more than in previous novels nor did he give the detective
a girlfriend.

Critical reaction to The Little Sister proved less
favorable than to Chandler's previous works. When praise
did come, more often than not it favored Chandler himself,
not his latest novel. Reviewers felt, for example, that
Chandler had "overextended himself ... with an elaborate
and too pretentious prose style."[4] One critic remarked
that Chandler was in danger "of becoming a gifted hack."[5]
Others discussed Chandler's prose style or his use of dialogue, but few took time to praise the book.

The critics were essentially right in some of their
negative reactions. A careful reading of the novel reveals
several flaws, not the least of which relates to organization. Anything Chandler learned about plot structure in his
previous novels seems to have been forgotten. For some
reason, Chandler felt compelled to design the most complex
plot of his career, far exceeding the intricacies of The Big
Sleep. (A fanciful speculator might propose that Chandler,
unhappy with his experience in Hollywood, tried to develop
a plot unadaptable to the screen, but there is no proof of

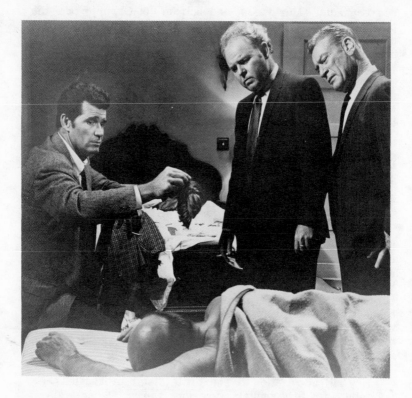

Marlowe (James Garner) removes Hicks' (Jackie Coogan) toupee and Lt. Christy French (Carroll O'Conner, center) and Sgt. Fred Beifus (Kenneth Tobey) recognize that Hicks is really Mileaway Marston. All photos in this chapter are from Marlowe (MGM, 1969).

---

this.) The basic complexity lies not in something simple, such as who killed whom, but in insufficiently explained relationships between characters. When one tries to sort out the actions of Dolores, Lagardie, Orrin, and Orfamay a confused, tangled web emerges. This situation is, perhaps, one of the most confusing blackmail schemes ever developed.

Chandler used The Little Sister to attack the Hollywood system he had grown to dislike, a system only lightly jabbed at in The High Window. There he had only commented on the false atmosphere of a movie set; here he

leveled his barbs against the people who made these movies.
First came the high-powered agents, represented by Sheri-
dan Ballou. Here was where Chandler felt the power of
Hollywood lay, not in the hands of the studio heads.   It
could take six months to see Ballou and his office "had
everything in it but a swimming pool. "[6] When Marlowe
talks back to Ballou and the agent's assistant says the detective "can't talk like that in here," Marlowe replies, "I
forgot to bring my prayer book.   This is the first time I
knew God worked on commission. "[7]

In Jules Oppenheimer, Chandler embodied the quality
he apparently felt essential for a successful studio mogul:
casual insanity.   Oppenheimer's chief interest in life is his
three dogs: Masie, Mack, and Jock.   These boxers have
the unique attribute of always peeing in order, everywhere,
it seems, including Oppenheimer's office (it drives the
secretary crazy).   In addition, Oppenheimer has little to do
with the studio he heads; he hasn't talked with one of the
assistants in five years and never goes into many of the offices because he can't stand the constant redecorations.
Finally, Oppenheimer is one of the old school of studio
heads whose power is being cut out from under them.   He
assures Marlowe that all you need to be successful in the
movie business is 1500 theatres.   (This was written at the
time the United States government was divesting the studios
of their theatre chains.)

Many of the actors in Chandler's Hollywood make
perfect companions for Jules Oppenheimer.   Marlowe's
opinion of these people is none too flattering: "More movie
stars.   More pink and blue bathtubs.   More tufted beds.
More Chanel No. 5.   More Lincoln Continentals and Cadil-
lacs.   More wind-blown hair and sunglasses and attitudes
and pseudo-refined voices and waterfront morals. "[8] For a
minute Marlowe catches himself.   "Now, wait a minute.
Lots of nice people work in pictures.   You've got the wrong
attitude, Marlowe. "[9] But the momentary burst of optimism
is short lived.   He attends a film and observes:

> The leading man was an amiable ham with a
> lot of charm, some of it turning a little yellow at
> the edges.   The star was a bad-tempered brun-
> ette with contemptuous eyes and a couple of bad
> close-ups that showed her pushing forty-five back-
> wards almost hard enough to break a wrist.
> Mavis Weld played second lead and ... she was

Marlowe (Garner) takes his girl friend, Jule (Corinne Camacho), to Steelgrave's club, "The Dancers."

---

good, but she could have been ten times better. But if she had been ten times better half her scenes would have been yanked out to protect the star. 10

Marlowe's convictions are reinforced when he visits the movie set.   The actors take verbal pot shots at each other and Mavis does have to contain her acting.   One of the actors bears the nickname "Mister Thirteen ... because any time [he plays] a part it means twelve other guys have turned it down."11   Mavis sums up the nature of movie actors: "We're all bitches.   Some smile more than others, that's all.   Show business.   There's something cheap about it.   There always has been.   There was a time when actors went in at the back door.   Most of them still should."12

But it wasn't only Hollywood that disenchanted Marlowe; he had come to hate California and his once-magical city.   Constantly reminding himself that "You're not human tonight, Marlowe" he rides along the Pacific:

> I drove on to the Oxnard cut-off and turned
> back along the ocean. The big eight-wheelers
> and sixteen-wheelers were streaming north, all
> hung over with orange lights. On the right the
> great fat solid Pacific trudging into shore like a
> scrubwoman going home. No moon, no fuss,
> hardly a sound of the surf. No smell. None
> of the harsh wild smell of the sea. A California
> ocean. California, the department-store state. [13]

Later Marlowe tells Dolores:

> I used to like this town.... A long time ago.
> There were trees along Wilshire Boulevard. Bev-
> erly Hills was a country town. Westwood was
> bare hills and lots offering at eleven hundred dol-
> lars and no takers. Hollywood was a bunch of
> frame houses on the interurban line. Los Ange-
> les was just a big dry sunny place with ugly
> homes and no style, but goodhearted and peaceful.
> It had the climate they just yap about now. Peo-
> ple used to sleep out on porches. Little groups
> who thought they were intellectual used to call it
> the Athens of America. It wasn't that, but it
> wasn't a neon-lighted slum either. [14]

But even Marlowe must sometimes change with the times,
and he has now upped his fee from twenty-five to forty dollars a day.

In spite of its plot weaknesses and note of pessimism, however, The Little Sister contains characters that
are undeniably Chandleresque, and they help to compensate
for the novel's inadequacies.

Metro-Goldwyn-Mayer, the studio that produced Lady
in the Lake, purchased the rights to The Little Sister and
The Long Goodbye and hired one of Hollywood's top screenwriters, Sterling Silliphant to do the scripts. (Chapter 7
deals with Silliphant's work on The Long Goodbye.) Silliphant faced one major problem in adapting The Little Sister:
how to update a topical 1949 popular literary work into a
relevant 1969 film experience. Primarily, this involved
reworking the plot into cinematic terms and modernizing
the book's post-war situations. Thoroughness typified Silliphant's screenwriting approach. He read the book a dozen
times to learn it by heart and discover where, if at all,

Chandler failed to communicate a point. Silliphant also
studied the author "to assimilate everything about [him]--
his attitudes toward life, his feelings about his characters--
and put myself onto his stage, see where he went, move
along in his footsteps."[15] Having done this, Silliphant re-
focused the characters "to heighten dramatic tension or reveal more of [the] central character in the reaction of [the]
central character to the minor character."[16] Where necessary, story elements were rearranged to heighten suspense.

Table 10 reveals Silliphant's reworking of the plot.
Concentrating on the visual, Silliphant has tightened material from the book and quickened the story's pace. True
to the pattern established in most screen adaptions of novels
and plays, Silliphant simplified his material to meet anti-
cipated audience needs. In this instance, the screenwriter's
major change involves eliminating a double blackmail plot
and focusing attention on the blackmail of Mavis. In the
novel, for example, Lagardie tries to blackmail Steelgrave
because Lagardie's wife, Dolores, ran off with Steelgrave.
Dolores attempts to blackmail Steelgrave because he left
her for Mavis. So, ironically, estranged husband and wife
work toward the same end. In addition, Orfamay and Orrin
try to blackmail Mavis for money, but the film retains only
the latter scheme.

Marlowe went into production with Paul Bogart as director. A veteran television director and Emmy Award
winner, Bogart chose Marlowe as his first feature film.
He began at NBC-TV in the late 1940's and learned television directing on the job. He won his first Emmy for a
segment of CBS's "The Defenders," his second for "Dear
Friends" in 1968. The fifth Marlowe film was the first to
be shot in color and largely on location. Academy Award-
winning William H. Daniels moved his camera to over
twenty locations, including Los Angeles International Air-
port, Sunset Strip's Large Burlesque, Mount Wilson, and
Malibu.[17]

Mixed critical reaction greeted Marlowe. Some reviewers were decidedly negative, feeling the picture was
unevenly made and Garner could not make up his mind
whether to play Marlowe with comedy or serious style.
Roger Greenspun called the film "the most promising sleep-
er of 1946...."[18] But some liked Garner and Paul Bogart
for not betraying the Chandler spirit. Charles Gregory felt
the film possessed "a style based on characterizations and
visuals harking back to the forties' film noir."[19]

Marlowe (Garner) is about to pass out from one of Dr.
Vincent Lagardie's (Paul Stevens) doped cigarettes.

Just as The Brasher Doubloon reflected John Brahm's
German origins, Marlowe mirrors Bogart's television experience. The picture, although competently filmed, sets
no cinematic landmarks. It displays, in fact, what audiences have come to expect of their television shows: technical competence devoid of creative genius. The color and
location shooting add nothing to the creation of Chandler-
like atmosphere that had not already been done in previous
Marlowe films. Thus, although these two elements do not
detract from the total film, neither do they add greatly to
it. Bogart himself admitted he did not dabble in unusual
technical filmmaking. "In 'Marlowe' there are no camera
tricks. If the story doesn't have it neither does the camera. There must be a real issue, completely played. A
good show, whatever the media, demands content."[20] What
Bogart overlooks, of course, is that creative filming can
greatly enhance a good story.

Marlowe introduces two'filmic devices not seen before in Chandler films.   The first, creative use of titles,
makes this picture the most interesting "Marlowe" film in
terms of opening credits.   The previous films' titles were
routine, but here we have important information conveyed
during display of the credits.   The photographing of Mavis
and Steelgrave by Orrin, of course, triggers the events that
follow throughout the film, and these are the scenes presented under the credits.   The second device is the use of
a theme song, another "first" for a "Marlowe" picture.
The theme, "Little Sister," in various versions, appears
throughout the film, particularly on Marlowe's car radio,
on Mavis' stereo, and as music for a television show dance
number.   This theme foreshadowed the use of music in The
Long Goodbye, which attempted to satirize film music.

Marlowe, as Bogart states, depends on its content to
sustain the picture.   Silliphant's plot alterations have already
been discussed.   Besides simplifying the plot, the screenwriter felt obliged to alter some of the characters.   According to Silliphant: "THE LITTLE SISTER has a lot of
people from past time ... moving around in present time.
It's one thing to be able to explain all this in narrative,
another to have to SHOW it.... [A]n update in certain
areas was essential."[21]   One aspect of this updating process involved eliminating certain minor figures.   Thus the
Maltese Falconish fat man, Joseph P. Toad, and young
punk kid, Alfred, were done away with "... because they
had become, through time and plagerism, parody figures."[22]
In their place came smartly-dressed foot-kicking Winslow
Wong, played by Bruce Lee.   Interestingly enough, not only
the character but also the actor foreshadowed the martial
art films that became so popular in the seventies.   Also
updated were the film studio characters.   The film mogul
of Chandler's novel has been replaced by the high-powered
television executive.   It is interesting to note the bitchy
actors in the book have been eliminated from the film, for
Silliphant has none of Chandler's bitterness toward Hollywood.

Two minor characters not in the book were included
in the movie.   The first is a homosexual hairdresser
named Chuck.   As Silliphant explains:

I put him in because Marlowe needed an office
and we wanted to situate it somewhere in reality--
we decided to put him on Hollywood Boulevard--and

Marlowe (Garner) asks Dolores (Rita Moreno, right) where
Mavis is, as she and a friend (Nicole Jaffey) patch him up
after he's been lightly stabbed by the dying Orrin Quest.

> the place we found as a live location was in a
> hairdressing salon where nobody was 'straight.'
> We simply took a slice from life--and made
> Chuck the message drop.... [H]e is simply a
> prop of Marlowe's office. [23]

Of all the characters in the film, only Chuck violates the
spirit of Chandler, for, as Durham puts it, "One of Chandler's particular anathemas was homosexuals: they offended
his idea of manhood and his sense of virility."[24] Only
once, in Playback, did Chandler include a sympathetic homosexual in one of his novels, and even then the character was
eliminated from the book's final draft. [25]

The other character not in the novel is Marlowe's girl friend, Julie. In her Silliphant scored a brilliant writing coup. Although Chandler's Marlowe never has a girl friend, the makers of the "Marlowe" films always gave him one. As was shown, these love interests have always been modifications of characters that existed in the novels. But in making these modifications sometimes Chandler's expert character sketches were damaged beyond repair, as in the case of Merle Davis. With three possible love interests to draw from, Orfamay, Mavis, and Dolores, Silliphant instead creates a new character. Thus he accomplishes his desire of giving Marlowe a girl friend while at the same time allowing the other three women to remain as Chandler depicted them.

The major characters rank among the best in any "Marlowe" film. Orfamay captures all the ill-disguised beauty and treachery of her novel counterpart. Mavis emerges exactly as she does in the book: a beautiful decent actress who is able to survive in a sordid world with a little help from our hero. Dolores captures the dangerous beauty and cold-at-heart character of Chandler's creation. Christy French and Fred Beifus accurately reflect the cops of the novel, good policemen stuck with a dirty job. And Lagardie, too, fits Chandler's specifications; an evil man who is somewhat ill at ease with his criminal status. But Silliphant doesn't just transpose the characters from novel to script, he makes them live in subtle ways. For example, the evil Lagardie hides among the innocence of a children's clinic. And Marlowe and Orfamay discuss Orrin's death while a bystander stuck between them flounders in a conversation she is physically part of, but in which she does not belong.

To portray Silliphant's Marlowe, the filmmakers chose James Garner. The Marlowe character fitted Garner's screen image, an image that developed largely out of his role in the late 1950's television series, "Maverick." There he played a smooth-talking somewhat cowardly gambler, an image that carried over to many of his subsequent roles. This screen character helped develop Garner into a top film and television star. Garner has some of Dick Powell's boyish charm which he uses to good advantage in scenes like the one where he mimics Mr. Crowell's behavior. The actor has some of Humphrey Bogart's or Powell's flair for comedy, delivering lines like "The jam I'm in is nothing to the jam your star in your

Marlowe (Garner) sends Mavis Wald (Gayle Hunnicutt) away
from Steelgrave's house before calling the police.

show would be in if I hadn't done the thing that put me in
the jam in the first place" with careless aplomb.   Physically, he more closely matches Chandler's detective than any
other actor who has played the detective.   Garner viewed
Marlowe as "A bit of a cynic, a tough guy with a spot for
the underdog."[26] That is how Garner played him.

The most important element of this discussion is,
of course, the character of Marlowe.

Marlowe of the film essentially captures the Marlowe
of the novel.   Silliphant said:

> ... I tried sincerely to keep the Marlowe char-
> acter as Chandler wrote and felt him.   I think I
> know what Ray intended, because I met him a
> couple of times in La Jolla and we talked--and I
> read everything he wrote twenty-two and a half
> times--and all his essays--and what people wrote
> about him--and I was and am a Chandler buff and
> fan--so I cared about preserving the spirit of
> him. ... 27

Silliphant did preserve the spirit of Marlowe.   Only
in a few ways do the two Marlowes differ.   Silliphant's
Marlowe is more self-assured than Chandler's; he never
puts himself down.   The film Marlowe is more literary; his
apartment contains numerous books.   The movie version of
the detective feels comfortable in Los Angeles; Chandler's
hero rebelled against the modernization of the city.   And,
of course, the film Marlowe has a girl friend.   But basically Silliphant's Marlowe remains as Chandler drew him:
a knight fighting, and winning, in a society that can be a
match for any man.

The production of Marlowe raised serious questions
about Marlowe's relevance.   The chief criticism of the film
was that Chandler's Marlowe and what he stood for were
out of date when the film was made.   There existed no
possibility for such a romantic hero to survive the transition to a modern day society.   Chandler's Marlowe functions
under a strict code; he is impeccably honest in a world
gone mad with deceit and corruption.   But that was in 1949.
Twenty years later it seemed to many that the corruption
Marlowe fought had engulfed society.   In films, this feeling
manifested itself in the anti-hero, a character who looked
out only for himself and held in contempt all the traditional
heroic values.   Thus Marlowe no longer had any relevance
because he no longer represented society.   (This debate in-
tensified with the making of The Long Goodbye.)

Silliphant, on the other hand, felt Marlowe was relevant to today's society:

> ... Marlowe seemed ... to work even better
> today--his shabby knight with all kinds of chinks
> in his worn armor--seemed even more vulnerable
> --more noble, somehow--in today's society than
> in the forties.   I would have proved it too had
> God kept Bogie among us.   And if Bogart were

Marlowe (Garner) struggles to separate the battling sisters Orfamay Quest (Sharon Farrell, top) and Mavis (Hunnicutt).

> alive today and playing Marlowe you couldn't get
> near the theaters the lines would be so long.
>   ... I do not agree with the critics who say that
> Marlowe's attitudes do not fit in with contemporary
> society. I say, rather, that contemporary soci-
> ety's attitudes do not fit in with Marlowe's atti-
> tudes, but that Marlowe's are more enduring--
> and that this difference should be a plus, not a
> criticism--and all the more reason to have pre-
> served the purity of the original character. [28]

Silliphant's analysis concisely answers the question of Marlowe's relevance. When a person's moral structure is built
on the prevailing attitudes of society and not on his conscience, the individual becomes something less than a complete thinking being. What made Chandler's Marlowe a
strong character was his determination to stand up for what
he believed in, no matter what the price. Such strength of
character, and the fundamental goodness of Chandler's Marlowe, remains relevant no matter how society changes. In
summary, although Silliphant's Marlowe is not totally integrated with his society (he doesn't know sitcom is the ab-
breviation for situation comedy and is more interested in a
Garbo film than a television show in production), he nevertheless survives the transition from 1949 to 1969 while re-
taining all of Chandler's hero's strength of character.

Marlowe accurately captures the mood of The Little
Sister and remains faithful to the novel in terms of Marlowe's character. The film is, in fact, the most under-
rated "Marlowe" picture. Certainly not one of the all-time
great detective films, Marlowe nevertheless possesses a
style that makes it an enjoyable one.

TABLE 10.   PLOT COMPARISON

The Little Sister / Marlowe

NOVEL	FILM
1. Orfamay Quest hires Marlowe to find her missing brother, Orrin.	
2. Marlowe goes to a Bay City hotel looking for Orrin. He questions the manager, Lester B. Clausen, who tries to call a man named "Doc." Marlowe finds a man, George W. Hicks, in Orrin's room. Hicks says Orrin is gone. Marlowe discovers Clausen has been murdered with an ice pick in the back of the neck.	Marlowe goes to a Bay City hotel looking for Orrin. He questions the manager, Haven Clausen, who tries to call a man named "Doc." Marlowe finds a man, Grant W. Hicks, in Orrin's room. Hicks says Orrin is gone. Marlowe discovers Clausen has been murdered with an ice pick in the back of the neck.
3. Back in his office, Marlowe tells Orfamay he hasn't found Orrin. He learns "Doc" is Dr. Vincent Lagardie and calls him, using Hicks' name. Lagardie denies knowledge of Clausen.	Back in his office, Marlowe tells his client, Orfamay, Orrin's brother, he hasn't found Orrin. He learns "Doc" is Dr. Vincent Lagardie and calls him, using Hicks' name. Lagardie denies knowledge of Clausen.
4. Marlowe is summoned to the Van Nuys Hotel by a mysterious caller. Marlowe finds a woman in the caller's room. She hits Marlowe on the head and escapes. The caller, George Hicks, has been murdered with an ice pick. Marlowe finds a photo claim check under Hicks' toupee and calls the police. Detective Lieutenant Christy French and Fred Beifus investigate.	Marlowe is summoned to the Alvarado Hotel by Grant Hicks. Marlowe finds a woman in Hicks' room. She hits Marlowe on the head and escapes. Hicks has been murdered with an ice pick. Marlowe finds a photo claim check under Hicks' toupee and calls the police. Detective Lieutenant Christy French and Fred Beifus investigate.

(TABLE 10 cont.)

5. French mentions the ice
   pick was the trademark of
   Sunny Moe Stein's mob.
   Stein had recently been
   killed in Los Angeles and
   suspicion fell on Weepy
   Moyer, whose possible
   alias is Steelgrave. Steelgrave, however, was in
   jail when the crime was
   committed.

6.   Marlowe mentions Sonny Steel-
                                              grave's gang used the ice pick
                                              murder method.

7. Marlowe learns the woman   Marlowe learns the woman in
   in Hicks' room is a movie   Hicks' room is a television
   actress, Mavis Weld.   actress, Mavis Wald.

8.   Marlowe claims the photographs
                                              which show Mavis and Steelgrave
                                              together.

9. Marlowe goes to see Mavis   Marlowe goes to see Mavis and
   and meets Dolores Gon-   meets Dolores Gonzales. Mar-
   zales. Marlowe offers   lowe offers Mavis his help, but
   Mavis his help and she   she refuses it.
   throws him out.

10. On his way out, Marlowe
    meets Steelgrave going in
    to see Mavis.

11.   On his way out, Marlowe meets
                                              Steelgrave. Steelgrave's men
                                              search Marlowe and beat him up.

12. Back in his office, Mar-
    lowe is visited by Joseph
    P. Toad and Alfred, who
    offer him $500 to stop
    working on the case.
    Marlowe refuses and learns
    they were sent by Mavis'
    agent, Sheridan Ballou.

13.   Back in his office, Marlowe is
                                              visited by Winslow Wong, who
                                              offers him $500 to stop working
                                              on the case. Marlowe refuses
                                              and Wong demolishes the office.

14. Marlowe claims the photo-
    graphs which show Mavis
    and Steelgrave at Steel-
    grave's club, The Dancers.
    A newspaper in the photo
    places the date as Febru-
    ary 20, the day Sunny Moe
    Stein was killed. This is
    proof Steelgrave was not
    in jail on that day. Mar-
    lowe reasons the photos
    were taken by Orrin Quest.

15.   Marlowe and his girl friend,
                                  Julie, go to Steelgrave's club,
                                  The Dancers, where Wong tries
                                  to kill Marlowe. Wong falls
                                  to his death instead.

16.   Orfamay visits Marlowe and
                                  tells him Orrin is staying with
                                  Dr. Lagardie. She wants Mar-
                                  lowe to go there because she is
                                  afraid her brother will be killed.

17. Marlowe visits Ballou,   Marlowe visits Mavis' agent,
    persuading Ballou to hire   Mr. Crowell, persuading Crowell
    him to protect Mavis'   to hire him to protect Mavis'
    career.   career.

18. Marlowe has deduced
    Mavis is Orrin's sister
    and goes to see Dr. La-
    gardie. Marlowe sug-
    gests Lagardie used to be
    the doctor for Steelgrave's
    mob. Marlowe says Hicks
    was killed because he tried
    to take over someone's
    racket. Clausen was killed
    because he knew who might
    want to kill Hicks. Mar-
    lowe speculates that not
    only does Lagardie know
    for sure Steelgrave is
    Moyer, but also that La-
    gardie persuaded Orrin
    to take the picture for re-
    venge against Steelgrave.

19.   Marlowe goes to see Dr. La-
                                  gardie. Marlowe speculates
                                  that Clausen was killed because

(TABLE 10 cont.)

someone was afraid he would talk and Hicks was killed because he tried to muscle in on the blackmail scheme. Marlowe reasons Orrin took the photographs and he is Mavis' sister. Marlowe suggests Lagardie used to be the doctor for Steelgrave's mob.

20. Marlowe passes out from a doped cigarette and awakens to find Orrin shot. Orrin tries to stick Marlowe with an ice pick as he dies.

Marlowe passes out from a doped cigarette and awakens to find Orrin shot. Orrin tries to stick Marlowe with an ice pick as he dies.

21. Marlowe returns to his office and is visited by Dolores. She used to be Steelgrave's girl and suggests Marlowe use the photos to blackmail Mavis. Marlowe refuses. Orfamay calls and says she went into Lagardie's after Marlowe left. She called the police.

22.

Marlowe tells Mavis and Orfamay that Orrin is dead. Orfamay tells a policeman about her brother's murder.

23. French and Beifus questions Marlowe; they believe Orrin did the ice pick murders. They release Marlowe.

French and Beifus question Marlowe; they believe Orrin did the ice pick murders. They release Marlowe.

24.

Marlowe returns to his office and burns the pictures and the negatives.

25. Dolores says Mavis is in trouble and takes Marlowe to Steelgrave's house. Marlowe finds Mavis and Steelgrave, who is dead. Mavis says she shot Steelgrave because he had

Dolores says Mavis is in trouble and takes Marlowe to Steelgrave's house. Marlowe has guessed Dolores used to be Steelgrave's girl friend, before Mavis took him. Marlowe finds Mavis and Steelgrave, who is dead. Mavis

Orrin killed.   Marlowe
sends her home and calls
the police.

says she shot Steelgrave because he had Orrin killed.
Marlowe sends her home and
calls the police.

26. The police take Marlowe
    in, but release him.   He
    and Mavis talk with the
    District Attorney and are
    both allowed to go free.

27. Orfamay comes to Mar-
    lowe's office and he learns
    she was Orrin's partner in
    the attempt to blackmail
    Mavis, their sister, but Or-
    rin double-crossed her.
    Orfamay told Steelgrave
    where Orrin was hiding.
    Marlowe burns the pictures
    and she leaves.

28.

Marlowe goes to his apartment
and finds Orfamay searching it.
He tells her he burned the
photographs.   Mavis joins them
and Marlowe learns Orfamay
was Orrin's partner in the attempt to blackmail Mavis, their
sister, but Orrin double-crossed
her.   Orfamay told Steelgrave
where Orrin was hiding.   Mavis
and Orfamay fight and Marlowe
separates them, telling Orfamay
to go home.

29. Marlowe visits Dolores and
    sorts out the puzzle.   Do-
    lores, Lagardie's ex-wife,
    persuaded Orrin to take the
    photographs.   Later she
    killed Sunny Moe Stein to
    strengthen the blackmail
    scheme.   She killed Orrin
    because he was becoming
    a nuisance and killed Steel-
    grave because she didn't
    want Mavis to have him.
    Marlowe can't tell the po-
    lice without ruining Mavis'
    career, so he leaves.
    Lagardie comes and Mar-
    lowe calls the police.

They arrive too late to
prevent Lagardie from killing Dolores.

30.   Marlowe goes to the strip club
                             where Dolores works. She ad-
                             mits killing Steelgrave to keep
                             Mavis from having him and that
                             she is Lagardie's former wife.
                             Marlowe can't tell the police
                             without ruining Mavis' career.
                             Lagardie comes and Marlowe
                             starts to call the police, but
                             Lagardie kills Dolores and then
                             shoots himself.

Chapter 7

THE LONG GOODBYE

Chandler's sixth novel, The Long Goodbye, differed
markedly from the author's previous works. First, Chandler altered his tone and style. This book unfolded at a
slower pace than the others and primarily concerned itself
with the concept of friendship rather than plot or the writer's usual forte, characters. Carefully crafted, the novel
nevertheless contains no unusual literary brilliance. But,
more important, Marlowe himself had changed. Although
subtle, this change existed nevertheless. In truth Marlowe
had begun to die a little: to retreat from his former self
and sink into sentimentality. The change benefited no one
and served as a warning of Marlowe's later near-total col-
lapse in Playback.

Chandler opens The Long Goodbye with Marlowe helping a drunk, Terry Lennox. They become friends. Terry
comes to Marlowe and asks to be driven to Tijuana. Marlowe agrees on the condition he not be told anything, although
he guesses that Terry's wife, Sylvia, has been murdered.
The police question Marlowe when he returns to Los Angeles. He refuses to talk and is jailed. He is later released
when the police consider the case closed. Terry writes a
confession and kills himself in Otatoclan, Mexico.

Marlowe receives a visit from one of Terry's World
War II army buddies, Menendez, a gangster. Terry once
saved Menendez's life and the gangster warns Marlowe to
have nothing more to do with the case, even though Marlowe
thinks Terry was innocent. Marlowe receives a letter from
Terry, written before he died, and a $5000 bill.

Howard Spenser, a literary agent, asks Marlowe to
help a drunken writer, Roger Wade. At first the detective
refuses, but when Wade disappears, Mrs. Eileen Wade persuades Marlowe to look for Roger. Marlowe locates Wade
in the custody of a disreputable doctor, Dr. Verringer, and
takes him home.

Later Wade calls Marlowe for help.   Wade is drunk
and makes a feeble attempt to kill himself.   Linda Loring,
Sylvia's sister, takes Marlowe to see her millionaire father.
He warns Marlowe to stop investigating the Lennox case.

Wade was having an affair with Sylvia and there exists a possibility he killed her in a drunken fit.   Marlowe
finds Wade shot to death in circumstances that could either
be suicide or murder.

Marlowe, who has figured the case out, takes Spenser to see Eileen.   At first Eileen says Roger killed Sylvia
and she saw him do it.   Marlowe exposes her lie.   He has
discovered that Eileen and Terry were married in England
during World War II and Terry dropped out of sight when
the Germans captured him.   Later, Terry turned up married to Sylvia.   Eileen killed Sylvia out of jealousy and
killed Roger because he suspected what she had done.   Eileen
writes a confession of the murders and kills herself.   Marlowe leaks a copy of the confession to a newspaper to clear
Terry.

A Señor Maioranos visits Marlowe, claiming to have
knowledge of Terry's death.   But Marlowe soon realizes the
man is Terry, disguised by plastic surgery.   Terry faked
the suicide to get out of the trouble caused by Sylvia's
murder.   Marlowe and Terry part, Marlowe refusing to re-
new their friendship.

The Long Goodbye (originally titled Summer in Idle
Valley), first published in 1953, was Chandler's third, and
last, "original" novel, although the small part where Terry,
disguised, comes to Marlowe's after Sylvia's death did
come from a previous short story, "The Curtain" (Black
Mask, September, 1936).[1] Written at a difficult time in
Chandler's life (his wife was ill and would die on December
12, 1954[2]), The Long Goodbye was not only Chandler's
longest novel, but also perhaps stands as one of the longest
private-eye books ever written (125,000 words).[3] In 1955
The Long Goodbye earned Chandler the Mystery Writers of
America Award for the "Best Mystery Novel" of 1954.[4]

Critics regarded the story in different ways.   Some
thought it was one of Chandler's best works, while others
did not care for it.   But most accepted the novel, with
reservations.   They thought the meticulous plotting, coupled
with the author's effective prose style, enhanced the book.

But at the same time, these critics felt The Long Goodbye
had "not quite the same sparkle and bounce as Chandler's
earlier novels" and that it had a "jarring note of sentimentality.... [A]nd signs of strain...."5

     As he had done in his other novels, Chandler used
The Long Goodbye to attack things that displeased him.
Whereas The Little Sister had criticized Hollywood, Chandler's sixth novel took on the literary world.   The publisher, Howard Spenser, knows he is going to reject novels
before he has even read them because they were handed to
him in person, not supplied by a New York agent.   But
writers are no better than agents.   Roger Wade writes
"tripe" that makes money because "he's an automatic best
seller.   And every publisher has to have a couple with the
way costs are now."6

     Chandler also used the book to comment on his most
hated class of people: the rich.   Before, this segment of
society had merely been wealthy, their money being counted
in the single millions.   But now Marlowe had met the man
who could buy and sell all the wealthy people of the previous
five novels, Harlan Potter, "worth a hundred million or
so...."7   Potter had his own philosophy about money:
"There's a peculiar thing about money....   In large quan-
tities it tends to have a life of its own, even a conscience
of its own.   The power of money becomes very difficult to
control."8   Potter's power is so great that he is able to
tell Marlowe: "And don't go away thinking I buy politicians
or law enforcement officers.   I don't have to."9   Not only
is Potter able to exercise his will over governmental and
civil officials, but he also controls the press as well.   The
Lennox case, prime newspaper material, dies after only a
couple of days in the papers because Potter wants it that
way.   Lonnie Morgan explains it to Marlowe:

          Newspapers are owned and published by rich
          men.   Rich men all belong to the same club.
          Sure there's competition--hard tough competition
          for circulation, for newsbeats, for exclusive
          stories.   Just so long as it doesn't damage the
          prestige and privilege and position of the owners.
          If it does, down comes the lid. 10

(The only paper that will publish Eileen's confession is inde-
pendently owned.)   Marlowe's assessment of Potter, of
course, is unflattering:

TABLE 11.   THE LONG GOODBYE

Cast		Credits	
Philip Marlowe	Elliott Gould	Executive Producer	Elliott Kastner
Eileen Wade	Nina Van Pallandt	Produced by	Jerry Bick
Roger Wade	Sterling Hayden	Directed by	Robert Altman
Marty Augustine	Mark Rydell	Screenplay by	Leigh Brackett
Dr. Verringer	Henry Gibson	Based on novel by	Raymond Chandler
Harry	David Arkin	Dir. of Photog.	Vilmostz Sigmond
Terry Lennox	Jim Bouton	Sound	John V. Speak
Morgan	Warren Berlinger	Music by	John Williams
Jo Ann Eggenweiler	Jo An Brody	Title Song: Lyrics	Johnny Mercer
Hood	Jack Knight	Music	John Williams
Pepe	Pepe Callahan	Edited by	Lou Lombardo
Hood	Vince Palmieri	Wardrobe (Male)	Keny James
Hood	Arnold Strong	(Female)	Majorie Wahl
Marlowe's neighbor	Rutanya Alda	Make-up by	Bill Miller
Marlowe's neighbor	Tammy Shaw		
Piano Player	Jack Riley		
Colony Guard	Ken Sansom	Camera and Lenses by Panavision	
Bartender	Danny Goldman	A United Artists picture	
Real Estate Lady	Sybil Scotford		
Detective Farmer	Steve Coit	Running time: 112 minutes	
Detective	Tracy Harris	Release date: March, 1973	
Detective Green	Jerry Jones		
Clerk	Rodney Moss	Rated R	

> He hated everything.... He explained civiliza-
> tion to me. I mean how it looks to him. He's
> going to let it go on for a little while longer.
> But it better be careful and not interfere with his
> private life. If it does, he's apt to make a phone
> call to God and cancel the order. [11]

Throughout the novel, Chandler also criticizes other
aspects of Marlowe's world; e.g., Los Angeles, gangsters,
and the police. But somehow these negative comments,
when taken individually like the two above, seem less force-
ful than similar criticisms in previous novels. Collectively, however, these attacks against Marlowe's environment
produce a new note of pessimism not evident in Chandler's
previous novels. In the earlier books, amid deceit and
corruption, some good managed to survive. For example,
although General Sternwood is wealthy, Marlowe takes a
liking to the old man. And amid all the shallowness of
Hollywood, Mavis Weld is a decent person well worth Marlowe's efforts to save her. But in The Long Goodbye there
exist no such cases of optimism. Before, Chandler seemed
to be commenting on society's flaws while at the same time
expressing a glimmer of hope. In the author's sixth novel,
however, that hope has disappeared, and this makes the
book a depressing one.

The Long Goodbye's plot quality falls somewhere between Chandler's best and his worst.   The main problem
with the plot is some poorly explained character actions.
For instance, Chandler never satisfactorily describes why
Eileen, a murderess, should want Marlowe around when
sooner or later he would find the connection between Roger
and Sylvia.   Also, it is hinted that Candy is blackmailing
Roger.   Yet at the book's end, Candy wants revenge against
Eileen for killing her husband.   Likewise, the characterizations are neither among the best or worst in Chandler.
They can be best summed up by what the author said about
The High Window: it had "no likeable characters...."[12]
Each character seems to be interested only in what he can
get for himself, usually at Marlowe's expense.   For example, Bernie Ohls allows Marlowe to leak the copy of Eileen's
confession to the press not to clear Terry, but to nail
Menendez.   And this is not because Menendez had a cop
beaten up, but because Ohls hates gamblers.

    Our primary concern lies with Marlowe's character,
and this character has changed in The Long Goodbye.   On
the surface this change is barely noticeable, but if one examines Marlowe more closely, he finds the hero has undergone an alteration for the worse.

    From the beginning, problems existed with this latest
Marlowe.   Chandler sent his agents, Brandt and Brandt, a
copy of the novel and asked for criticism.   He got it, and
it was not favorable.   Bernice Baumgarten and Carl Brandt
did not like the new Marlowe: they felt "he had gone sentimental and become Christ-like."[13]   As Durham explains:

> Chandler had sent along with the manuscript a
> letter explaining that he did not care whether the
> mystery was fairly obvious, 'but I cared about
> people, about this strange corrupt world we live
> in, and how any man who tried to be honest looks
> in the end either sentimental or plain foolish.'[14]

The agents did not care for this explanation and Chandler
asked the novel be returned, "explaining that the lack of
'gusto' in the book was caused by his [Chandler's] bitter
struggle and lack of cheerfulness."[15]   Chandler spent months
rewriting but never could bring himself to accept his agents'
criticism and finally broke contact with them.[16]

    However unwilling Chandler may have been to realize

Terry Lennox (Jim Bouton) asks Marlowe for a ride to
Mexico. All photos in this chapter are from The Long
Goodbye (UA, 1973).

---

it, Marlowe had indeed changed. For one thing, the author
chose to make him less effective as a detective. Marlowe
goes to another detective agency, the Carne Organization,
for help in locating Roger Wade. For the first time we
meet several average Marlowe clients. In one day he has
a man come whose neighbor is trying to poison his dog, a
woman who says her roommate steals money from her purse,
and a fifty-year-old Jew married to a twenty-four-year-old
Gentile, who constantly runs away from him. Marlowe
takes only this last case, which he farms out. While these
characters may serve to illustrate the shabbiness of a detective's day, they never appeared in previous novels, sug-
gesting the disenchantment Marlowe felt with the detective
business.

Durham described how Marlowe felt about his business:

> In The Long Goodbye [Marlowe] was old, tired,
> and bored. As an old man of forty-two the private
> eye began thinking of the trouble business as a
> dull business. Every other month he thought
> about giving it up to look for a 'sensible occupa-
> tion.' But, of course, he did not; instead he
> went out into the 'tired evening' to give to soci-
> ety as he always had--justice, courage, and loyal-
> ty--yet the fun had gone out of it. At times, in
> fact, he gave way to despair.... [17]

The one straw that Marlowe clung to to see him
through this time of disillusionment was his unshakable faith
in Terry Lennox and even that deserted him at the book's
end. There exists one problem concerning Lennox that
serves to illustrate Marlowe's character alteration. Like
the Marlowe of old, the sleuth stands by his friend, believ-
ing in him and not allowing him to tell anything about Sylvia.
Even though Marlowe knows she's dead, he trusts Terry,
and therefore Terry need not explain. In addition, of
course, Marlowe sets himself up so that if he is questioned
by the police, he cannot be implicated in a murder; he
merely drove Terry somewhere. Having done all this, why,
then, does Marlowe refuse to tell the police anything? He
was seen at Tijuana and can certainly admit to driving there
without compromising himself or his friend. The police
may not believe it, but that is not Marlowe's problem.
Marlowe says if he talks, no one will hire him; but he has
told half-truths to the law before without risking losing clients.

The answer to this question is that Marlowe has become a sentimentalist and does, in fact, look slightly foolish. He apparently wants nothing to stain his memory of
Terry and somehow feels any discussion of his friend with
the police would do just that.

The above discussion of Marlowe treats subtle aspects of the hero's character. These may be open to different interpretations and, perhaps, can be explained away
in such a manner as to allow Marlowe to remain his old
self. But one thing cannot be so dismissed: the fact that
Marlowe breaks his own code and goes to bed with a woman.
This is a serious violation of the hero's ethics, because

abstinence from sex is the only aspect of Marlowe's code
not generally subject to variation (see Durham's comment,
quoted on page 9).   Chandler held what can be called an
atypical attitude toward women.   He lived with his mother
until he was thirty-five and immediately after her death
married a woman eighteen years older than himself.   He
revered women and appeared to feel secure only in the
company of females older than himself.   Although Marlowe
does not seek out older women, he nevertheless maintains
his creator's reverence for the opposite sex.   The inclusion
of this sexual encounter in The Long Goodbye, therefore,
indicates a basic change in Marlowe's once-cherished ideals.

/Chandler worked hard to develop the right girl for
Marlowe, Linda Loring.   On the surface she seems incom-
patible with our hero.   She is married, rich, and not in
love with him.   But she isn't a virgin nor overly promis-
cuous, two extremes that Marlowe would certainly avoid.
Her character is carefully built up through the latter part
of the novel.   Her husband, one of Chandler's unethical
doctors, accuses her of being a tramp, but she does not
have that reputation, and even Eileen Wade says she's not
the tramp her husband thinks she is.   She is rich, the
daughter of Harlan Potter, but she remains untouched by the
corruption money can bring.   Marlowe refuses her proposal
of marriage, saying that it wouldn't last six months and
he'd rather be remembered as the only man to refuse her
rather than as a discarded husband, but the encounter shows
her attentions are honorable.   Her age, thirty-six (six
years younger than Marlowe) makes her worldly enough for
Marlowe without making her seem too old (in contrast to
Chandler's tastes in women).   In short, she is just right
for a brief encounter before she goes on to her divorce in
Paris and Marlowe goes back to his sleuthing.

The Long Goodbye, then, represents a change in the
basic Marlowe character, a change toward sentimentality
and sex that was not for the better.   As Marlowe puts it,
"The French have a phrase for it.   The bastards have a
phrase for everything and they are always right.   To say
goodbye is to die a little."[18]   To read The Long Goodbye
after studying the other "Marlowe" novels is also to die a
little, to say goodbye to an old and dying friend.

Like The Little Sister before it, The Long Goodbye
was not released as a film until twenty years after the
novel appeared, and it took at least five years to get it on

Detective Dayton (Tracy Harris) questions Marlowe (Elliott Gould) about Terry Lennox.

---

the screen.   Metro-Goldwyn-Mayer purchased the rights to the book and commissioned Stirling Silliphant to do the script (along with The Little Sister, as discussed in the previous chapter).

The same problems that Silliphant encountered in doing The Little Sister, the need for simplification and a time update, repeated themselves in The Long Goodbye.   Silliphant simplified this novel in the same manner as the previous one; he tightened the plot and condensed the characters.   He overcame the time difference by moving the war-related subplot from World War II to the Korean War and streamlined and modernized other parts of the novel. (Many of Silliphant's statements about his adaption technique for

The Little Sister apply to The Long Goodbye.)   The resulting plot was very faithful to Chandler's, more so in fact than
Marlowe had been to The Little Sister.   (Table 12 compares
the plots of the novel, Silliphant's script, and the film.)
Silliphant completed a revised first draft of the script in
October, 1968.   MGM, however, lost interest in the project
and dropped the idea of filming Silliphant's script.   The
studio sold Elliott Kastner the filming rights to the book.

Leigh Brackett, co-author of The Big Sleep script,
was selected by executive producer Elliott Kastner to adapt
the novel.   She chose to write a totally new script and
faced the same problems Silliphant had encountered; the
need for simplification and the great time difference between
the novel and the production of the film.   Brackett explained:

> The first script was a compromise. . . .   We
> tried to keep the 'flavour' of the original, the
> true Chandler touch, while streamlining and try-
> ing to inject a little excitement.   But we got in-
> volved with a plot premise that simply did not
> work; the idea that Terry Lennox had plotted,
> planned, and premeditated Sylvia's murder,
> framed Roger for it, split for Mexico when something
> slipped up and simply waited to reappear, know-
> ing exactly what everybody was going to do to
> clear him; Marlowe would do thus-and-such, Eileen
> would obligingly murder her husband, and etc. . . .
> Our only achievements were two: Terry Lennox
> had become a clear-cut villain, and it seemed
> that the only satisfactory ending was for the cru-
> elly-diddled Marlowe to blow Terry's guts out. . . .
> The story line of the Roger Wade portion of the
> novel was greatly simplified.   Much of it would
> have been unusable in any case because of the
> WW II time-frame involved in the original rela-
> tionship between Eileen and Terry. . . .   We re-
> lieved Eileen of all crimes except adultery, sim-
> plified the motives all round, made the murder
> of Roger a suicide, gave the gambler a satchelful
> of money to tie things together and stayed with
> the brutal ending. [19]

Unlike Silliphant, Brackett found the time difference
irreconcilable.   Whereas Silliphant merely updated the

novel, Brackett did not think such a modernization possible,
for she felt Marlowe could not be separated from his outdated environment. She said:

> By Chandler's own definition, Marlowe was a
> fantasy. . . .   He existed only in the context of the
> Raymond Chandler world especially invented for
> him. . . . Take away that context, and who is Mar-
> lowe?
> Time had removed the context. . . .   We've got
> a whole new generation and a whole new bag of
> cliches--just as phony but different.   The private
> eye is alive and well on television, and he exists
> in a new context and the corruptions he fights have
> new faces. [20]

Thus Brackett's approach and philosophy can be seen to be
directly opposite that of Silliphant's.

In all the furor that surrounded The Long Goodbye
(discussed later), very few bothered to closely examine the
film's plot.   Such an examination reveals that the plot does
not make sense in places and is, in fact, the poorest Marlowe film storyline.   In spite of Brackett's statement, the
improbabilities concerning the Terry-Eileen-Roger relationship were not resolved in the film.   For example, Terry
kills Sylvia and runs away with Augustine's money.   Eileen
was having an affair with Terry.   She not only knows where
he is (she returns the money to Augustine) but has made
plans to join him.   Terry says he has a girl who loves him,
Eileen, and Marlowe meets Eileen on her way to Terry after
Marlowe has killed him.   So, then, if Eileen loves Terry and
is going away with him, why does she hire Marlowe to find
Roger?   (This was also a weakness in the book.)   But an
even more serious flaw is the timing of Roger's suicide.
It comes at the perfect moment and yet is apparently un-
motivated by anything that happens in the picture.   It would
have been better for the storyline if, indeed, Eileen had
murdered her husband.   The coincidence that Roger dies,
and in doing so frees Eileen just when she is about to go off
with Terry, is hard to accept.   One might argue that she
hadn't planned to leave her husband, but his death changed
the circumstances of her relation with Terry.   In that event,
Terry is a very lucky fellow.

There are other flaws in the film as well.   For example, why does Terry take Augustine's money instead of

giving it to Marlowe to return? Terry doesn't need it,
Eileen has "more money than Sylvia and Augustine put together," he knows Augustine won't rest until he gets it,
and surely Marlowe can be trusted. In sum, The Long
Goodbye clearly contains weaknesses in its plot line.

It should be pointed out that many of these plot in-
consistencies were not in the original script or, in some
cases, even in the first rough cut of the film. Brackett
explains:

> [Eileen] did not know where Terry was. She
> had no plan to go to him. At the time she hired
> Marlowe, she thought that Terry was dead, a sui-
> cide. She did not learn that he was alive and in
> Mexico until she received from him a message
> and the suitcase containing the money, which she
> was to return to the gangster in order to get
> Terry off the hook. This scene was written,
> this scene was shot, this scene was in the rough
> cut. It was the reason for Eileen's abrupt de-
> parture from the house. This scene had, unac-
> countably, vanished from the print I saw in the
> theatre.
> There were other things, small things. A
> scene between Roger Wade and Marlowe in which
> they discuss suicide, which led up to Roger's
> demise.... The gangster's girl was not in the
> script, nor was the coke-bottle scene. [21]

It is unfortunate that some of Brackett's material was
omitted from the final print of the film, for it would have
helped to clarify some of the characters' action and rectify
the plotting weaknesses.

Problems arose in forming a crew to film the script.
First choice for director was Peter Bogdanovich, who was
going to do the picture with Robert Mitchum playing Marlowe. (Mitchum got his chance to play Marlowe in the latest Chandler film, Farewell My Lovely, as discussed in the
next chapter.) But it was decided that Elliott Gould should
play Marlowe. Bogdanovich, however, refused to do the
film with Gould. Brian Hutton next received the directorial
chores and script writing went ahead. But the film was de-
layed, and Hutton's services lost, when another commitment
made him unavailable. Then Robert Altman was approached
and asked if he thought Gould would be good for the part.

Marlowe (Gould), just released from jail, meets a newspaper man, Lonnie Morgan (Warren Berlinger).

Altman replied only Gould could play Marlowe, so he became director.[22] But another problem developed. Altman's close friend, Dan Blocker (Hoss Cartwright of Bonanza), selected for the role of Roger Wade, died in May, 1972, and the death unsettled Altman. Altman recalls, "I didn't know whether I would do the film or not. His death was the biggest loss I've ever had."[23] The film ends with a credit, "With Special Rememberance for DAN BLOCKER." Sterling Hayden replaced Blocker.

Production of the film involved three interesting aspects. First, the picture was shot entirely on location (no sound stages were used). Scenes in Los Angeles included Marlowe's house in back of the Hollywood Bowl; the Malibu

Beach Colony (the new skyscraper at 9000 Sunset Boule-
vard); a $65,000 per-client, per-year Pasadena rest home,
Westwood and Hollywood offices; the now-unused Lincoln
Heights jail in East Los Angeles; a piano bar on Ventura
Boulevard in San Fernando Valley, and an all-night super-
market on Lankersheim Boulevard in the Valley. The Mexi-
can scenes were filmed in the villages of Tepoztlan and
Chiconcuac. [24]

Second, the entire film's negative was exposed to
varying amounts of light after exposure and before develop-
ing, a technique called post-flashing. Perfected by director
of photography Vilmos Zsigmond and Technicolor labs, this
process had the effect of reducing color intensities to pastel
levels. Zsigmond explained it:

> We were making a today picture, but we wanted
> the look of twenty years ago. It is very difficult
> to talk about it in words, but we did not want to
> recreate the Fifties, but to remember them....
> So what we decided to do was to put the picture
> into pastels, with a shading toward the blue side.
> Pastels are for memory.... It is also a sad and
> funny movie--Chaplinesque. You feel sorry for
> Gould, and that also works in pastels. The blue
> shading in night effects also will give a feeling of
> the Fifties. [25]

In addition, post-flashing serves several other functions. It
increases the film's speed, making possible the filming of
large night exteriors with little additional light. Flashing
controls contrast, and in doing so adds white light to all
areas, which lightens all the colors. It brings out shadow
detail where there was none before. And it can give a sur-
realistic quality to the film, which is the case in the Mexican forest scenes where 50 per cent flash was used. [26]

Thirdly, Zsigmond used a constantly moving camera
which one critic likened to an incessantly stalking panther. [27]

> Every shot was a moving shot. The camera
> was constantly in motion, slowly dollying back and
> forth along the track without apparent rhyme or
> reason during both the masters and the close-ups.
> Vilmos admitted that the moves were only occa-
> sionally legitimate, i.e., justified by the action.
> He maintained that these slight moves, coupled

with very slow zooms in and out, gave a feeling
of improvisation and a 3-dimensional quality as
objects and people changed their relationships to
one another. He likened it to a controlled hand-
held or cinema verite technique....
    Although he admitted that most cameramen will
find it obtrusive and pretentious, he urged them
to see for themselves. Vilmos feels that it is
not obtrusive if the speed of the move is slow,
and that the movement will help the picture.
'The audience will like it better because it's not
perfect. The "mistakes" are making it better,'
he maintained. [28]

     Release of The Long Goodbye came in March, 1973,
and moviegoers had only time to say a short hello to it before United Artists withdrew it from the theatres. The
movie appeared to be a complete financial disaster. A
film whose weekly receipts fall below $15,000 or $20,000
in Los Angeles is considered a poor picture. In Chandler's
city, the movie opened at the Village Theatre in Westwood.
The Long Goodbye made $10,800 the first week and was down
to $4300 by the third week. Grauman's Chinese, another
example, reported $10,800 the first week and $4600 the
third. Similar poor earnings occurred in other cities.
United Artists withdrew the picture amid speculation it
would be re-edited, shortened, or abandoned altogether. [29]

     Initial critical reaction paralleled the lukewarm box
office receipts. Variety called it "an uneven mixture of in-
sider satire on the gumshoe film genre ... [and a] handsome production ... [that] features a strong cast and an
improbable plot ... [which] can be enjoyed on several
levels."[30] Time said "Altman's lazy, haphazard putdown
is without affection or understanding, a nose-thumb not only
at the idea of Philip Marlowe but at the genre that his
tough-guy--soft-heart character epitomized. It is a curious
spectacle to see Altman mocking a level of achievement to
which, at best, he could only aspire."[31] Charles Champlin,
writing in the Los Angeles Times, found the movie distasteful and concluded his review by stating, "You don't have to
admire Chandler to regret the movie, but it helps."[32]

     Despite the poor financial and critical response,
United Artists refused to abandon the film. The company
had over $1,700,000 invested and so they decided to devise
a new advertising campaign and re-issue the film, without

Marlowe (Gould) is held at bay by Eileen and Roger Wade's dog.

cuts or other changes, in the fall. The original ads showed
Gould holding a can of cat food and with a cat on his shoul-
der. The copy ran "I have two friends in this world. One
is a cat. The other is a murderer."[33] Altman said, "Before, they tried to sell it as though it was a detective
story, some blood-and-guts thing like 'Shamus.'"[34] Three
new advertising schemes intrigued United Artists. The
first, partially developed by Altman, was a satirical approach. The other two were "a straight photographic approach that [involved] a montage of action" and "a totally
non-specific, symbolic approach, in which ... one symbol
[would] represent the film."[35] The company gingerly chose
the first approach, but at that time they were not hopeful.
"It's a 90-10 shot now against us," said Altman. [36] The ad
campaign designed to turn a box-office disaster into a popular success was that of a Mad magazine type movie satire.

        The Long Goodbye's re-release came in October,
1973. Favorable critical comments abounded. Ten out of
fifteen New York critics reviewed it favorably. [37] Judith
Crist designated it the eighth best film of the year. [38]
Pauline Kael stated:

          'The Long Goodbye' reaches a satirical dead
          end that kisses off the private-eye form ... grace-
          fully.... It's a knockout of a movie ... probably
          the best American movie ever made that almost
          didn't open in New York.... What separates Alt-
          man from other directors is that time after time
          he can attain crowning visual effects like this and
          they're so elusive they're never precious. They're
          like ribbons tying up the whole history of movie.
          It seems unbelievable that people who looked at
          this picture could have given it the reviews they
          did. [39]

Vincent Canby was equally lavish in his praise:

          In 'The Long Goodbye' Robert Altman ... at-
          tempts the impossible and pulls it off.... The
          film ... is Altman's most entertaining, most
          richly complex film since 'M*A*S*H' and 'McCabe
          and Mrs. Miller.' It's so good that I don't know
          where to begin describing it.... Don't be misled
          by the ads. 'The Long Goodbye' is not a put-on.
          It's great fun and it's funny, but it's a serious,
          unique work. [40]

Finally, one Chicago critic, David Elliot, chose it as the
number one picture of 1973. [41]

Some critics, however, still disparaged the film.
One was Andrew Sarris.

> 'The Long Goodbye' seems to be admired by
> many critics whom I admire ... which goes to
> prove only that even my dearest friends can make
> grave errors of judgment on occasion. I have
> never denied that 'The Long Goodbye' contains
> some incidental virtues, but I think it takes more
> ingenuity than my friends possess either individu-
> ally or in tandem to make all the jagged edges of
> the film fit into one coherent picture.... 'The
> Long Goodbye' rides off furiously in too many
> different directions with too many gratuitously
> Godardian camera movements to make even a
> good movie. And I don't think I am entirely
> alone on 'The Long Goodbye.' Indeed, I detect a
> note of defensiveness in all the huzzahs for the
> film. [42]

These quotations, when compared to those uttered
after the film's March release, illustrate the change in the
critical climate that had occurred. Earlier, the reviewers
were negative or only mildly positive. But the later reviews either heralded The Long Goodbye as a masterpiece
or credited it with being grossly overrated. This polariza-
tion of the critics sparked many debates about the picture,
resulting in a wealth of critical commentary on the film,
some of it dealing with the film's satire.

More than any other "Marlowe" picture, The Long
Goodbye relied heavily on "in" jokes and satire of previous
films. Much of the movie, in fact, was derived from other
sources, although a few of these sequences are linked to
other motion pictures only by coincidence. Some of the
more obvious and noted allusions are the following:

The film has Marlowe a cat fancier. In addition, our
hero is also afraid of dogs. Marlowe's cat-dog relationship comes straight from Shamus, the picture that "lifted"
two scenes from The Big Sleep. In Shamus, Burt Reynolds, the detective hero, has a cat (Morris, from the
Nine Lives cat food commercials) and fears the dogs the
millionaire villain uses to guard his house. The Long

Marlowe's (Gould) first encounter with Marty Augustine (Mark Rydell).

Goodbye, however, turns the cat sequences around: Marlowe has trouble feeding his cat and the animal leaves shortly after the film starts. In Shamus, Reynolds has no trouble feeding his pet, which is missing at the start of the film and does not appear until the picture is well underway. In addition, Chandler himself was very fond of cats.

The 1948 Lincoln Continental Marlowe drives is Gould's own car. (Ironically, it is the same make and model year that Marlowe talks about in The Little Sister when he complains about movie stars and their Lincoln Continentals.)

The Wade beach house belongs to Altman.

The Malibu gatekeeper does an imitation of Barbara Stanwyck in Double Indemnity, Chandler's first screen-writing job.   He also does an imitation of Cary Grant, Chandler's choice for the Marlowe role. 43

"Terry Lennox ... becomes the Harry Lime in Mar-lowe's life, and the final sequence is a variation of 'The Third Man,' with the very last shot a riff on the leave-making scenes of the movies' most famous clown. "44

A reference to Dashiel Hammett's The Thin Man oc-curs when Marlowe calls a dog "Asta."

The music satirizes film musical themes used in pic-tures like Marlowe.   "The John Wililams [sic]-Johnny Mercer title tune recurs in every conceivable tempo and arrangement, including a Mexican street band format. "45 And never once is this tune played all the way through uninterrupted.

The scene where Marlowe asks Eileen about Augustine just as they are becoming friends parallels a scene in Murder, My Sweet and one in The Big Sleep when Marlowe makes a probing statement just as a romantic mood has been established.

Interestingly enough, several scenes in The Long Goodbye are "opposites" to similar scenes in Marlowe. For instance, a scene in Marlowe has Marlowe see the reflection of Wong in a telephone booth door.   In The Long Goodbye Marlowe sees Eileen, talking on the tele-phone, reflected in a wall decoration.   In Marlowe, the camera is inside a room looking out through sliding glass doors at Marlowe.   In The Long Goodbye the camera is outside, looking in through glass walls at Roger and Eileen.   Reflected in the glass are Marlowe and the ocean.

Marlowe featured Bruce Lee, later the biggest star of the Kung Fu films.   Marlowe's cellmate in The Long Goodbye is David Carradine, star of the television series, "Kung Fu."

In a scene in Marlowe, Christy French hits his part-ner by mistake and the partner says, "Sure, it's a new

kind of third degree.   The cops beat the hell out of each
other and the suspect cracks up from the agony of watch-
ing. "   Marty Augustine of The Long Goodbye breaks a
Coke bottle over his girl friend's nose and says to Marlowe: "Her I love.   You I don't even like. "

Roger repeatedly calls Marlowe "The Marlboro Man. "
The ads for Marlowe were a take-off on the Marlboro
cigarette commercials.

Finally James Garner watches Greta Garbo on a television monitor and says, "She was great, wasn't she?"
Gould says of Al Jolson, "He was okay. "

As can be readily seen, these frequently obscure
and trivial satirical references are not always the ingredi-
ents of great comedy.   Aimed at the select group who can
recognize them, these references are not effective in most
cases because the audience at large has no idea they exist.
Critics often deplore a film like Shamus because of its pre-
tentiousness in using allusions to other popular films.   Yet
here many reviewers, particularly Pauline Kael, loved these
satirical bits, demonstrating the faulty reasoning of the
critics and filmmakers who feel a plethora of trivial references an adequate substitute for good filmmaking.   Used
sparingly, these bits can add greatly to a picture, but here
Altman has been driven to an excess that hurts the film.

More than any other "Marlowe" film, The Long Goodbye is a manufactured "masterpiece. "   As Stephen Farber
points out, critics who decry the publicity surrounding a
film like The Great Gatsby often are easily taken in by
more subtle promotion efforts. 46   It is doubtful the new advertising campaign designed for The Long Goodbye helped
the film to any degree.   Far more effective was the publicity
surrounding the film's withdrawal and subsequent re-issue.
This, along with the name of Robert Altman, the inside
satire discussed above, and the supposed "laying to rest" of
Marlowe, thoroughly convinced reviewers like Pauline Kael
they were in the presence of greatness.   The Long Goodbye
certainly has its good points, but in no way stands out as a
cinematic masterpiece.

Although the film had a great impact on the critics,
The Long Goodbye received little attention from the public.
The picture may well be the least successful of all the
"Marlowe" films, for it failed to earn $1,000,000 in box

office rentals during 1973,[47] far below the amount needed
to show a profit.

The secondary characters in The Long Goodbye bear
no resemblance to Chandler's characters. In Silliphant's
unproduced script, these characters have remained within
the bounds of Chandler's world, with the only major character change being the fusion of Eileen Wade and Linda
Loring into Linda Wade. But Brackett and Altman opted
for a different approach, making the characters reflections
on modern society. This is particularly evident in the case
of Marty Augustine, one of the least Chandler-like gangsters
to grace a "Marlowe" film. This Jewish mobster has an
internationally integrated mob, three children at an exclusive
camp, a wife at a thousand-dollar-a-day health club, a
house full of servants, and a girl friend: in short, what
every well-rounded 1970's gangster should have. Augustine
is a character that beautifully illustrates Brackett's statement that "we've got ... a whole new bag of cliches ... and
the corruptions [the private eye] fights have new faces."[48]

Eileen Wade is also far removed from Chandler's
world. She has undergone a complete, radical change when
compared to the character in the novel. From the unprin-
cipled, brutal character of the book she has become the
least deceitful and most sincere "villainess" of any "Marlowe" film. As Brackett stated, her only crime is adultery
and her basically unselfish nature makes her one of the
most sympathetic women in any "Marlowe" picture.

In Roger Wade, Altman saw a personification of
Chandler himself. The director gave each member of the
crew a copy of Raymond Chandler Speaking so they could
read about Chandler's fascination with suicide. Altman said
"Roger Wade was in a sense Chandler. He was the sort
of hero who gave up the struggle. He just didn't want to
deal with it any more. I think he just wanted to escape....
Our adaption is really much more about suicide than it is
about murder."[49]

These two characters do serve to illustrate that the
secondary characters, as well as Marlowe, have lost touch
with contemporary society. Altman stated that except for
their behavior the characters were cut off from everything
before 1973. But their behavior indicated they weren't
really 1973 people because they had attitudes belonging to
other times. Roger Wade, for example, had an out-of-date

Roger Wade (Sterling Hayden) fights with his wife, Eileen
(Nina Van Pallandt).

---

hard-drinking masculine attitude.   Altman also believed the
characters were frustrated and they wondered what had happened to them: "Like Eileen Wade: you never see her in
a miniskirt, or a low-cut blouse, or with her shirt off like
the girls ... across from Marlowe."[50]

Of all the film's characters, Terry Lennox is the
most poorly done.   By making him Marlowe's long-time
friend, instead of a new acquaintance, as in the book, all
of the critical relationship between Marlowe and Terry has
been destroyed.   The point of the novel is that Marlowe
helps Terry, even though he hardly knows him, because he
believes in Terry and Marlowe's code states such a belief

carries with it an obligation not to betray a friend. That's
the kind of guy Marlowe is. In the film, however, it's not
Marlowe's code that makes him help Terry, for many people would stick by a long-time close friend. This, however, poses another problem: why would Marlowe be a
long-time friend of Terry? From the first time we meet
him we can tell Terry Lennox is a creep with a capital
"C." Even Gould's Marlowe would be able to see this and
would certainly have an idea that Terry had no moral
scruples.

At the heart of this discussion, of course, lies the
character of Marlowe. Because Altman was a primary factor in determining the character of Marlowe, a discussion
of the director has been left until now. Altman looked to
the picture as a comeback vehicle. The director hoped to
recapture the superdirector status he achieved after
M*A*S*H, for although his post-M*A*S*H films were interesting, they were not big money-makers. The road to this
comeback was to be a new and different interpretation of
Chandler's hero. Altman had very definite ideas about
Marlowe:

> ... [W]e literally called him Rip Van Marlowe,
> as if he had just woken up twenty years later and
> found out that there was absolutely no way to ac-
> commodate himself.... The only real thing he
> ever did was to believe in his friend--falsely.
> Everything else he did was an absolute mistake....
> It's true that our Marlowe doesn't have any
> of the heroics of the earlier movie Marlowes. I
> don't have any trust or distrust of heroics....
> Most people who are considered heroes are al-
> ways to be found messing about in someone else's
> affairs, and I don't think that's very heroic....
> You could say the real mystery of The Long
> Goodbye is where Marlowe's cat had gotten to.
> I shot the film in sequence; and I think that the
> most important thing we do in the film is to set
> up the whole cat sequence at the beginning. That,
> I think, tells the audiences that this isn't going to
> be Humphrey Bogart....
> So I think Marlowe's dead. I think that was
> 'the long goodbye.' I think it's a goodbye to that
> genre--a genre that I don't think is going to be
> acceptable any more. [51]

Altman and Brackett concentrated on two basic aspects of Marlowe's character: his position in time and his code of honor. Altman stated, "Marlowe is a Fifties character who has survived unchanged into the Seventies. He's a man out of time, out of place. He wears white shirts, narrow ties, and rumpled blue suits with brown shoes. He is the only one in the whole picture who smokes constantly puffing on Camels or Luckies. [Chandler once wrote that Marlowe smoked Camels and used stick matches of the kind that Gould strikes on every available surface.[52]] For him, the last fifteen or twenty years never happened."[53]

Even more important to the filmmakers than "Rip Van Marlowe" was the belief that what Chandler's Marlowe stood for no longer had any validity. Brackett said:

> Gould's Marlowe is a man of simple faith, honesty, trust, and complete integrity. All we did was strip him of the fake hero attributes. Chandler's Marlowe always knew more than the cops. He could be beaten to a pulp, but he always came out one way or another. By sheer force of personality, professional expertise, and gall, he always had an edge. We said, 'A man like this hasn't got an edge. He gets kicked around. People don't take him seriously. They don't know what he's all about, and they don't care. So instead of being the tough-guy, Marlowe became the patsy.'[54]

Altman said that the film would cast doubts on the "Marlowe" values of loyalty, honor, and duty[55] and that "I see Marlowe the way Chandler saw him, a loser. But a real loser, not the fake winner that Chandler made him out to be. A loser all the way."[56] (This contrasts sharply with Silliphant's Long Goodbye Marlowe, a self-assured winner.) The person chosen to "put Marlowe to rest for good"[57] and show what a loser he really was, of course, turned out to be Elliott Gould.

Like Altman, Gould hoped The Long Goodbye would be a comeback film. Gould, who starred in M*A*S*H, "plummeted from the exalted position of superstar to has-been in the absurdly brief span of two years."[58] Some say this was due to Gould's mental condition. Warner Bros. had collected on an insurance policy, saying the actor was crazy (what Warners meant by "crazy," Gould did not

Roger Wade (Hayden), Marlowe (Gould), Eileen Wade (Van Pallandt), and Dr. Verringer (Henry Gibson) in a heated discussion that will break up the beach party.

---

explain), and United Artists wanted proof he was sane.   A mental test convinced the studio that Gould was, indeed, sane. [59]

Gould agreed with Brackett's and Altman's interpretation of Marlowe and played him perfectly in keeping with their ideas.   Gould, then, becomes a new Marlowe: a loser whose outdated morals make him out of place in contemporary society.   He shrugs off society's rebuffs with an "I don't know" or a "That's okay."   He is totally asexual, going against the established "Marlowe" film image.   (Cut out of the final print was a scene in which Marlowe and Terry leave Marlowe's apartment and pass the bare-breasted girls next door.   Marlowe remarks that "It just doesn't work for me if you can't take their bras off."[60])   But worst of all, Gould spends the whole film trying to prove his guilty friend innocent, and is one step behind the police throughout most of the picture.

Gould's Marlowe remains faithful to one Chandler
tradition: the use of witty dialogue. In this, Marlowe is
the equal of his predecessors.   For example, Marlowe asks
if Roger Wade is Eileen's husband's real name.   When she
asks him why he wants to know, he says, "Because if
Roger Wade isn't his real name, I thought he might be using his real name."   When a policeman picks up a large
bronzed shoe in Marlowe's apartment and asks what it is,
Marlowe replies, "A baby shoe."   The picture also contains
some clever puns.   For example, when Marlowe goes to
Otatoclan to learn the details of Terry's death, the Mexican
coroner characterizes the detective as "a friend of the
diseased."

So far we have seen how this Marlowe goes against
the established Chandler tradition.   It is important to remember that by the time we reach the film version of The
Long Goodbye we are dealing with several Marlowes:
Chandler's Marlowe in his first five novels; the author's
hero in The Long Goodbye; the screen image of the detective in the first five "Marlowe" pictures (and in Silliphant's
script of The Long Goodbye); and Altman's Marlowe.   Altman set out to lay Marlowe to rest, but even he had his
Marlowes confused.   He tried to satirize the novel and film
image of Marlowe up to The Long Goodbye and in doing so
failed to capitalize on the flaws of the detective (discussed
earlier) as he appeared in Chandler's sixth novel.

The bitterly ironic thing about the picture, and something few, if any, critics have commented on, is that Brackett's, Altman's and Gould's Marlowe is a more effective,
less pessimistic character than Chandler's.   For instance,
Gould has no trouble finding Dr. Verringer, does not have
to go to the Carne Organization for help, is not sentimental
about Terry (he never pours an extra cup of coffee, lights
an extra cigarette, or orders an extra gimlet in remem-
brance of his friend), had a natural belief in a long-time
friend, does not break Marlowe's moral code by sleeping
with a woman, sees justice done in the end, is not used as
bait by the police to catch a gangster, is not beaten up as
much as the book Marlowe, and never expresses the pessimism of the literary hero.   Chandler aficionados might argue that the writer's hero would never have murdered his
friend.   Of course he wouldn't have.   But Marlowe's primary concern was always to see justice done.   Had Terry
been guilty, the detective would have taken him to the police, shot him in self defense, or left Terry to be killed or
commit suicide.   The result would have been the same, and

the killing of Terry is not, therefore, as much of a de-
parture from Chandler as one might imagine.

Gould's Marlowe is, of course, largely an ineffectual
character out of place in society, but it doesn't bother him;
he survives. He has physically, if not spiritually, made it
from the fifties into the seventies. The sentimental, pessimistic Marlowe of the novel probably would never have survived the transition. Altman intended the film to "put Marlowe to rest for good," but he need not have bothered to
try. Chandler did that better than anybody else, and a
straight film version of the depressing novel would have
laid our hero to rest far more effectively than the attempt
made here.

The Long Goodbye, then, is an uneven film generally
well scripted, acted, and photographed, but marred by its
illogical plot (the result of editing which caused Brackett to
comment that she was "thoroughly confused" by the rough
cut[61]) and inside satire. Although it is definitely not a bad
film, it can by no stretch of the imagination be called a
masterpiece, and even Altman has come to concede that the
picture is one of his least satisfying films.[62] Certainly it
is the most over-rated Marlowe picture.

TABLE 12.   PLOT COMPARISON

<u>THE LONG GOODBYE</u>

NOVEL	SILLIPHANT'S SCRIPT	FILM
1. Marlowe meets a drunk, Terry Lennox, helps him out, and they become friends.	Marlowe meets a drunk, Terry Lennox, helps him out, and they become friends.	
2.		Marlowe makes an unsuccessful attempt to feed his hungry cat and the animal runs away.
3. Terry comes to Marlowe upset and asks to be driven to Tijuana. Marlowe agrees on the condition he not be told anything, because Marlowe knows Terry's wife, Sylvia, is dead.	Terry comes to Marlowe upset and asks to be driven to Tijuana. Marlowe agrees on the condition he not be told anything, because Marlowe knows Terry's wife, Sylvia, is dead.	
4.		Marlowe is asked by his long-time friend, Terry Lennox, to drive him to Tijuana. Terry has just had a fight with his wife, Sylvia. Marlowe agrees.
5. When Marlowe returns to Los Angeles, he is questioned by the police because Sylvia has been brutally murdered.	When Marlowe returns to Los Angeles, he is questioned by the police because Sylvia has been brutally murdered.	When Marlowe returns to Los Angeles, he is questioned by the police because Sylvia has been brutally murdered.
6. Marlowe refuses to talk and is arrested. Marlowe is visited in jail by a lawyer, Sewell Endicott, but Marlowe refuses his help.	Marlowe refuses to talk and is arrested. Marlowe is visited in jail by a lawyer, Sewell Endicott, but Marlowe refuses his help.	Marlowe refuses to talk and is arrested.

(TABLE 12 cont.)

7.	Marlowe is released because the police consider the case closed. Terry wrote a confession and killed himself in Otatoclan, Mexico.	Marlowe is released because the police consider the case closed. Terry wrote a confession and killed himself in Otatoclan, Mexico.	Marlowe is released because the police consider the case closed. Terry wrote a confession and killed himself in Otatoclan, Mexico.
8.	Marlowe is visited by one of Terry's WW II army buddies, Menendez, a gangster. (The other buddy is Randy Star, a gambler.) Terry saved their lives during the war. Menendez tells Marlowe to lay off the Lennox case.	Marlowe is visited by one of Terry's Korean War army buddies, Blitz Bellson, a gangster. (The other buddy is Randy Starr, a gambler.) Terry saved their lives during the war. Bellson tells Marlowe to lay off the Lennox case.	
9.		Marlowe goes to the Carne Organization for help and learns Terry was once called Paul Marston.	
10.	Marlowe receives a letter from Terry, explaining his actions, and a $5000 bill.	Marlowe receives a letter from Terry, explaining his actions, and a $5000 bill.	Marlowe receives a note from Terry and a $5000 bill.
11.	Marlowe is asked by a literary agent, Howard Spenser, to help one of his writers, Roger Wade, a drunk. Marlowe refuses.		
12.	Eileen Wade, Roger's wife, asks Marlowe to find her husband, who is missing. Marlowe accepts.		Marlowe is asked by Eileen Wade to find her husband, Roger, a writer. Marlowe accepts.
13.		Marlowe meets Linda Wade, Sylvia Lennox's sister. She takes him to her millionaire	

		father, Harlan Potter. He warns Marlowe off the Lennox case.
14. Marlowe gets the names of three dope doctors from the Carne Organization, thinking Roger may be with one of them.		
15. Marlowe finds Roger with one of the doctors, Dr. Verringer. Marlowe takes Roger home. Marlowe meets Linda Loring, Sylvia's sister. He suggests her millionaire father, Harlan Potter, suppressed the murder investigation.		Marlowe finds Roger at a disreputable clinic run by a Dr. Verringer. Marlowe takes Roger home.
16. Roger calls Marlowe for help. Marlowe finds the writer unconscious and later Roger half-heartedly tries to kill himself.		
17.	Linda asks Marlowe to help her with her drunken husband, Roger, a geologist. Marlowe refuses.	
18.		Marlowe is visited by a gangster, Marty Augustine. Marty says Terry had $355,000 of Marty's money when he went to Mexico. Marty orders Marlowe to find the money.
19.		Marlowe follows Augustine to the Wades' house and sees, but cannot hear, him talking to Eileen.
20. Linda takes Marlowe to see her father. He warns		

(TABLE 12 cont.)

Marlowe to stop
investigating the
Lennox case.

21.   Linda tells Marlowe
             that Roger was sleep-
             ing with Sylvia. They
             are called to Linda's
             house because Roger
             is unconscious. Lat-
             er Roger tries to
             kill himself because
             he thinks he may
             have killed Sylvia.

22.   Roger tells Marlowe Au-
                                               gustine owes him
                                               $50,000.

23.   Marlowe goes to
             Otatoclan and finds
             inconsistencies in
             the details of Ter-
             ry's death. One of
             Blitz' men tries to
             kill Marlowe, but
             Marlowe kills him
             instead.

24.   Marlowe goes to Otato-
                                               clan to learn the details
                                               of Terry's death.

25.   Marlowe visits Starr   Marlowe goes to a party
             and suggests he and   at the Wades'. Dr. Ver-
             Blitz had Terry   ringer comes and de-
             killed to appease   mands and gets $4400
             Harlan Potter.   he says Roger owes him.

26. Marlowe goes to the   Marlowe goes to the
    Wades' house and   Wades' house and
    Roger is shot. It   Roger is shot. It
    may be suicide or   may be suicide or
    murder.   murder.

27.   Marlowe goes to   Marlowe questions Eileen
             Harlan Potter and   about Augustine's visit
             says Linda killed   and she says Roger owes
             Roger.   him $10,000. Roger
                                       commits suicide by walk-
                                       ing into the ocean.

28. A Vice Squad cop,
    Big Willie Magoon
    is beaten up by
    Menendez's men.

29.

Marlowe learns Roger
was sleeping with Sylvia
and could have killed
her.   He tells the po-
lice, but they already
know Roger left Sylvia's
house before she was
killed.

30. Marlowe and Howard
Spenser go to see
Eileen.   Marlowe
has learned that
Eileen and Terry
were married dur-
ing WW II and that
she lost track of
him when he was
captured.   Later
he turned up mar-
ried to Sylvia.   At
first Eileen says
she saw Roger mur-
der Sylvia and she
covered up for him.
But Marlowe ex-
poses her.   She
killed Sylvia.   Roger
suspected and that's
why he drank.   She
killed Roger.

31.

Marlowe has learned
that Linda and Terry
were married during
the Korean War, and
that she lost track of
him when he was
captured.   Later
Terry turned up
married to Sylvia.
At first Linda says
she saw Roger kill
Sylvia and she cov-
ered up for him.
But Marlowe exposes
her.   She killed both
Sylvia and Roger.

32.

Marlowe is being ques-
tioned by Augustine when
the missing money is
mysteriously returned.

33. Eileen writes a con-
fession of the two
murders and kills
herself.

Linda writes a con-
fession of the two
murders and kills
herself.

(TABLE 12 cont.)

34.   Marlowe sees and chases
                                                                 Eileen outside of Augus-
                                                                 tine's but he is hit by a
                                                                 car and taken to the
                                                                 hospital.

35. Marlowe gets a copy   Marlowe gets a copy
    of Eileen's confession   of Linda's confession
    from the police and   from the police and
    leaks it to a news-   leaks it to a news-
    paper.   paper.

36. Menendez comes and   Blitz comes and
    beats up Marlowe,   beats up Marlowe,
    but it is a police   but it is a police
    trap. They let Mar-   trap. They let
    lowe have a copy of   Marlowe have a copy
    the confession so   of the confession so
    they could catch   they could catch
    Menendez, partly   Blitz because of
    because of what he   what he did to Cap-
    did to Willie Ma-   tain Gregorious.
    goon and partly be-
    cause the police
    hate gamblers.

37. Marlowe sleeps with
    Linda Loring and re-
    fuses her marriage
    offer.

38. Marlowe is visited   Marlowe is visited
    by a Señor Maior-   by a Señor Maranos,
    anos, who claims to   who claims to have
    have knowledge of   knowledge of Terry's
    Terry's death. Mar-   death. Marlowe
    lowe realized the   realizes the man is
    man is really Terry.   really Terry. The
    The suicide was   suicide was faked to
    faked to get Terry   get Terry out of the
    out of the jam with   jam with Sylvia.
    Sylvia. They part,   They part, Marlowe
    Marlowe unwilling   unwilling to renew
    to renew their   their friendship.
    friendship.

39.   Marlowe goes to Otatoclan
                                                                 and learns the suicide
                                                                 was faked. Terry killed
                                                                 Sylvia because Roger told
                                                                 Sylvia that Terry was
                                                                 having an affair with
                                                                 Eileen. Sylvia knew
                                                                 Terry was carrying money
                                                                 for Augustine and was
                                                                 going to tell the police.

After the murder, Terry
had to get away. Terry
and Eileen are now going
to be together. Marlowe
kills Terry.

Chapter 8

FAREWELL, MY LOVELY

The filming of The Long Goodbye marked the end of
a twenty-nine-year process of converting Chandler's six
major novels into feature films. It is fitting, then, that
the next Marlowe picture should be a remake of the first
film starring the detective. But Farewell, My Lovely stands
out as more than a simple attempt to redo Murder, My
Sweet; rather, it represents an interesting venture in "Marlowe" filmmaking that takes a different approach in present-
ing Chandler's hero.

The history of the latest Marlowe film began when
executive producer Elliott Kastner purchased the filming
rights to The Long Goodbye and Farewell, My Lovely.
Some time after the release of The Long Goodbye, Kastner
and executive producer Jerry Bick began plans to film
Farewell, My Lovely. The picture was to be a joint Elliott
Kastner/Independent Television Corp. production with the
British entertainment tycoon Sir Lew Grade putting up part
of the several million dollars necessary to shoot the picture. [1] (The involvement of I. T. C. , a British company,
made Farewell, My Lovely the only Marlowe film produced
in part by an English organization.)

George Pappas and Jerry Bruckheimer signed as co-
producers of the picture. Pappas, a long associate of
Kastner, won the New Directors Award at Cannes for
Jeremy (1973), served as associate producer on Cops and
Robbers (1973), and produced 92 in the Shade (1975), another
Kastner film. Bruckheimer worked in a Detroit advertizing
agency before going to the BBD&C agency in New York.
He created commercials for Gillette, Campbell's Soup, and
Breck Shampoo and has won several Cannes Film Festival
Awards, several Clios (for excellence in advertising), and
the Hollywood Film Board Award. [2]

Kastner's choice for director was Dick Richards, and

Richards agreed to do the picture if Robert Mitchum played
Marlowe. (This presented no problem, for Kastner was also anxious to have the actor for the part, and Mitchum had
been an early contender for the part of Marlowe in The
Long Goodbye). Richards, 45, is a former photographer
and ad man turned filmmaker. He attended several Ivy
League schools, but knew that his real interest lay in
photography. He served in the Army as a photo-journalist
(part of the time in Korea) and covered presidents Kennedy
and Johnson. Richards' photographs appeared in Life,
Look, Vogue, Time, Esquire, and other magazines. He
started doing commercials and did advertisements for Volks-
wagen, General Motors, Coca Cola, Kellogg, Alka Seltzer,
and Pepsi Cola. For these commercials he won over one
hundred world-wide awards, among them a Clio and prizes
at the Cannes, New York, and Hollywood film festivals.

Richards began in feature films by directing The
Culpepper Cattle Company (1972), which developed out of
research on cowboys he did for a soup commercial. He followed that film with Rafferty and the Gold Dust Twins
(1974). (Bruckheimer also worked on both of these pictures.)

Richards feels his advertising experience has been
valuable for filmmaking:

> Commercials are a microcosm of feature
> films.... You tell a story, create a character,
> sell an idea or product in 30 or 60 seconds.
> You must communicate within that framework and
> that time span--or you're out.
> Frequently you'll spend more on a one-minute
> commercial than on an entire week of filming for
> a feature movie. And, because so much must be
> accomplished in so little time, new editing tech-
> niques have been developed in commercials which
> are now widely used in theatrical films, such as
> cuts in the midst of a zoom or pan, or direct cut
> time lapse [interval between consecutive scenes].
> ... [M]ore care goes into most commercials
> than into many movies. I feel good when I hear
> people say, as they sometimes do, that the best
> things on TV are the blurbs. [3]

Bruckheimer, too, feels commercials have helped his filmmaking. "Art has been described as getting to the

TABLE 13.   FAREWELL, MY LOVELY (1975)

Cast

Philip Marlowe	Robert Mitchum
Mrs. Grayle (Velma)	Charlotte Rampling
Nulty	John Ireland
Mrs. Florian	Sylvia Miles
Moose Malloy	Jack O'Halloran
Brunette	Anthony Zerbe
Billy Rolfe	Harry Dean Stanton
Mr. Grayle	Jim Thompson
Marriott	John O'Leary
Amthor	Kate Murtagh
Tommy Ray	Walter McGinn
Georgie	Jimmy Archer
Nick	Joe Spinell
Kelly/Jonnie	Sylvester Stallone
Cowboy	Burt Gilliam

An EK ITC Production
Fujicolor
An Avco Embassy Release
Running time: 97 min.
Release date: August 13, 1975
Rated R (an appeal to have this rating
   changed to PG was rejected by the
   Motion Picture Association of
   America)

Credits

Exec. Producers	Elliott Kastner
	Jerry Bick
Produced by	George Pappas
	Jerry Bruckheimer
Directed by	Dick Richards
Screenplay by	David Zelag Goodman
Based on novel by	Raymond Chandler
Dir. of Photog.	John Alonzo
Art Director	Angelo Graham
Set Decorations	Bob Nelson
Sound Mixer	Tom Overton
Music by	David Shire
Costumers	Tony Scarano
	Sandy Berke
Edited by	Walter Thompson
	Joel Cox
Asst. Directors	Henry Lange
	David Sonsa
Makeup	Frank Westmore
Production Mgr.	Tim Zinnemann
Prod. Designer	Dean Tavoularis
Hairdresser	Judy Alexander

essentials, and you learn to do this in making ads for
TV. "[4]

The first problem the filmmakers faced was how to
handle the story.   They wanted to do it differently from
The Long Goodbye, principally to be able to film a faithful
version of Chandler's novel, particularly in terms of atmosphere.   So Kastner, Richards, and Mitchum agreed the picture should be made as a period piece and decided to set
the film in Los Angeles in 1941.   This proved to be a cru-
cial decision for several reasons.   It meant shooting would
be much more difficult than if the film had been set in
contemporary Los Angeles.   Marlowe would now be operating in a different atmosphere than in the film The Long
Goodbye, and thus the problem of Marlowe's relevance to
contemporary society was circumvented (but not, of course,
the problem of whether Marlowe would be popular with today's film audience).   Setting the picture in 1941 made
Farewell, My Lovely the only Marlowe film not set in the
time it was produced, and the filmmakers, therefore, would
have to try to capture the "spirit" of the era.

The filmmakers hired David Zelag Goodman to write the script, which was a year in preparation. Goodman has scripted Monte Walsh (1970), Lovers and Other Strangers (1970), for which he received Academy Award and Writers Guild of America Award nominations, Straw Dogs (1971), and Logan's Run (1976).

Goodman enjoyed Murder, My Sweet, but chose not to model the new film on that picture because he felt Murder, My Sweet was outmoded by today's standards. "There was something slow and naive (in the sense of being simple) about Murder, My Sweet. The story lacked substance and depth. The period in which it was made was more innocent. It was not possible to do an innocent adaptation today, and the story doesn't really fit into today's time period."5 To help establish the correct time period and capture the mood of 1941, Goodman chose for a frame of reference Joe DiMaggio's 56-game hitting streak.

Goodman did not face the major problem of Stirling Silliphant and Leigh Brackett: compensating for a twenty-year time difference between the novel and the setting of the film. But he did face the usual problems of adapting Chandler's long descriptive passages while still keeping the Chandler spirit. Like John Paxton, Goodman used narration to incorporate some of these descriptive passages into film.

In our conversation, Goodman brought up another problem not previously mentioned in dealing with Chandler on screen. He said: "You don't have a ready-made audience in dealing with a classic writer. If all the people who ever read Farewell, My Lovely saw the movie, it still wouldn't be a very large audience by movie standards."6 Thus the picture would have to be made so it appealed to the audience at large, as well as detective film fans.

The plot of Farewell, My Lovely remains reasonably faithful to that of the novel. Like the previous Marlowe film screenwriters, Goodman found it necessary to simplify Chandler's complex plot. He explained: "Without injuring Chandler we made the plot simpler, but with great respect for Chandler. You can't use a lot of Chandler because in film everything has to tie in somehow. But the nice part of Chandler is that he has good parts you can use."7

Like Murder, My Sweet, Farewell, My Lovely begins

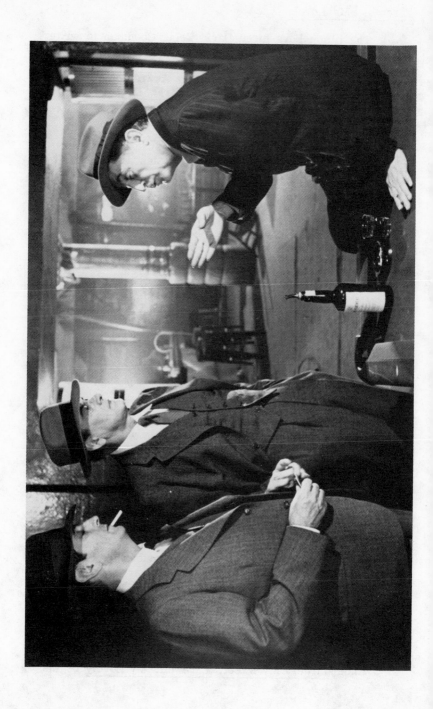

with a flashback. Following the opening, it becomes quickly apparent that the focus of the picture is upon Moose
Malloy. In the novel, the subplots of Malloy-Velma and
the missing jade share roughly equal time. The book begins with Malloy and Velma, shifts to the jade, and then the
subplots come together near the end of the story. In the
film, however, the jade serves only to introduce Marlowe
to Marriott and the Grayles. The search for Velma occu-
pies more time than the jade, but the primary concern rests
in the reason for the attempts on Malloy's life. Also, the
importance of Laird Brunette's political connections has
been increased in the film.

The characters of Farewell, My Lovely underwent a
greater alteration than the plot. The major character
change proved to be the total elimination of Anne Riordan
from the story, thus following the trend of removing Marlowe's love interest started in the film The Long Goodbye.
Dr. Sonderborg and Jules Amthor were combined into the
lesbian brothel owner, Frances Amthor. The major character additions were Tommy Ray, the former band leader
at Florian's; Billy Rolfe, a thoroughly corrupt cop; and Geor-
gie, Marlowe's local newsboy, who functions as a message
drop something in the manner of Chuck in Marlowe. In addition, the black characters in the novel, excluded from Murder, My Sweet, once again became part of the story.

Interestingly enough, some parts of the novel that
appeared in Murder, My Sweet were excluded from Farewell, My Lovely and vice versa. For example, Murder,
My Sweet devotes considerable attention to Anne Riordan,
while Farewell, My Lovely eliminates her. Farewell, My
Lovely, on the other hand, includes the character of Laird
Brunette, who was not in Murder, My Sweet.

The decision to shoot the picture in 1941 Los Angeles meant Richards concentrated on a different area of film
than had his immediate predecessor, Robert Altman. Whereas Altman's primary concern lay in the character of Marlowe in The Long Goodbye, Richards, having hired Mitchum,
turned his attention to faithfully recreating Chandler's
mileau. "Richards figured such realism could only be put

Facing page: Marlowe (Robert Mitchum, right) has summoned police detectives Billy Rolfe (Harry Dean Stanton,
left) and Lieut. Nulty (John Ireland) to Florian's. All photos
in this chapter are from Farewell, My Lovely (Avco Embassy, 1975).

on film if the company worked in places evocative of the
same somber, sometimes violent moods Chandler's genius
brought to life on paper."[8]

The filmmakers hired Academy Award-winning art
director Dean Tavoularis as set designer and John Alonzo
as cinematographer. Tavoularis worked on such pictures
as Bonnie and Clyde (1967), Little Big Man (1970), Zabriskie
Point (1970), The Conversation (1974), and both Godfather
pictures. He won an Oscar for The Godfather Part II
(1974). John Alonzo worked on Lady Sings the Blues (1972)
and Sounder (1972) and won an Oscar nomination for his
work on Chinatown (1974). (The great success of Chinatown, set in 1930's Los Angeles and praised by many critics
as having recaptured the Chandler atmosphere, may have
been part of the reason the filmmakers elected to film
Farewell, My Lovely as a period picture.) Almost the entire film was shot on location.

Richards and Bruckheimer felt the visual aspects
should be as important as the story line. "Long before the
full cast was even assembled for 'Farewell, My Lovely,'
they worked out rough camera approaches to key sequences
using a portable home-type video-tape set.... 'We talked
things out for weeks before we began to shoot [Richards
said]. It's the proper blending of the two [visuals and
story].'"[9]

Filming began on February 18, 1975, in Los Angeles
and lasted for about three months or forty shooting days. [10]
Both the exterior and interior shots were filmed on location.
Myron's, a period ballroom in downtown Los Angeles where
people who remember the '40's still dance to the big band
sounds, served as the location for the opening sequence. A
house, vacant pending the settlement of an estate, in the
Wilshire district near Vermont Avenue became Mrs. Florian's home. Frances Amthor's brothel was located in a run-
down million dollar mansion and many scenes took place in
a location familiar to Chandler, Echo Park. The climax
of the film comes on board a luxurious gambling ship, for
which Chandler may have had in mind the Rex, a popular
casino ship of the 1940's. No trace of the original vessel
could be found, so the filmmakers had the Queen Mary removed from its drydock, had its machinery overhauled, and
redecorated it. Pier sequences were shot in Long Beach. [11]

Naturally, this exterior shooting involved considerable

difficulties and the crew never spent more than two days in one spot. One difficult sequence had Marlowe following a suspect on foot through the streets of Los Angeles. Richards explained:

> ... [T]here were no reflectors marking traffic
> lanes at that time.... There were no red-painted
> curbs to restrict parking. Even the traffic lights
> and corner stop signs were of a different design.
> The fire hydrants in 1941 were unlike those we
> use today. We had to rip out all the modern
> stuff so nothing would seem incongruous--and then
> we had to replace it when we were through.
> We had to remove all TV anntennae [sic], all
> shop signs or advertising that didn't fit the period.
> We had to reroute all traffic blocks away so that
> only 1941 and earlier model autos would be in
> camera range.
> And obviously, we had to choose our camera
> angles very carefully so that we didn't photograph
> any modern buildings.
> In fact, what appears in the movie to be a
> single continuing walk down a couple of blocks is,
> in actuality, a compendium of maybe 10 to 15
> briefer shots, photographed at separate locations
> in order to avoid the intrusion of visuals that
> wouldn't fit the period. [12]

The interior scenes involved equal difficulty. The filmmakers rented locations bare of all furnishings and then dressed them with period items in an effort to match Chandler's descriptions. But finding the right interiors often proved difficult. For example, the crew went to Skid Row and shot in actual hotel rooms in the area. Richards described the difficulty in locating the appropriate site for Florian's. :

> We must have looked at 50 places before we
> settled on an upstairs room over Jack's Bar on
> 6th Street. Although we had to decorate it our-
> selves with peeling wallpaper, plaster hanging
> loose from the ceilings, crummy furnishings and
> the like, the very fact that it was where it was--
> the fact that when you went downstairs or stepped
> into the street you might well get knifed for the
> two bucks in your pocket--produced the kind of
> performances we needed. [13]

Mrs. Grayle (Charlotte Rampling) makes a play for Marlowe (Mitchum).

The total intent of location shooting was to try to capture as much of the Chandler atmosphere as possible. Richards remarked: "We had to get the real smell of the Los Angeles of the period ... and the real sounds, too.... And the real language. Chandler wrote dialogue the way people really spoke.... [Chandler] wrote what critics call the classic detective story. We have tried to be faithful to his legacy and his style by creating the basic classic detective movie."14

The filming problems may well make Farewell, My Lovely one of the last 1930's/1940's period films to be shot in Los Angeles. After Chinatown and Farewell, My Lovely, Alonzo plans to shot 98 per cent of his next film, I Will, I Will ... For Now, on a sound stage. He said:

> I came out of the documentary school ... but
> I'm reverting to the old tradition that many things
> can be better done on a sound stage....
>   All of the location problems in Los Angeles
> have gotten worse. Even Hancock Park, which
> you could always rely on for period houses, now
> has new signs and modern houses interspersed.
> And the television crews are eating up what loca-
> tions are left.
>   Logistics are also getting to be a worse prob-
> lem. With all the truck and trailers, moving the
> caravan eats up a lot of time. So now I'm think-
> ing, if it can be done on the back lot, do it. [15]

As publicity material for Farewell, My Lovely pointed out,
"It is simpler today for a motion picture producer to shoot
a Biblical spectacle against authentic backgrounds still
available in Egypt, Israel and the environs of Rome than to
photograph a story set in the late 1940s in Los Angeles in
the same city only 35 or so years later."[16] Richards concluded: "unless there is a radical change in public policy,
a few years hence it will be utterly impossible to film a
1940s story in the streets of Los Angeles.... Architectural
remnants of the era are fast disappearing along with open
spaces and clean air."[17]

Farewell, My Lovely was one of the first American
films to use a Japanese film stock called Fujicolor, which
Alonzo chose for its pastel effect. In addition, it cost 3
1/2 cents a foot less than regular film stock. The film's
stiffer emulsion caused some problems going through the
camera gate, but Panovision modified the equipment. [18]

John St. John served as technical advisor to the picture. St. John, a detective loaned to the filmmakers by the
Los Angeles Police Department, was the officer in charge
of the investigation of the Skid Row "slasher" murders.
And for trivia fans, we have Elliott Carpenter, who appears
in the film playing the piano in a cafe. It was his piano
that was heard when Dooley Wilson "played" "As Time
Goes By" in Casablanca. [19]

Farewell, My Lovely premiered on August 13, 1975,
in New York at the Loews State 1 and Loews Tower East
theatres. Both the public and critics generally responded
favorably to the picture. The film broke house records at
the Tower East on August 16 and 17 and thirteen out of

eighteen New York critics gave it favorable reviews. 20   The
critics praised the movie on three counts: the acting, the
set design, and the fidelity to Chandler.   Rex Reed said:
"I think it's the kind of movie Bogart would have stood in
line to see" while Bob Salmaggi touted it as "fascinating
and thoroughly engrossing. "21

 Other reviewers liked the picture, but with reservations.   Variety praised the quality of the production but
labeled Farewell, My Lovely "a lethargic, vaguely campy
tribute to Hollywood's private eye mellers of the 1940's and
to writer Raymond Chandler [that] fails to generate much
suspense or excitement.... "22   Richard Eder thought the
picture was simply a new version of an old film dressed up
for modern audiences and, like Murder, My Sweet critics
before him, found the film's plot confusing. 23   Eder felt the
best aspect of the movie lay in the original Chandler material: "The strengths of this movie are in Chandler and the
high quality of the acting.   The author's lines, tough, funny
and baroque, get full value. "24

 A small number of reviewers gave Farewell, My
Lovely completely negative reviews.   Charles Michener believed the film was ruined by "gumshoe-ese that echoes
Chandler's language without its hallucinatory sparkle. "25
Jay Cocks stated the film made a mockery of "the traditions
of Raymond Chandler and the hard-boiled melodrama" and
wondered "How can anyone take such an enterprise serious-
ly, after all, when the detective runs around in a trench
coat six inches too short and 25 years too new for him?"26

 The effort the filmmakers invested in Farewell, My
Lovely proved worthwhile.   Although the Chandler atmosphere can be captured on a sound stage (as Hawks proved),
the location shooting, coupled with narration of Chandler's
lines, recreates Marlowe's mileau with a fidelity that
makes the picture exciting to watch.   From Florian's bar
to the Grayle house, the viewer is made to feel he is actually tramping the streets of Chandler's Los Angeles.   None
of the recent Marlowe films and only two of the older ones,
Murder, My Sweet and The Big Sleep, match Farewell, My
Lovely in terms of set design.   It is fortunate that filmmakers had enough faith in Chandler to invest the extra
money needed to set the picture in 1941, for they may be
the last moviemakers to have the opportunity to present
Marlowe's world as Chandler knew it.

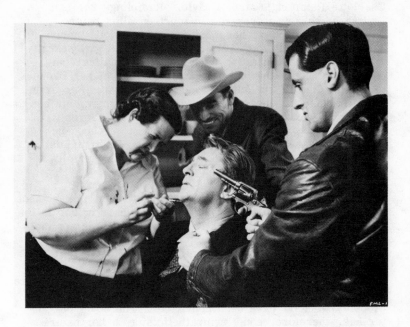

Frances Amthor (Kate Murtagh) drugs Marlowe (Mitchum)
with the help of Cowboy (Burt Gilliam) and Jonnie (Sylvester
Stallone).

For the most part the secondary characters of Farewell, My Lovely accurately reflect those of the novel.   John
Ireland's Lieutenant Nulty is a classic Chandler cop, frustrated by the restrictions placed on him by crooked politicians and finally doing what his conscience dictates, regard-
less of the consequences.   Jack O'Halloran is as effective
as Mike Mazurki was in the Moose Malloy role and Silvia
Miles ably recreates the drunken Mrs. Florian of the novel.
The major change in the secondary character lies with Frances Amthor.   Although nothing like her ever appeared in
Chandler, it proved an interesting idea to turn Amthor into
a woman, and she doesn't seem out of place.   A lesbian
brothel owner is far removed from the psychic consultant
Jules Amthor of the novel, but the complete tone and idea
of the character remains the same.

The major problem in characterization lies with
Charlotte Rampling's Mrs. Grayle. Rampling, 29, is a
British actress who appeared in fourteen films before
Farewell, My Lovely, her most famous previous picture
being The Night Porter (1974), the story of a girl sexually
tortured in a concentration camp. Several critics complained that Rampling had been cast because of her likeness
to Lauren Bacall and felt this hurt the picture. For example, Charles Michener stated. "Cast, seemingly, for her
superficial vocal and physical resemblence to Lauren Bacall, Rampling comes across as merely a scrubbed-up
mannequin of her smoky predecessor."[27] Richard Eder
called Rampling's relationship to Bacall "both painfully intentional and painfully bad."[28]

Although Rampling's obviously intentional resemblance
to Bacall (especially the first glimpse we have of her in the
Grayle Mansion) does detract from her role, it is not the
main fault of the Grayle characterization. The major problem concerns the hardness Rampling brings to the part, a
coldness not found in the book character. At the end of the
novel, Marlowe speculates Mrs. Grayle shot herself to spare
her ailing husband the agony of a trial, even though she
probably wouldn't have been convicted. The novel character has, therefore, some sympathetic side to her nature
that Marlowe could detect. But the film character is a one-
dimensional person ranking far below Claire Trevor's expert
Mrs. Grayle characterization.

The major concern with Farewell, My Lovely lies,
of course, in the character of Marlowe. Robert Mitchum
was born in Bridgeport, Connecticut on August 6, 1917.
His father died when he was eighteen months old and he
was raised by his mother and grandparents. He ran away
to his sister in New York at 13 and learned to survive the
street life of Hell's Kitchen. Not wishing to burden his
mother or sister, he quit school when he was 14 and hit the
road. When he was 16, he was arrested for vagrancy in
Savannah, Georgia, and later charged with robbery, even
though he had been in jail when the robbery took place.
He escaped from a Georgia chain gang after a week and
still doesn't know whether he's wanted in Georgia.

Mitchum went to California at 20, helped out in the
Little Theatre in Long Beach, and returned to Delaware to
marry Dorothy Spense in 1940. They went back to California and Mitchum got a job in a factory. When his wife

became pregnant, Mitchum went looking for extra money and
found a job riding a horse in a Hopalong Cassidy film,
where he was almost stomped to death. He got several
more acting jobs and when the supply of leading actors was
depleted by the war (Mitchum had tried to enlist but was
rejected) he got bigger roles in such films as Corvette K-
225 (1943) and Thirty Seconds Over Tokyo (1944). In 1945
Mitchum starred in The Story of G. I. Joe and won his only
Oscar nomination. Later in the year the Army accepted
him, and he spent eight months helping process men out of
the Army. He returned to feature films after being discharged and has remained in pictures ever since. Although
he has acted in over a hundred films, Farewell, My Lovely
is his first detective role. [29]

Mitchum is an actor who doesn't worry about his
work. "Mostly, it's just a matter of turning up on time
for work.... I always suggest that they get someone else
for the part. Nobody can convince me, no matter what the
film, that it should be me.... [Acting] sure beats the hell
out of working."[30]

Richards has stated, "The part of Philip Marlowe
... has been waiting 30 years for Robert Mitchum to claim
it"[31] and obviously felt Mitchum made an excellent Marlowe. Many of the critics agreed. Rex Reed said Mitchum
"gives strength, credence and sympathy to his Marlowe,"[32]
Bob Salmaggi said "we couldn't have a better choice...,"[33]
and Bernard Drew stated, "Mitchum is altogether superb,
possibly the best Marlowe of all."[34]

Other critics, however, disliked Mitchum. Variety
felt he "ambles through the role without conviction."[35]
More scathing was Jay Cocks' comments. "[Mitchum] is
all wrong. For Chandler, Marlowe was a kind of rogue
knight. Mitchum plays him with the same sloppy self-loath-
ing that he has frequently used to demonstrate his superior-
ity to a role. If this contempt suits Mitchum, it ill becomes Marlowe."[36] Lastly, Michener liked neither Mitchum
nor the overall treatment of Marlowe. He called Mitchum
"little more than an evocation of himself in the 1940s"[37]
and complained:

... Richards and ... Goodman inject Marlowe
with an updated social conscience. Having mut-
tered 'What a world,' he gives his fee to the
fatherless son of one of the murder victims, a

Jesse Florian (Sylvia Miles) tells Marlowe (Mitchum) she's had a call from Velma.

---

little boy who happens to be black.   By doing so, this Marlowe unwittingly commits the movie's final 'unspeakable' horror: he turns Chandler's hard-boiled hero into a soft-boiled liberal. [38]

In spite of the critics' negative comments, Mitchum does make an excellent Marlowe.   More than any other film Marlowe except Bogart, Mitchum has a "lived-in" look and a matter-of-fact manner that capture the essence of Chandler's hero.   From the droop of his cigarette to the unconcerned delivery of his lines, Mitchum embodies the best aspects of the detective hero.   He delivers wisecracks like "I don't accept tips for finding kids.   Pets, yes: five dollars for dogs and cats; ten dollars for elephants" in classic Marlowe style.   And often his facial expressions perfectly recapture Marlowe's reactions in the novel.   For example, Mitchum's expression when Judge Grayle finds him kissing

Mrs. Grayle expertly matches Marlowe's feeling in the
novel, where he says, "I felt as cold as Finnegan's feet,
the day they buried him." On the negative side, Mitchum's
major failing is that he occasionally says his lines as
though he doesn't believe them (his complaint to Nulty about
what he needs, for example, seems a little forced) and on
rare occasions, therefore, is not up to his usual standard
of excellence.

Part of Marlowe's character in Farewell, My Lovely
emerges as a decided change from Chandler's Marlowe: the
involvement in violence. Farewell, My Lovely is the most
violent "Marlowe" film, with a total of eleven corpses strewn
throughout the picture, three of them done in by our hero
in self-defense. Not only does Farewell, My Lovely present Marlowe at his most violent, but also he shoots a
woman, something the literary Marlowe would never do.
Although nothing existed in the detective's code forbidding
him to kill a woman in self-defense, when Marlowe did come
up against a gun-toting female, Chandler had him escape
through foresight or good luck. In The Big Sleep, Carmen
tried to shoot the detective, but he had loaded her gun with
blanks. And in the novel Farewell, My Lovely, Marlowe
escapes being shot by Mrs. Grayle only because she has
already emptied her gun into Mosse Malloy. Thus Marlowe's shooting of Mrs. Grayle in the film Farewell, My
Lovely, however much she deserved it, is uncharacteristic
for our hero.

Farewell, My Lovely stands out as an excellent "Marlowe" film. Its few faults are far outweighed by its many
virtues, and it certainly comes close to realizing Richards'
goal of creating "the basic classic detective movie."

TABLE 14.   PLOT COMPARISON

Farewell, My Lovely

NOVEL	FILM

1.

It is 1941. Marlowe telephones Detective Lieutenant Nulty to come and meet him so Marlowe can explain about his involvement in seven unsolved murders. Nulty arrives and Marlowe explains after he found a runaway girl and returned her to her wealthy parents he was grabbed by a large man, Moose Malloy.

2.   Marlowe is dragged into Florian's, an all-black bar, by a large man, Moose Malloy. Malloy is looking for a girl named Velma, whom he hasn't seen since he went to prison eight years ago. Velma used to sing at Florian's when it was white. No one remembers Velma and Malloy runs into trouble. He kills the owner of the bar and leaves. Marlowe calls the police. A detective lieutenant named Nulty gets the case. Nulty asks Marlowe to look for Velma and Marlowe agrees.

3.

Three shots are fired at Malloy from a passing car, but the bullets miss. Malloy offers to hire Marlowe to find Velma, whom he hasn't seen since he went to prison seven years ago.

4.

Marlowe and Malloy go to

Florian's, an all-black bar.
Velma used to sing at Florian's
when it was white. No one
remembers Velma and Malloy
runs into trouble. He kills the
owner of the bar and Marlowe
tells Malloy to leave. Malloy
says he will keep in touch.
Nulty and Detective Lieutenant
Billy Rolfe arrive and Marlowe
explains the killing was self
defense. Nulty tells Marlowe
to bring Malloy in and sign a
deposition.

5. Marlowe learns that the   Marlowe learns that the former
    former owner of Florian's   owner of Florian's is dead but
    is dead but his widow,   his alcoholic widow, Jessie,
    Jessie, is still alive.   is still alive.

6. Marlowe goes to see Jessie
    and finds she is a drunk.
    He plies her with liquor
    and asks her about Velma.
    She gives Marlowe some
    photographs but tries to
    hide a picture of Velma.
    She refuses to say why she
    hid it and says Velma is
    dead.

7.   Marlowe goes to see Jessie.
                                     She doesn't know where Velma
                                     is, but says she will try and
                                     find out.

8.   Marlowe gets a photograph of
                                     Velma from Tommy Ray, the
                                     former band leader at Flori-
                                     an's. But Marlowe learns the
                                     photo is a fake, and that Nulty
                                     is anxious to find Malloy.

9. Marlowe sees Nulty and tells
    what happened with Jessie.
    Marlowe suggests Nulty
    should find out who turned
    Malloy in for the reward
    when he was sent to jail.
    Nulty asks Marlowe if
    Jessie paid him to lay off.

10. Marlowe goes to his office

(TABLE 14 cont.)

and gets a call from a man
named Lindsay Marriott,
asking him to come and
see Marriott. Marlowe
agrees.

11. Nulty calls and says Malloy
    went to see Jessie. He
    asks Marlowe for more
    help, but Marlowe refuses.

12.

A man named Lindsay Marriott
contacts Marlowe. Marriott
says a very rare jade necklace
was stolen from a friend. He
is going to buy it back and
wants Marlowe to go along.

13. Marlowe goes to see Mar-
    riott. Marriott says a
    very rare jade necklace was
    stolen in a hold-up from
    one of his friends. He is
    going to buy it back and
    wants Marlowe to go along.
    He says he picked Mar-
    lowe's name out of the
    phone book. Marlowe says
    he doesn't think he can
    help Marriott, but that
    he'll go along anyway.

14. Marlowe and Marriott drive
    to the rendezvous spot and
    find it deserted. Marlowe
    leaves the car to investi-
    gate, but finds no one. He
    returns to the car and is
    knocked out.

Marlowe and Marriott drive to
the rendezvous spot. Marlowe
gets out of the car and is
knocked out.

15. Marlowe awakens to find
    the car gone. He follows
    its tracks and finds it
    empty. A girl comes.
    She tells Marlowe that
    Marriott is dead and leads
    him to the body. Mar-
    riott has been beaten to
    death. Marlowe searches
    the body and finds an
    extra cigarette case. The

girl, Anne Riordan, tells
Marlowe she happened to
be driving by and spotted
Marlowe's flashlight. Marlowe tells Anne to take
him back to his car.

16.   Marlowe awakens to find Mar-
                                             riott murdered. Nulty tells
                                             the detective to forget about
                                             finding Malloy.

17. Marlowe goes to the police
     and is questioned by Lieu-
     tenant Randall. Randall
     suggests Marriott planned
     to steal the money but was
     killed by an accomplice.
     Marlowe doesn't like that
     idea. Randall shows Mar-
     lowe the extra cigarette
     case. The cigarettes that
     were in it are gone.

18. Marlowe goes to his office
     and finds Anne waiting for
     him. She says she knows
     who the necklace belongs
     to. She says her father
     was Bay City police chief
     until a mob of gamblers
     led by Laird Brunette had
     him fired. The necklace
     belongs to the very rich
     Mrs. Lewin Lockridge
     Grayle. Anne says Mrs.
     Grayle will talk with Mar-
     lowe. Marlowe says the
     jade is probably lost be-
     cause of Marriott's death.
     Anne gives Marlowe the
     cigarettes she took from
     Marriott's cigarette case.

19.   Marlowe learns the necklace
                                             probably belongs to Judge Bax-
                                             ter Wilson Grayle and Marlowe
                                             visits him. He meets Mrs.
                                             Grayle and her husband tells
                                             Marlowe nothing is missing
                                             from his jade collection. Mrs.
                                             Grayle says she will pay Mar-
                                             lowe to find Marriott's killer.

(TABLE 14 cont.)

20. Marlowe finds a card that
     says "Jules Amthor Psy-
     chic Consultant" in Mar-
     riott's cigarette mouth-
     piece. Marlowe calls
     Amthor and arranges to
     see him. Marlowe learns
     Marriott holds a trust deed
     to Jessie Florian's house.

21. Marlowe goes to see Jes-
     sie. A neighbor tells
     Marlowe Jessie gets a
     registered letter every
     month. Marlowe tells
     Jessie she knows about
     Marriott's trust deed.
     She pulls a gun on Mar-
     lowe and he leaves.

22. Marlowe gets a call ask-
     ing him to come to the
     Grayle house.

23. Marlowe sees Mrs. Grayle.
     She explains about the
     robbery and says Marriott
     was a blackmailer of
     women.

24.   Marlowe goes to his office and
                                           is knocked unconscious.

25. An Indian named Second
     Planting takes Marlowe to
     see Amthor. Marlowe asks
     why Amthor's cards were
     in the cigarette holders but
     Amthor says he doesn't
     know. Marlowe suggests
     Amthor told Marriott what
     women to date so they
     could be set up for rob-
     bery. Amthor and Plant-
     ing beat up Marlowe.

26.   Marlowe awakes to find himself
                                           in a brothel run by Frances
                                           Amthor. She wants to know
                                           where Malloy is and beats
                                           Marlowe and drugs him to find

out but Marlowe says he
doesn't know where Malloy is.

27. When Marlowe comes to,
two Bay City policemen
are there. They drive
him away from Amthor's
and knock him out.

28. Marlowe wakes up three
days later to find himself
in a locked room, drugged.
He regains his senses and
breaks out of the room.

29.   Marlowe overpowers one of
                                       Amthor's thugs and searches
                                       the brothel. He finds Tommy
                                       Ray dead, shot twice in the
                                       head. Marlowe finds Amthor
                                       in her office.

30. Marlowe discovers Malloy
in another room but doesn't
let Malloy see him.

31. Marlowe confronts the man
in charge, Dr. Sonderborg,
who says the Bay City po-
lice brought him there.
Marlowe goes to Anne's.

32.   Marlowe asks Amthor why
                                       Malloy is so important, but
                                       she won't tell him. Amthor
                                       is shot and killed by one of
                                       her men and Marlowe goes to
                                       a friend's to recover from the
                                       effects of the drugs.

33. Marlowe tells Anne what
happened and says he
doesn't think Amthor is
the leader of a jewel robbery gang.

34.   Mrs. Grayle calls and invites
                                       Marlowe to a political party
                                       for her husband.

35. Randall comes to see Marlowe and he tells Randall
what happened.   Marlowe

(TABLE 14 cont.)

tells Randall that Mar-
riott blackmailed women
and was the finger man
for a jewel mob. Mar-
riott was killed because
he had outlived his useful-
ness. Randall knows that
Marriott held the trust
deed and has found out
about Marlowe's interest
in Malloy and Velma.
Marlowe tells Randall he
saw Malloy at Sonder-
borg's.

36.   At the party, Marlowe meets
                                  a gambler, Laird Brunette.
                                  Brunette wants to hire Marlowe
                                  to find Malloy. Marlowe
                                  agrees.

37. Marlowe and Randall go
    to see Jessie Florian and
    find her dead. Her neck
    has been broken by Mal-
    loy, but Marlowe says
    Malloy didn't mean to kill
    her. Randall says Amthor
    and Sonderborg have left
    town.

38.   Mrs. Florian calls Marlowe
                                  and says she has been in touch
                                  with Velma and Velma wants
                                  to talk to Malloy. Velma sets
                                  up a meeting with Marlowe
                                  and Malloy in her motel.

39. Marlowe goes to the Bay
    City police chief to find
    the two men, Blane and
    Galbraith, who took him
    to Sonderborg's. Galbraith
    tells Marlowe he and Blane
    kept people from bothering
    Amthor and he doesn't
    know what Sonderborg's
    racket is. But Galbraith
    thinks and Marlowe agrees,
    Sonderborg hid men on
    the run. Marlowe wants

to know where a man on
the run might go after
leaving Sonderborg's.
Galbraith suggests the
gambling ships Laird
Brunette owns.

40.   When Marlowe and Malloy go
                                        to the motel, Malloy is am-
                                        bushed but Marlowe saves
                                        him.   Marlowe kills the two
                                        men sent to shoot Malloy.
                                        Velma is nowhere around.
                                        Marlowe wonders who is try-
                                        ing to kill Malloy, and calls
                                        Nulty.   Nulty is upset because
                                        Marlowe did not tell him
                                        where Malloy was.

41.   Marlowe and Nulty go to Mrs.
                                        Florian's and find her dead.

42. After some difficulty,
    Marlowe gets on board one
    of Brunette's gambling
    ships.   He confronts Brun-
    ette, tells him some of
    what has happened, and
    says he wants to see Mal-
    loy.   Brunette denies know-
    ing Malloy but agrees to
    see Malloy gets a message
    from Marlowe.

43.   Marlowe tells Nulty he is go-
                                        ing to take Malloy on board
                                        Brunette's gambling ship and
                                        try to solve the murders that
                                        have been committed.   Nulty
                                        says he is under orders to
                                        bring Marlowe in and refuses
                                        to go to the ship because of
                                        Brunette's political connections.
                                        Nulty lets Marlowe go and the
                                        detective and Malloy go to the
                                        ship.   They fight their way to
                                        Brunette's cabin and the gam-
                                        bler says he never heard of
                                        Velma.

44. Marlowe returns to his
    apartment and calls Mrs.
    Grayle.   She agrees to

(TABLE 14 cont.)

come over. Malloy comes
and Marlowe says Malloy
didn't mean to kill Jessie
Florian. Mrs. Grayle
comes and Malloy hides
in another room.

45. Marlowe tells Mrs. Grayle
that he doesn't think Marriott was involved with
jewel robbers and that the
jade necklace was never
stolen. Marriott went to
the rendezvous thinking he
was going to kill Marlowe.
Marlowe says Jessie and
Marriott knew about Mrs.
Grayle's past. Marriott
was dangerous to Mrs.
Grayle, so she killed him.
Mrs. Grayle draws a gun
on Marlowe.

46. Malloy enters the room.
Mrs. Grayle is Velma.
She shoots Malloy and tries
to shoot Marlowe, but the
gun is empty. She leaves,
Marlowe calls the police
and Malloy dies.

47.

Mrs. Grayle enters the cabin.
She is Velma and she tries to
get Malloy to help her, but
Marlowe explains the case.
Velma was a prostitute who
married a millionaire who
didn't know her past and didn't
know she let Malloy take the
rap for a bank robbery. But
Amthor and Brunette knew
Velma's past. Brunette, with
Velma's help, was going to
use Mr. Grayle for political
protection for Brunette's
rackets. The plan was spoiled
when Malloy was paroled and
came looking for Velma. Marriott was killed because he was
a weak link and Brunette also
had Tommy Ray and Mrs.
Florian killed.

48. Marlowe is with Anne.
    Mrs. Grayle has escaped.
    The photo Jessie gave
    Marlowe is false.   Velma
    had turned Malloy in eight
    years ago.   Amthor was
    an international con man
    but had nothing to do with
    the murders or Sonderborg.
    Velma is discovered by a
    detective in Baltimore.
    She kills him and shoots
    herself.   She never could
    have been prosecuted, but
    Marlowe says she shot
    herself to spare her hus-
    band the trial.

49.   Mrs. Grayle shoots and kills
                                       Malloy.   Marlowe kills Mrs.
                                       Grayle.   Nulty breaks in,
                                       having decided to go against
                                       Brunette's political pull.

Chapter 9

CONCLUSION

In the preceding pages we have examined the process and results of several screen adaptations of Raymond Chandler's novels. In addition, the character of Marlowe in the novels and films has been compared and contrasted. From these analyses, two general patterns emerge. One deals with the process of transforming a detective novel into a film; the other reflects the differences in a literary hero and the screen image of him.

In the part of this study treating novels and films, a central trend runs through all the Marlowe films, and this pattern appears applicable to other film adaptations of books as well. In the case of each Marlowe film, the screenwriter passed through three basic steps: simplifying the plot, intensifying the characters, and finding filmic equivalents of key passages in Chandler's writing.

Simplification of the plot collectively resulted in several basic changes. Elimination of minor incidents not pertinent to the major thread of the story was accomplished. The major portions of the plot were condensed and shortened to better fit the filmmaker's time limitations. Paradoxically, this "simplification" did not always make the story easier to understand. In The Big Sleep, for example, the storyline was simplified and shortened at the expense of some necessary explanations concerning the action found in the novel. The complete elimination of these pieces of information did not make the screen version of the novel any easier to understand. In general, however, these condensations and shortenings resulted in less complex plots than in the novels.

The film intensification of certain characters also helped to shorten and tighten the story. Many minor characters in the six novels were dropped, and only a few new ones were added to the Marlowe films. Moose Malloy in

198

Murder, My Sweet, a composite of the book characters of Malloy and Second Planting, and Linda Wade in Silliphant's Long Goodbye script, a fusion of the novel's Linda Loring and Eileen Wade, illustrate how aspects of several characters were sometimes combined into one, much in the same way Chandler combined his short story characters when he included them in a novel. Ann Grayle in Murder, My Sweet, who was a member of the family and therefore had a personal interest in the case, is an example of how screen character changes resulted in a tightening of relationships. In addition, a character's importance was sometimes increased or diminished. All these character changes served to make the films more unified than the novels.

Visual equivalents of some of Chandler's passages were harder to accomplish than plot or character changes. Most filmmakers used standard photographic methods to accomplish their aims, but others embellished on ordinary cinematic techniques. Robert Montgomery, for example, tried to capture the Chandler spirit by total use of the subjective camera. On the other hand, the makers of Murder, My Sweet mixed a few subjective shots with narration. And the creators of Farewell, My Lovely combined narration with a recreation of the actual Los Angeles Chandler wrote about. However it was done, each group of filmmakers tried to capture the Chandler spirit the author had conveyed so well in his descriptive passages.

The second major pattern to emerge from this study concerns the Philip Marlowe filmic image. Throughout the Marlowe pictures, as well as the unproduced version of The Long Goodbye, Marlowe is more personally involved with violence than his novel counterpart. Chandler's Marlowe is a relatively nonviolent person. He moves within a violent world, but rarely is he the perpetrator of violence or its victim. In the first five Marlowe pictures, however, our hero suffers far more beatings than in the original sources. In this case we see a traditional Hollywood attitude toward the filmic tough guy image: the hero can take physical punishment without serious injury. In the Silliphant script and the final movie version of The Long Goodbye and in the film Farewell, My Lovely, Marlowe is not subject to these extra beatings. But the detective metes out violence in incidents not in the novels. In Silliphant's Long Goodbye script (never shot), Marlowe kills Chick Agostino in self defense; in the filmed version, the hero murders Terry Lennox. And in Farewell, My Lovely, Marlowe shoots and

and kills Mrs. Grayle as well as a couple of thugs.   These
incidents run contrary to the Chandler originals, for his
Marlowe never killed anyone after The Big Sleep.

Another principal difference between the book and
screen versions of the Marlowe character concerns sex.
The filmic Marlowe on the whole takes far more interest
in women than Chandler's original hero, and each of the
first five Marlowe pictures has a romantic encounter.   The
Brasher Doubloon and Marlowe are, in fact, heavily laced
with sex.   George Montgomery goes to the Murdock mansion because he likes Merle's voice and stays on the case
because of her.   James Garner, in the sexiest Marlowe
film, has a steady girl friend who spends the night in his
apartment, the closest we ever come to seeing Marlowe in
bed with a woman.   Interestingly, the films, The Long
Goodbye and Farewell, My Lovely, as well as Silliphant's
Long Goodbye script, do not hold true to this pattern.   The
absence of any romantic adventures for Marlowe in The
Long Goodbye is in this case contrary to Chandler, for that
is the only novel under discussion in which the detective
does engage in sex.   Farewell, My Lovely, however, does
remain faithful to its source by not giving Marlowe a girl
friend.   The last two Marlowe pictures, then, show a
break in the romantic aspect of Marlowe's character established in the first five films.

The filmic Marlowe has distinct traits and it is now
appropriate to summarize the movie version of the hero.
This character is relatively poor, kept that way by his
moral code which does not allow him to accept unearned
money.   This code, of course, also compels the detective
to seek the truth and see justice done no matter what the
personal risk.   The filmic sleuth rebounds quickly from
physical injury and sometimes commits violent acts.   Although he operates alone, he frequently carries on a romantic relationship.   Generally, the film Marlowe operates
without harassment from the police and is far ahead of them
in finding the truth.   The emergent image, then, is that of
a violent, sexually successful, self-assured individual.

Still another aspect of the screen Marlowes concerns
the question of who best personified the hero in film.
Serious students of the Marlowe movies automatically dis-
miss the two Montgomerys as the worst of the Marlowes.
Not one published critical examination of Marlowe films
read for this book placed them above the bottom slot.   Both

Robert Montgomery and George Montgomery are ill-suited
to portray Marlowe; Robert because he better fits gentle-
men-type roles and in no way physically seems like a tough
detective, and George because his slick and almost lecher-
ous nature is far removed from Chandler's Marlowe.   Elliott Gould, James Garner, and Robert Mitchum fall in the
middle category.   Most of the attention concerning The Long
Goodbye focused, of course, on the off-beat nature of Marlowe and some critics have praised Gould for this interpretation of Chandler's hero.   Gould, while not as effective
as these critics seem to think, is at least passable as
Marlowe.   James Garner, on the other hand, turns in a
very effective performance and was considerably under-
rated by the critics.   He has some of the boyish nature of
Dick Powell, but without the innocence that seems out of
place in the Powell portrayal.   Overall, however, he is not
as accomplished an actor as Powell.   Mitchum is the best
of the three and makes a most effective Marlowe.   His
violent nature, however, is somewhat against him and he
occasionally relies solely on his physical appearance, rather
than his acting, to carry him through a scene.

     The two actors who have garnered the most support
as the best Marlowe are Dick Powell and Humphrey Bogart.
Those that favor Powell, such as William K. Everson, feel
this actor is superior because he was new to the detective
genre and didn't have the competing screen tough-guy images
Bogart had to contend with. [1]   Paul Jensen also felt that
Powell's boyishness and innocence perfectly fitted in with
the Marlowe character, while Bogart was too violent, particularly in the scene where he hits Carol Lundgren. [2]
While there is merit in both arguments, my opinion remains
that Bogart is superior to Powell.

     The major criticisms against Bogart can be easily
countered.   Bogart's superb acting ability allowed him to
"become" the character he played in a film but, at the
same time, prevented him from being stereotyped as a particular character.   Thus his portrayal as Rick in Casablanca
does not in any way detract from his personification of
Marlowe in The Big Sleep.   Powell does not have this violent streak but, as Jensen fails to point out, Bogart's violent handling of Carol Lundgren comes straight out of the
novel, so certainly Bogart is in keeping with Chandler's
hero.   Powell is less violent simply because Chandler presented his hero that way in Farewell, My Lovely.   One
factor working slightly against Powell is that he misjudges

Mrs. Grayle's character. When she asks him to help her
kill Amthor, Powell overfills his glass in surprise, something Chandler's hero would not do. Chandler's Marlowe
had too much experience with people for a thing like that
to surprise him.

More than any other actor, Bogart captures the true
spirit of Marlowe and, as Stirling Silliphant suggested, if
Bogart were still alive people would be flocking to Marlowe
pictures starring the actor. Everything about Bogart's performance is superb: the fast-paced way he delivers his
lines, coupled with his skill at verbal fencing, expertly
conveys Chandler's crackling dialogue; the way Bogart moves
his hands--for instance, tugging at his ear--adds interesting
bits of business to the picture; the actor's "lived in" face
and rumpled appearance make him seem the perfect visual
equivalent of Chandler's detective; and Bogart's ability to
seem tough just by his presence, rather than by his actions, all combined to make Humphrey Bogart the best of
the screen Marlowes.

An assessment of the best Marlowe picture produces
evaluations similar to those reached in the discussion of the
best Marlowe. Without question, The Brasher Doubloon is
the worst of the Marlowe films. This picture has almost
no redeeming qualities to compensate for its flaws in acting, direction, script, and set design. The occasional
bright spots, such as Florence Bates' performance, are
lost in the vastness of overall poor filmmaking. Lady in
the Lake, Marlowe, and The Long Goodbye rank about even
with each other. Each has its strong points, but each contains flaws that prevent its being classified as a classic
motion picture. Lady in the Lake has a good script and
several interesting subjective camera sequences, but Montgomery's performance and the overuse of the first-person
camera detract from the overall effect of the film. Marlowe
also displays a good script, as well as some deft performances, but its routine photography keeps the picture from
being visually exciting. The Long Goodbye sports some
good acting and interesting photography, but it is flawed by
poor editing and excessive use of inside satire. Farewell,
My Lovely's set design makes it better than the above
films, and only the Mrs. Grayle character ranks it below
Murder, My Sweet. Again, therefore, we are left with
Murder, My Sweet and The Big Sleep.

Murder, My Sweet and The Big Sleep are, without

doubt, the two best Marlowe films.   Both effectively capture the Chandler spirit and both present excellent screen
personifications of the author's hero.   To choose one above
the other is a difficult, and perhaps not entirely necessary,
task at best.   But I believe The Big Sleep stands out as the
most effective Marlowe picture.   Murder, My Sweet is certainly well acted, directed, scripted, and photographed.
The Big Sleep, however, has all of these qualities and
more.   What sets The Big Sleep apart has not so much to
do with Chandler, as it has with the Bogart-Bacall-Hawks
team.   This trio infused the picture with a mystique not
found in the other Marlowe films.   The overall acting talents
of Bogart and Bacall, under the direction of Hawks, was a
dynamic combination hardly, if ever, surpassed in the private eye film genre.   This explains why The Big Sleep can
be watched over and over, and still leave the viewer with
the impression he is seeing it for the first time.   It is
truly a film that remains today as exciting and dynamic as
it was thirty years ago.

     Table 15 summarizes the major production facts of
the Marlowe films.   One factor not yet discussed concerns
the relationship between the Marlowe pictures and the times
in which they were made.   This is always an important
concern when examining the history of motion pictures, for
the prevailing attitudes of society will affect the film's treatment of material.   The first two Marlowe films, Murder,
My Sweet and The Big Sleep were made during approximate-
ly the same period, roughly the second half of 1944.   In
spite of World War II, however, almost no references to
the nation's overseas conflict are made.   In Murder, My
Sweet, only a gas ration sticker on Marriott's car windshield
(he has an "A" rating) serves to indicate a war is being
fought.   In The Big Sleep, Marlowe, too has a ration card
(he's more fortunate than Marriott, his is a "B" sticker).
Twice in The Big Sleep, Marlowe asks Bernie Ohls how he's
fixed for "red points" (ration coupons).   No other mention
of the Second World War is made in these two films, and
there aren't even any servicemen in evidence in bars and
nightclubs.   Clearly these two films were made to provide
the audience with action and violence, while at the same
time taking their minds off the war by omitting mention of
it.   (This was fortunate in the case of The Big Sleep, which
was not released in the United States until well after the
war was over.)

     Lady in the Lake and The Brasher Doubloon were

TABLE 15. MARLOWE FILMS SUMMARY

Film/Novel	Screenwriter(s)	Director	"Marlowe"
Murder My Sweet (1945)/ Farewell, My Lovely (1940)	John Paxton	Edward Dmytryk	Dick Powell
The Big Sleep (1946)/ The Big Sleep (1939)	Leigh Brackett William Faulkner Jules Furthman	Howard Hawks	Humphrey Bogart
Lady in the Lake (1947)/ The Lady in the Lake (1943)	Steve Fisher	Robert Montgomery	Robert Montgomery
The Brasher Doubloon (1947)/ The High Window (1942)	Dorothy Hannah Leonard Praskins	John Brahm	George Montgomery
Marlowe (1969)/ The Little Sister (1949)	Stirling Silliphant	Paul Bogart	James Garner
The Long Goodbye (1973)/ The Long Goodbye (1953)	Leigh Brackett	Robert Altman	Elliott Gould
Farewell, My Lovely (1975)/ Farewell, My Lovely (1940)	David Zelag Goodman	Dick Richards	Robert Mitchum

also produced at nearly the same time, at the end of 1946
and the beginning of 1947. (It is interesting to note that
the two novels Chandler wrote before the United States en-
tered World War II, The Big Sleep and Farewell, My Lovely, were filmed during the war, while the two novels he
wrote when the war was in progress, The High Window and
The Lady in the Lake, were not filmed as Marlowe adventures until after the war's end.) Both these films express
a pessimism not found in their source novels, perhaps a
result of a "let down" feeling in the country after the war.
Lady in the Lake makes repeated references to how bad the
detective business is and Robert Montgomery tries to escape
his profession by becoming a writer. George Montgomery,
too, seems to care little for his business and he takes the
Murdock case only to be around Merle.

The last three Marlowe pictures reflect on more
contemporary society. Optimism characterizes Marlowe,
and 1969 seems like a good year for both Marlowe and society at large. Garner's Marlowe is generally at home in
his environment. The Long Goodbye, on the other hand,
illustrates how a man of honor looks foolish in the 1973
world, perhaps reflecting the Watergate-related idea that
honor is a thing of the past. In addition, The Long Goodbye
caters to sensationalism in the unnecessary episode where
Marty Augustine breaks his girl friend's nose, the sequences
with Marlowe's bare-breasted neighbors (Gould calls them a
"melon convention"), and the use of four-letter words.
Needless sex, violence, and profanity were used by many
1970's films to supply audiences with something they could
not get on television. Farewell, My Lovely, too, has some
unnecessary nudity (when Mitchum searches Amthor's
brothel), but the film also reflects one aspect of 1970's society: preoccupation with nostalgia. The 1941 setting of
the picture takes the viewer back to a simpler time when
the enemies of society were clear-cut and athletes were
simple heroes, not temperamental superstars going on strike
and demanding huge salaries.

Obviously this book is not the last word on Chandler,
Marlowe, or the detective film. Much more study needs to
be done in these areas. For example, Chandler had very
definite ideas about women. Current interest in women and
film would make an examination of the women in Chandler's
novels and their counterparts in the Marlowe films both interesting and valuable. Chandler also had strong opinions
about the police. The law enforcement officers in the

author's writings were nearly always corrupt. Some were personally corrupted by money, but most were simply subject to the whims of politicians and powerful gangsters, being unable to operate with a free hand. This is what allowed Marlowe to hold back information from the police. Until they could be open and honest in every case they investigated, Chandler felt Marlowe had the right to operate according to his own code, even when it violated the letter of the law. An interesting study could be done on the relationship between private detectives and the police, not only in relation to Chandler but also in connection with other detective novels and films. And finally, more work needs to be done on the history of detective films, particularly in relation to the silent era.

Marlowe remains as popular today as he was when Chandler created him and the Marlowe films have helped to maintain and even increase that popularity. These novels and films allow the reader or viewer to slip from his everyday existence into the half-real, half-fantasy realm of Chandler's detective, to become, for a few short hours, "the best private eye in the business."

NOTES

INTRODUCTION

1. Theodore Strauss, "The Falcon Takes Over," reprinted
    in The New York Times Film Reviews 1913-1968,
    Vol. III, 1930-1948 (New York: New York Times &
    Arno Press, 1970), p. 1870.

2. Strauss, "Time to Kill," Ibid., p. 1910.

3. Brian Davis, The Thriller (New York: E. P. Dutton,
    1973), p. 32.

4. Charles Gregory, "Knight Without Meaning?" Sight and
    Sound, Summer, 1973, p. 157.

5. James Robert Parish, Actors Television Credits, 1950-
    1972 (Metuchen, N. J.: Scarecrow Press, 1973), p.
    664; Arthur Shulman and Roger Youman, How Sweet
    It Was (New York: Bonanza Books, 1966), p. 224.

6. Dorothy Gardiner and Katherine Sorley Walker, eds.,
    Raymond Chandler Speaking (Boston: Houghton Mif-
    flin, 1967), p. 143.

7. Parish, p. 128; Shulman and Youman, p. 270.

8. Edward Lipnick, "Creative Post-Flashing Technique for
    'The long Goodbye'," American Cinematographer,
    March, 1973, p. 278; "MGM's 'Marlowe', Based on
    Raymond Chandler Mystery Hit at Local Theatre,"
    Exhibitor's Merchandising Manual from MGM (Mar-
    lowe) (Metro-Goldwyn-Mayer, 1969), p. 1.

9. Nick, "Harry O," Variety, September 18, 1974, p. 72,
    col. 2.

10. Bill, "The Rockford Files," <u>Ibid</u>., p. 42, col. 2.

11. <u>Ibid</u>.

12. Clifford D. May, "Whatever Happened To Sam Spade?,"
     <u>Atlantic Monthly</u>, August 1975, pp. 30, 31.

CHAPTER 1

1.   Howard Haycraft, <u>Murder for Pleasure</u> (New York:
     D. Appleton-Century, 1941).

2.   Everson, <u>The Detective in Film</u> (Secaucus, N. J.:
     Citadel Press, 1972).

3.   Quoted in Haycraft, p. 6.

4.   <u>Ibid</u>., p. 29.

5.   <u>Ibid</u>., p. 7.

6.   Edgar Allan Poe, "The Murders in the Rue Morgue,"
     reprinted in <u>Complete Stories and Poems of Edgar
     Allan Poe</u> (New York: Doubleday, 1966), p. 19.

7.   May, "Whatever Happened To Sam Spade?," <u>Atlantic
     Monthly</u>, August 1975, p. 30.

8.   Haycraft, p. 54.

9.   A. Conan Doyle, "A Scandal in Bohemia," reprinted
     in <u>The Complete Sherlock Holmes</u> (New York: Lit-
     erary Guild, 1936), p. 177.

10. Haycraft, p. 112.

11. <u>Ibid</u>., p. 166.

12. <u>Ibid</u>., p. 169.

13. Quoted in Ron Goulart, <u>An Informal History of the
     Pulp Magazines</u> (New York: Ace Books, 1972), p.
     121.

14. Quoted in Goulart.

15.   Everson, p. 5.

16.   Ibid., p. 23.

17.   Ibid., p. 26.

18.   Ibid., p. 34.

19.   Ibid.

20.   Ibid., p. 51.

21.   Ibid., p. 52.

22.   Ibid., p. 56.

23.   James Robert Parish, editor-in-chief, The Great
        Movie Series (New York: A. S. Barnes, 1971),
        p. 269.

24.   Ibid., p. 324.

25.   Leonard Maltin, ed., TV Movies (2d ed.; New York:
        New American Library, 1974), p. 581.

26.   Philip Durham, Down These Mean Streets a Man Must
        Go: Raymond Chandler's Knight (Chapel Hill: Uni-
        versity of North Carolina Press, 1963), pp. 16-22.

27.   Ibid., p. 89.

28.   Ibid., pp. 59, 60.

29.   Ibid., p. 142.

30.   Ibid., pp. 80-86.

31.   Chandler quoted in Raymond Chandler Speaking (Boston:
        Houghton Mifflin, 1972), p. 70.

32.   Ibid., p. 89.

33.   Ibid., pp. 86-89.

34.   Raymond Chandler, The Big Sleep (1939: rpt. New
        York: Ballantine Books, 1971), p. 141.

35.   Chandler, "The Simple Art of Murder," quoted in Dur-
      ham, Down These Mean Streets, pp. 95, 96.

CHAPTER 2

1.   Dorothy Gardiner and Katherine Sorley Walker, eds.,
      Raymond Chandler Speaking (Boston: Houghton
      Mifflin, 1962), pp. 207, 210, 211.

2.   Philip Durham, "Introduction," Killer in the Rain
      (Cambridge, Mass.: Riverside Press, 1964), p.
      viii; Durham, Down These Mean Streets a Man
      Must Go: Raymond Chandler's Knight (Chapel Hill:
      University of North Carolina Press, 1963), p. 156.

3.   Mertice M. James and Dorothy Brown, eds., The
      Book Review Digest 1940 (New York: H. W. Wil-
      son, 1941), p. 163.

4.   Ibid.

5.   Durham, Down These Mean Streets, p. 38.

6.   Raymond Chandler, Farewell, My Lovely (1940; rpt.
      New York: Ballantine Books, 1971), p. 1.

7.   Ibid.

8.   Ibid., p. 4.

9.   Ibid., p. 103.

10.   Ibid., p. 113.

11.   Ibid., p. 12.

12.   Ibid., p. 14.

13.   Durham, Down These Mean Streets, p. 39.

14.   Chandler, p. 16.

15.   Durham, Down These Mean Streets, p. 42.

16.   Paul Jensen, "Raymond Chandler: The World You Live
      In," Film Comment, November-December, 1974, p.
      20.

17. Based on personal correspondence, John Paxton to the
    writer, June, 1973.

18. Ibid.

19. Ibid.

20. Ibid.

21. Ibid.

22. Ibid.

23. Ibid.

24. Ibid.

25. Ibid.

26. Romano Tozzi, "Edward Dmytryk," Films in Review,
    February, 1962, pp. 87-91.

27. Ibid., p. 91.

28. Thomas H. Pryor, "Murder, My Sweet," reprinted in
    The New York Times Film Reviews 1913-1968, Vol.
    III, 1939-1948 (New York: New York Times &
    Arno Press, 1970), p. 2052.

29. Personal correspondence, John Paxton to the
    writer, 1973.

30. Ibid.

31. Ibid.

32. Ray Hagen, "Claire Trevor," Films in Review, Novem-
    ber, 1973, p. 544.

33. Anne Rothe, ed., Current Biography 1948 (New York:
    H. W. Wilson, 1949), pp. 503, 504.

34. Personal correspondence, Paxton to the writer, 1973.

35. Quoted in Rothe, p. 504.

36. "Sweet and Lovely Mayhem," Newsweek, February 26,
    1945, p. 100.

37.   Ibid.

38.   William K. Everson, The Detective in Film (Secaucus,
      N. J. : Citadel Press, 1972), p. 231.

CHAPTER 3

1.   Philip Durham, Down These Mean Streets a Man Must
      Go: Raymond Chandler's Knight (Chapel Hill: Uni-
      versity of North Carolina Press, 1963), pp. 125,
      126, 155, 156.

2.   Ibid. , p. 126.

3.   Philip Durham, "Introduction," Killer in the Rain
      (Cambridge, Mass. : Riverside Press, 1964), pp.
      viii, x.

4.   Ibid. , p. ix, x.

5.   Mertice M. James and Dorothy Brown, eds. , The
      Book Review Digest 1939 (New York: H. W. Wil-
      son, 1940), p. 176.

6.   Ibid.

7.   Quoted in Durham, Down These Mean Streets, p. 33.

8.   Ibid.

9.   Raymond Chandler, The Big Sleep (1939; rpt. New
      York: Ballantine Books, 1971), p. 146.

10.   Chandler, quoted in Down These Mean Streets, p. 33.

11.   Quoted in ibid.

12.   Leigh Brackett, "From 'The Big Sleep' to 'The Long
      Goodbye' and More or Less How We Got There,"
      Take One, January 22, 1974, pp. 26, 27.

13.   Ibid. , p. 27.

14.   George P. Garrett, O. B. Hardison, Jr. , and Jane R.
      Gelfman, eds. , Film Scripts One (New York: Mere-
      dith Corp. , 1971).

15.   Quoted in Peter Bogdanovich, The Cinema of Howard
         Hawks (New York: Museum of Modern Art, 1962),
         p. 25.

16.   Chandler, The Big Sleep, p. 20.

17.   Paxton Davis, "Bogart, Hawks and The Big Sleep Re-
         visited--Frequently," The Film Journal, Summer,
         1971, p. 8.

18.   Bogdanovich, p. 25.

19.   Davis, p. 8.

20.   "'The Big Sleep' Trailer (1946)," Original Motion Pic-
         ture Soundtrack Recordings of the Great Scenes and
         Stars from the Warner Bros. Classics, 1923 to
         1973. (Warner Brothers, 1973), Side Four, Band
         7.

21.   Crowther, "The Big Sleep," reprinted in The New
         York Times Film Reviews 1913-1968, Vol. III,
         1939-1948 (New York: New York Times & Arno
         Press, 1970), pp. 2133-34.

22.   Quoted in Joseph McBride, ed., Focus on Howard
         Hawks (Englewood Cliffs, N.J.: Prentice-Hall,
         1972), p. 25.

23.   Garrett et al., p. 137.

24.   Wood, Howard Hawks (New York: Doubleday, 1968),
         p. 170.

25.   Sennett, Warner Brothers Presents (New Rochelle,
         N.Y.: Arlington House, 1971), pp. 212-13.

26.   Agee, Films, The Nation, August 31, 1946, p. 250.

27.   Bogdanovich, pp. 25, 26.

28.   Chandler, The Big Sleep, p. 5.

29.   Crowther, p. 2134.

30.   Farber, "Journey into the Night," New Republic,
         September 23, 1946, p. 351.

31.   Brian Davis, The Thriller (New York: E. P. Dutton,
       1973), p. 22.

32.   Chandler, The Big Sleep, p. 3.

33.   Farber, p. 351.

34.   Chandler, quoted in Film Scripts One, p. 138.

35.   Paxton Davis, p. 3.

CHAPTER 4

1.   Philip Durham, "Introduction," Killer in the Rain
       (Cambridge, Mass.: Riverside Press, 1964), p.
       viii.

2.   Philip Durham, Down These Mean Streets a Man Must
       Go: Raymond Chandler's Knight (Chapel Hill:
       University of North Carolina Press, 1963), p. 44.

3.   Mertice M. James and Dorothy Brown, eds., The
       Book Review Digest 1943 (New York: H. W. Wil-
       son, 1944), p. 141.

4.   Paul Jensen, "Raymond Chandler: The World You
       Live In," Film Comment, November-December,
       1974, p. 24.

5.   Based on personal correspondence, Steve Fisher to the
       writer, May 24, 1973.

6.   Ibid.

7.   "New Camera Technique," Variety, November 27,
       1946, p. 14, col. 5.

8.   Personal correspondence, Audrey Totter to the writer,
       April 3, 1975.

9.   Personal correspondence, Fisher to the author, 1973.

10.   Ibid.

11.   Quoted in ibid.

12.   Dorothy Gardiner and Katherine Sorley Walker, eds.,
      Raymond Chandler Speaking (Boston: Houghton
      Mifflin, 1962), p. 132.

13.   Personal correspondence, Fisher to the author, 1973.

14.   Jesse Zunser, "Revolution in Movies," Cue, January
      18, 1947, p. 14.

15.   Ibid., pp. 12-14.

16.   Personal correspondence, Fisher to the author, 1973.

17.   "The New Pictures," Time, January 27, 1947, p. 97.

18.   "Camera-Eye Montgomery," Newsweek, February 3,
      1947, p. 73.

19.   Pryor, "Lady in the Lake," reprinted in The New
      York Times Film Reviews 1913-1968, Vol. III,
      1939-1948 (New York: New York Times & Arno
      Press, 1970), p. 2162.

20.   Crowther, "Subjective Film," The New York Times,
      February 9, 1947, Sec. II, p. 1, col. 8.

21.   Ibid.

22.   Personal correspondence, Steve Fisher to the writer,
      February 3, 1975.

23.   Anne Rothe, ed., Current Biography 1948 (New York:
      H. W. Wilson, 1949), pp. 457-59.

24.   Raymond Chandler, The Lady in the Lake (1943; rpt.
      Ballantine Books, 1971), p. 6.

25.   Ibid.

CHAPTER 5

1.   Quoted in Raymond Chandler Speaking (Boston: Hough-
      ton Mifflin, 1962), p. 207.

2.   Ibid., pp. 211, 212.

3.   Ibid., p. 212.

4.   Philip Durham, Down These Mean Streets a Man Must
     Go: Raymond Chandler's Knight (Chapel Hill: Uni-
     versity of North Carolina Press, 1964), pp. 125-
     26.

5.   Ibid., p. 42.

6.   Mertice M. James and Dorothy Brown, eds., The
     Book Review Digest 1942 (New York: H. W. Wil-
     son, 1943), p. 135.

7.   Ibid.

8.   Quoted in Durham, p. 43.

9.   Raymond Chandler, The High Window (1942; rpt. New
     York: Ballantine Books, 1971), p. 80.

10. Ibid., p. 142.

11. Ibid., p. 168.

12. Ibid., p. 103.

13. Ibid.

14. Ibid., pp. 114-115.

15. Paul Jensen, "Raymond Chandler: The World You Live
     In," Film Comment, November-December, 1974, p.
     20.

16. "John Brahm," Films in Review, January, 1966, pp.
     58, 59.

17. Thomas M. Pryor, "The Brasher Doubloon," reprinted
     in The New York Times Film Reviews 1913-1968,
     Vol. III, 1939-1948 (New York: New York Times
     & Arno Press, 1970), p. 2182.

18. Charles Gregory, "Knight Without Meaning?" Sight and
     Sound, Summer, 1973, p. 158.

19. "John Brahm," p. 60.

CHAPTER 6

1. Chandler, quoted in Raymond Chandler Speaking (Boston: Houghton Mifflin, 1962), p. 148.

2. Ibid., p. 217.

3. Ibid., p. 220.

4. Mertice M. James, Dorothy Brown, and Gladys M. Dunn, eds., The Book Review Digest 1949 (New York: H. W. Wilson, 1950), p. 152.

5. Ibid.

6. Raymond Chandler, The Little Sister (1949; rpt. New York: Ballantine Books, 1971), p. 123.

7. Ibid., p. 125.

8. Ibid., p. 88.

9. Ibid., pp. 89, 90.

10. Ibid., p. 90.

11. Ibid., p. 141.

12. Ibid., p. 144.

13. Ibid., p. 88.

14. Ibid., p. 202.

15. Based on personal correspondence, Stirling Silliphant to the writer, September 10, 1973.

16. Ibid.

17. "MGM's 'Marlowe,' Based on Raymond Chandler Mystery Hit at Local Theatre," Exhibitors' Merchandising Manual from MGM (Marlowe) (Metro-Goldwyn-Mayer, 1969), p. 1; "Scorns Tricks," Exhibitors' Merchandising Manual, p. 6.

18. Roger Greenspun, "Marlowe," reprinted in The New York Times Reviews (1969-1970) (New York: New York Times, 1971), p. 9.

19. Charles Gregory, "Knight Without Meaning?" Sight and
     Sound, Summer, 1973, p. 158.

20. Exhibitors' Merchandising Manual, p. 6.

21. Personal correspondence, Silliphant to the writer,
     1973.

22. Ibid.

23. Ibid.

24. Philip Durham, Down These Mean Streets a Man Must
     Go: Raymond Chandler's Knight (Chapel Hill: Uni-
     versity of North Carolina Press, 1963), p. 140.

25. Ibid.

26. Personal correspondence, Silliphant to the writer,
     1973.

27. "Shuns 'Image'," Exhibitors' Merchandising Manual,
     p. 6.

28. Personal correspondence, Silliphant to the writer,
     1973.

CHAPTER 7

1.   Philip Durham, Down These Mean Streets a Man Must
     Go: Raymond Chandler's Knight (Chapel Hill: Uni-
     versity of North Carolina Press, 1963), p. 156.

2.   Ibid. , p. 104.

3.   Mertice M. James and Dorothy Brown, eds. , The
     Book Review Digest 1954 (New York: H. W. Wil-
     son, 1955), p. 165.

4.   Durham, p. 130.

5.   James and Brown, p. 165.

6.   Raymond Chandler, The Long Goodbye (1953; rpt. New
     York: Ballantine Books, 1971), p. 74.

7.   Ibid., p. 187.

8.   Ibid., p. 191.

9.   Ibid., p. 193.

10.   Ibid., p. 54.

11.   Ibid., pp. 191, 193.

12.   Durham, p. 43.

13.   Ibid., p. 101.

14.   Ibid.

15.   Ibid.

16.   Ibid.

17.   Ibid., pp. 100-01.

18.   Chandler, p. 300.

19.   Brackett, "From 'The Big Sleep' to 'The Long Good-
      bye' and More or Less How We Got There," Take
      One, January 22, 1974, pp. 27, 28.

20.   Ibid., p. 27.

21.   Personal correspondence, Leigh Brackett to the writ-
      er, February 27, 1975.

22.   Brackett, "From 'The Big Sleep ...," pp. 27, 28;
      Robert Altman, interview with David Steinberg,
      Movies, Movies, Movies ABC-TV, January 17,
      1974.

23.   Quoted in Eric Levin, "TV Teletype: New York,"
      TV Guide, January 26, 1974, p. 1.

24.   Edward Lipnick, "Creative Post-Flashing Technique
      for 'The Long Goodbye'," American Cinematog-
      rapher, March, 1973, pp. 278-79; United Artists
      Pressbook (The Long Goodbye) (United Artists,
      1973), p. 5.

25. Lipnick, p. 280.

26. Ibid. , pp. 234, 280-81.

27. Murf, "The Long Goodbye," Variety, March 7, 1973,
    p. 18, col. 3.

28. Lipnick, pp. 328-29.

29. Aljean Harmetz, "Why Don't People Go to the Movies
    They Don't Go to?" The New York Times, May 27,
    1973, Sec. II, p. 11, col. 4, 5.

30. Murf, p. 18, col. 3.

31. Jay Cocks, "A Curious Spectacle," Time, April 9,
    1973, p. 85.

32. Quoted in Harmetz, "Why People Don't Go to the
    Movies...," p. 11, col. 7.

33. Harmetz, p. 11, col. 4.

34. Altman, quoted in Harmetz, "Why People Don't Go to
    the Movies...," p. 11, col. 6.

35. Ibid. , col. 7.

36. Ibid. , col. 8.

37. "N.Y. Critics' Opinions," Variety, October 31, 1973,
    p. 34, col. 4.

38. "10 Best Films of '73: 5 Critics, Assorted Bags,"
    Variety, January 2, 1974, p. 5, col. 5.

39. Kael, "Movieland--The Bums' Paradise," The New
    Yorker, October 22, 1973, pp. 133, 137.

40. Canby, "Altman and Gould Make a Brilliant 'Long
    Goodbye'," The New York Times, October 29, 1973,
    p. 42, col. 1-3.

41. "'10 Best' of 1973 As Picked in Chi," Variety, Janu-
    ary 30, 1974, p. 4, col. 4.

42. Sarris, "'The Long Goodbye'," Village Voice, Novem-
    ber 29, 1973, p. 84, col. 4, 5.

43. Kael, p. 136.

44. Ibid. , p. 137.

45. Murf, p. 18, col. 3.

46. Farber, "L. A. Journal," Film Comment, November-
     December, 1974, p. 2.

47. "Big Rental Films of 1973," Variety, January 9, 1974,
     pp. 19, 60.

48. Brackett, "From 'The Big Sleep'...," p. 27.

49. Quoted in "Robert Altman Speaking," Film Comment,
     March-April, 1974, p. 40.

50. Ibid. , p. 41.

51. Ibid.

52. Dorothy Gardiner and Katherine Sorley Walker, eds. ,
     Raymond Chandler Speaking (Boston: Houghton Mif-
     flin, 1962), p. 728.

53. Robert Altman, quoted in "Creative Post-Flashing,"
     p. 279.

54. Brackett, p. 28.

55. Charles Gregory, "The Long Goodbye," Film Quarter-
     ly, Summer, 1973, p. 46.

56. Quoted in Brackett, "From 'The Big Sleep'...," p. 28.

57. Gregory, p. 46.

58. Guy Platley, "What Ever Happened to Elliott Gould?
     Plenty!" The New York Times, March 4, 1973, p.
     13, col. 1.

59. Ibid. , col. 3, 4.

60. Robert Altman, interview with David Steinberg, 1974
     [note 22].

61. Leigh Brackett, personal correspondence, to the writ-
     er, February 18, 1975.

62.   "From the Heartland," Time, June 16, 1975, p. 68.

CHAPTER 8

1.   "Feature [#1]," "Farewell, My Lovely" Press Infor-
       mation (New York: Avco Embassy Pictures, 1975),
       p. 1.

2.   "'Farewell, My Lovely' Production Notes: The Film-
       makers," "Farewell, My Lovely" Press Information,
       p. 13.

3.   "Feature [#2]," "Farewell, My Lovely" Press Infor-
       mation, pp. 2-4.

4.   Ibid. , p. 3.

5.   David Goodman, conversation with the writer, July 10,
       1975.

6.   Ibid.

7.   Ibid.

8.   "Feature [#3]," "Farewell, My Lovely" Press Infor-
       mation, p. 2.

9.   "Feature [#2]," pp. 3, 4.

10.   "'Farewell' to Location Shooting," Variety, April 30,
       1975, p. 30.

11.   "'Farewell, My Lovely' Production Notes: On the
       Movie," pp. 6-8.

12.   "Feature [#3]," p. 3.

13.   Ibid.

14.   Quoted in "Feature [#1]," p. 3; "Feature [#3]," p. 4.

15.   "'Farewell' to Location Shooting."

16.   "Feature [#3]," p. 1.

17.   Quoted in ibid.

18. "'Farewell' to Location Shooting."

19. "Short [#1]," "Farewell, My Lovely" Press Information; "Short [#2]," "Farewell, My Lovely" Press Information.

20. "Chandler's 'Farewell' in Strong N.Y. Start," Variety, August 20, 1975, p. 3; "N.Y. Critics' Opinions," Variety; August 20, 1975, p. 38.

21. "Farewell, My Lovely Advertisement," The New York Times, August 15, 1975, p. 27.

22. Verr, "Farewell, My Lovely," Variety, August 13, 1975, p. 16.

23. Eder, Screen, "Detective Yarn," The New York Times, August 14, 1975, p. 39.

24. Ibid.

25. Michener, "Marlowe Soft-Boiled," Newsweek, August 18, 1975, p. 73.

26. Cocks, "Soft-Boiled," Time, September 1, 1975, p. 44.

27. Michener.

28. Eder.

29. "Biography of Robert Mitchum," "Farewell, My Lovely" Press Information, pp. 1-8.

30. Quoted in "Feature [#4]," "Farewell, My Lovely" Press Information, pp. 1, 3.

31. "Biography of Dick Richards," "Farewell, My Lovely" Press Information, p. 2.

32. "Farewell, My Lovely" Advertisement (see note 21).

33. Ibid.

34. Bernard Drew, "Philip Marlowe Lives Again: Robert Mitchum Stars in Chandler's 'Farewell, My Lovely,'" The Burlington Free Press, August 28, 1975, p. 31.

35.   Verr.

36.   Cocks.

37.   Michener.

38.   Ibid.

CHAPTER 9

1.   Everson, The Detective in Film (Secaucus, N. J. :
        Citadel Press, 1972), p. 230.

2.   Jensen, "Raymond Chandler: The World You Live In,"
        Film Comment, November-December, 1974, p. 22.

BIBLIOGRAPHY*

PERIODICALS

Agee, James. Films, The Nation, August 31, 1946, p. 250.

Blades, John. "The Big Sleep," Film Heritage, Summer, 1970, pp. 7-15.

Brackett, Leigh. "From 'The Big Sleep' to 'The Long Goodbye' and More or Less How We Got There," Take One, January 22, 1974, pp. 26-28.

"Camera-Eye Montgomery," Newsweek, February 3, 1947, p. 73.

Canby, Vincent. "Altman and Gould Make A Brilliant 'Long Goodbye'," The New York Times, October 29, 1973.

"Chandler's 'Farewell' in Strong N.Y. Start," Variety, August 20, 1975, p. 3.

Cocks, Jay, "A Curious Spectacle," Time, April 19, 1973, pp. 83, 85.

_____. "Soft-Boiled," Time, September 1, 1975, pp. 44, 45.

Crowther, Bosley. "Subjective Film," The New York Times, February 9, 1947.

---

*Personal interviews, correspondence, and studio promotional literature are omitted in this listing; such material is cited throughout the Notes (see preceding section).

225

Davis, Paxton. "Bogart, Hawks and The Big Sleep Revisited Frequently," The Film Journal, Summer, 1971, pp. 3-9.

Dawson, Jan. "Robert Altman Speaking," Film Comment, March-April, 1974, pp. 40, 41.

Dempsey, Michael. "Altman: The Empty Staircase and the Chinese Princess," Film Comment, September-October, 1974, pp. 10-17.

Drew, Bernard. "Philip Marlowe Lives Again: Robert Mitchum Stars in Chandler's 'Farewell, My Lovely'," The Burlington Free Press, August 28, 1975.

Eder, Richard. "Detective Yarn," The New York Times, August 14, 1975, p. 39.

Farber, Manny. "Journey into the Night," The New Republic, September 23, 1946, p. 351.

_____. "Through Thin and Thick," The New Republic, March 26, 1945, p. 422.

Farber, Stephen. "L. A. Journal," Film Comment, November-December, 1974, pp. 2, 58.

"Farewell, My Lovely" advertisement, The New York Times, August 15, 1975, p. 27.

"'Farewell' to Location Shooting," Variety, April 30, 1975, p. 34.

"From the Heartland," Time, June 16, 1975, pp. 67, 68.

Gregory, Charles. "Knight Without Meaning?" Sight and Sound, Summer, 1973, pp. 155-59.

_____. "The Long Goodbye," Film Quarterly, Summer, 1973, pp. 46-48.

Grenier, Cynthia. "Hello, 'Goodbye'," The Village Voice, November 15, 1973.

Hagen, Ray. "Claire Trevor," Films in Review, November, 1963, pp. 541-52.

Hale, Wanda. "Capital Presents 'Lady in the Lake'," Daily News, January 24, 1947.

Harmetz, Aljean. "Why Don't People Go to the Movies They Don't Go to?" The New York Times, May 27, 1973.

"The Hazards of Humphrey B," Newsweek, September 2, 1946, pp. 77, 78.

Jameson, Richard. "Son of Noir," Film Comment, November-December, 1974, pp. 30-33.

Jensen, Paul. "Raymond Chandler: The World You Live In," Film Comment, November-December, 1974, pp. 18-26.

"John Brahm," Films in Review, January, 1966, pp. 58-61.

Kael, Pauline. The Current Cinema, "Movieland--The Bums' Paradise," New Yorker, October 22, 1973, pp. 133-39.

Levin, Eric. "TV Teletype: New York," TV Guide, January 16, 1974, p. 1.

Lipnick, Edward. "Creative Post-Flashing Technique for 'The Long Goodbye'," American Cinematographer, March, 1973, pp. 278-81, 328-29, 334-35.

"The Long Goodbye," Films in Review, August-September, 1973, p. 441.

McCarten, John. (The Current Cinema), "Florida, Montgomery, and No Bacall" New Yorker, February 1, 1947, pp. 56, 57.

McNulty, John. "Egypt, Gunfire, and Gossamer" (The Current Cinema), New Yorker, September 7, 1946, pp. 48-50.

May, Clifford D. "Whatever Happened to Sam Spade?" The Atlantic Monthly, August 1975, pp. 27-35.

Michener, Charles. "Marlowe Soft-Boiled," Newsweek, August 18, 1975, p. 73.

Monaco, James. "Notes on 'The Big Sleep,' Thirty Years

After," Sight and Sound, Winter 1974/75, pp. 34-38.

Murf. "The Long Goodbye," Variety, March 7, 1973.

"New Camera Technique," Variety, November 27, 1946.

"The New Pictures," Time, December 18, 1944, p. 94.

"The New Pictures," Time, August 26, 1946, pp. 77, 78.

"The New Pictures," Time, June 2, 1947, pp. 97, 98.

"N. Y. Critics' Opinions," Variety, October 31, 1973.

Platley, Guy. "What Ever Happened to Elliott Gould?
Plenty!" The New York Times, March 4, 1973.

O'Hara, Shirley. "Singing the Blues," New Republic, June
16, 1947, pp. 32, 33.

_____ "Techniques: New and Old," New Republic,
February 3, 1947, p. 42.

Sarris, Andrew. "'The Long Goodbye'," The Village Voice,
November 29, 1973.

Stewart, Garrett. "'The Long Goodbye' from 'Chinatown',"
Film Comment, Winter 1974-75, pp. 25-32.

"Sweet and Lovely Mayhem," Newsweek, February 26, 1945,
p. 100.

Symons, Julian. "The Case of Raymond Chandler," The
New York Times Magazine, December 23, 1973, pp. 13,
22, 25, 27.

Tarantino, Michael. "Movement as Metaphor: The Long
Goodbye," Sight and Sound, Spring 1975, pp. 98-102.

"10 Best Films of '73, Assorted Bags," Variety, January
2, 1974.

"'10 Best' of 1973 As Picked in Chi," Variety, January 30,
1974.

"They Died Like Flies [by G. W.]" (The Current Cinema),
New Yorker, March 17, 1945, p. 78.

"Thrice-Told Tale," Newsweek, April 21, 1947, p. 96.

Tozzi, Romano. "Edward Dmytryk," Films in Review, February, 1962, pp. 86-101.

Verr, "Farewell, My Lovely," Variety, August 13, 1975, p. 16.

"Warners' 'Big Sleep' Makes Patrons Wake Up and Sing," The Hollywood Reporter, August 8, 1946.

Williamson, Bruce. "Judith Crist's Magical Mystery Tour" (SR Up Front), Saturday Review of the Arts, March, 1973, pp. 7-10.

Zunser, Jesse. "Revolution in Movies," Cue, January 18, 1947, pp. 12-14.

BOOKS (and a dissertation)

Bogdanovich, Peter. The Cinema of Howard Hawks. New York: Museum of Modern Art, 1962.

_____. Pieces of Time. New York: Arbor House, 1973.

Chandler, Raymond. The Big Sleep. 1939; rpt. New York: Ballantine Books, 1971.

_____. Farewell, My Lovely. 1940; rpt. New York: Ballantine Books, 1971.

_____. The High Window. 1942; rpt. New York: Ballantine Books, 1971.

_____. Killer in the Rain. Cambridge, Mass.: Riverside Press, 1964.

_____. The Lady in the Lake. 1943; rpt. New York: Ballantine Books, 1971.

_____. The Little Sister. 1949; rpt. New York: Ballantine Books, 1971.

_____. The Long Goodbye. 1953; rpt. New York: Ballantine Books, 1971.

_____. Pickup on Noon Street. New York: Ballantine Books, 1972.

_____. Playback. Boston: Houghton Mifflin, 1958.

_____. The Raymond Chandler Omnibus. New York: Alfred A. Knopf, 1964.

_____. Trouble Is My Business. New York: Ballantine Books, 1972.

Davis, Brian. The Thriller. New York: E. P. Dutton, 1973.

Doyle, A. Conan. The Complete Sherlock Holmes. (Many editions.)

Durham, Philip. Down These Mean Streets a Man Must Go: Raymond Chandler's Knight. Chapel Hill: University of North Carolina Press, 1963.

Everson, William K. The Detective in Film. Secaucus, N.J.: Citadel Press, 1972.

Gabree, John. Gangsters: From Little Caesar to the Godfather. New York: Pyramid Publications, 1973.

Gardiner, Dorothy, and Katherine Solley Walker, eds. Raymond Chandler Speaking. Boston: Houghton Mifflin, 1962.

Garrett, George P., O. B. Hardison, Jr., and Jane R. Gelfman, eds., Film Scripts One. New York: Meredith Corp. 1971.

_____, _____, and _____. Suggestions for Instructors to Accompany Film Scripts One and Film Scripts Two. New York: Meredith Corp., 1971.

Goulart, Ron. An Informal History of the Pulp Magazines, New York: Ace Books, 1972.

Halliwell, Leslie. The Filmgoer's Companion. 2d ed. New York: Hill and Wang, 1967.

Haycraft, Howard. Murder for Pleasure. New York: Appleton-Century, 1941.

Higham, Charles, and Joel Greenberg. Hollywood in the Forties. New York: Paperback Library, 1970.

James, Mertice M., and Dorothy Brown, eds. The Book Review Digest 1939. New York: H. W. Wilson, 1940.

_____. The Book Review Digest 1940. New York: H. W. Wilson, 1941.

_____. The Book Review Digest 1942. New York: H. W. Wilson, 1943.

_____. The Book Review Digest 1943. New York: H. W. Wilson, 1944.

_____. The Book Review Digest 1954. New York: H. W. Wilson, 1955.

_____, _____, and Gladys M. Dunn, eds. The Book Review Digest 1949. New York: H. W. Wilson, 1950.

McArthur, Colin. Underworld USA. New York: Viking Press, 1972.

McBride, Joseph, ed. Focus on Howard Hawks. Englewood Cliffs, N.J.: Prentice-Hall, 1972.

Maltin, Leonard, ed. TV Movies. 2d ed. New York: New American Library, 1974.

Manchel, Frank. Film Study: A Resource Guide. Cranbury, N.J.: Associated University Press, 1973.

Michael, Paul. Humphrey Bogart: The Man and His Films. New York: Bonanza Books, 1965.

The New York Times Film Reviews 1912-1968. Vol. III, 1939-1948. New York: New York Times & Arno Press, 1970.

The New York Times Film Reviews (1969-1970). New York: New York Times, 1971.

Parish, James Robert. Actors' Television Credits 1950-1972. Metuchen, N.J.: Scarecrow Press, 1973.

_____, editor-in-chief. The Great Movie Series. New

York: A. S. Barnes, 1971.

Parker, Robert Brown. "The Violent Hero, Wilderness
    Heritage and Urban Reality: A Study of the Private Eye
    in the Novels of Dashiell Hammett, Raymond Chandler
    and Ross MacDonald." Unpublished PhD dissertation,
    Boston University, 1970.

Poe, Edgar Allan. Complete Stories and Poems of Edgar
    Allan Poe. New York: Doubleday, 1966.

Richardson, Robert. Literature and Film. Bloomington:
    Indiana University Press, 1972.

Rothe, Anne, ed. Current Biography 1948. New York:
    H. W. Wilson, 1949.

INDEX

Film titles are in capitals; book and magazine titles are underscored; stories and television shows are in quotation marks. Fictional characters are designated by a (c).